MICHAEL LEGAT

WRITER'S GUIDES

•

THE NUTS AND BOLTS OF WRITING

and

REVISION

Also by Michael Legat

non-fiction
Dear Author . . .
An Author's Guide to Publishing
Understanding Publishers' Contracts
Writing for Pleasure and Profit
How to Write Historical Novels
Plotting the Novel
Non-Fiction Books: A Writer's Guide
The Illustrated Dictionary of Western Literature
Putting on a Play
We Beheld His Glory

fiction
Mario's Vineyard
The Silver Fountain
The Shapiro Diamond
The Silk Maker
The Cast Iron Man

The Nuts and Bolts of Writing

Michael Legat

ROBERT HALE · LONDON

ISBN 0 7090 6443 8

Robert Hale Limited
Clerkenwell House
Clerkenwell Green
London EC1R 0HT

2 4 6 8 10 9 7 5 3 1

Printed in Great Britain by
St Edmundsbury Press Limited, Bury St Edmunds, Suffolk
and bound by
WBC Book Manufacturers Limited, Bridgend

Contents

This book is dedicated in friendship and gratitude
to John Hale
in the hope that it will achieve its aim
and also
to John McLaughlin
whose advice I so much appreciate

Introduction

This book originated in a cry of mixed irritation and despair from my publisher. 'You would not believe', he said, 'the poor standard of the typescripts submitted for our consideration. I don't mean the actual content of the books, but the spelling, the punctuation, the grammar, and the presentation. There are plenty of books which tell would-be writers how to write novels or non-fiction or articles, including your own *Writing for Pleasure and Profit*, but there's a real need for something on what I would call the nuts and bolts of writing.'

No sensible author ignores such a suggestion from a publisher, especially when he's right. Many excellent books on spelling, punctuation and grammar already exist, but most of them seem to have a strong flavour of the text book, rather than being aimed at someone who is trying to get work published, and certainly none of these specialist works also covers the way to submit a typescript or information on such subjects as literary agents and organizations for authors.

The Nuts and Bolts of Writing attempts to fill the gap.

M.L.

PART ONE

The Tools Of The Trade

Let us therefore agree ... that a reasonably good standard of writing is a mark not of preciosity but of good sense, not of prissiness but of efficiency; that such a standard can be attained by anyone with a little effort; that the effort will be worthwhile ...; that it requires neither hairsplitting nor self-consciousness but merely a willingness to acquire good habits.

Sir Ernest Gowers

1 Punctuation

When we speak we use pauses and inflexions to make our meaning clear. The pauses may be very slight – almost imperceptible – and the inflexions may be quite subtle variations in tone, but they can make a great difference to the sense of our words. For instance, if we say, 'He is tall and handsome,' we are making a straightforward statement in which neither his height nor his good looks takes precedence over the other. But if we say, 'He is tall *and* handsome,' the emphasis puts extra weight on the second adjective, and suggests as the thought behind the words, 'He is not only tall, but handsome, too.' Yet again, if we say, 'He is tall – (*slight pause*) and handsome,' we are expressing masculine beauty as a kind of extra piece of information, almost as an afterthought. Inflexions also make it clear whether we are making a statement or asking a question. If we say, 'The dog is trained' with a downward inflexion on the last word, it is a statement, but if there is an upward inflexion, it becomes a question. And by stressing certain words, we obtain yet other variations: 'The *dog* is trained' suggests that some other animal or person (perhaps the dog's owner) isn't trained; while 'The dog *is* trained' is a particularly emphatic statement.

In writing, these pauses and inflexions are replaced by punctuation, which makes sense of what we write, avoids confusion and indicates expression.

Take, for instance, the following unpunctuated passage:

He told me where he was going to see James and I replied that he might see Brenda there at the same time the dog started barking again I had to shout as I asked will you tell him I I tried to quieten the dog but I failed to shut him up of course I should have given him a bone I know Bill did not hear me I thought he smiled as he went away without my having had a chance to question him for the second time I went home dissatisfied.

11

As written it is impossible to tell how that is to be read, and although one can just about make sense of it, the addition of punctuation can not only clarify it, but can be used to give it different meanings.

For instance, it could be punctuated as follows:

> He told me where he was going – to see James – and I replied that he might see Brenda there. At the same time the dog started barking. Again I had to shout as I asked, 'Will you tell him I –?' I tried to quieten the dog, but I failed; to shut him up, of course, I should have given him a bone. I know Bill did not hear me. I thought he smiled as he went away, without my having had a chance to question him. For the second time, I went home dissatisfied.

Alternatively, it could be punctuated like this:

> He told me where he was going to see James, and I replied that he might see Brenda there at the same time. The dog started barking again. I had to shout as I asked, 'Will you tell him I ... I tried to quieten the dog, but I failed to shut him up? Of course, I should have given him a bone, I know.' Bill did not hear me, I thought. He smiled as he went away. Without my having had a chance to question him for the second time, I went home dissatisfied.

Several other variations are possible, especially if we add the underlining of certain words (which should really be considered as a form of punctuation) to give particular emphasis to them, and each new version will have its own shades of meaning.

In the course of this chapter so far half a dozen or so punctuation marks have been used. There are many more. In the following pages, each of them and its various functions will be examined.

The Full Stop

Full stops are used at the end of statements which are neither interrogatory nor exclamatory. They separate sentences, especially when the sentences present different ideas or thoughts: *The cat sat on the mat. The dog watched it. The cat purred. The dog growled.* Reading those four sentences aloud, you will probably insert a more-than-slight pause between each one; in writing, such pauses almost always demand a full stop (or at least a semi-colon – see below). They can be used in a somewhat unusual way to create a special effect, as in: *He was free. Rich. Happy. And very drunk.* This produces a quite different, more emphatic impression from the more conventional style of: *He was free, rich, happy, and very drunk.*

Full stops are also used in abbreviations: *U.N.O., B.B.C., etc., Mrs., Dr.* Increasingly, however, full stops are omitted in abbreviations, and *UNO, BBC, Mrs, Dr* are acceptable forms.

The Comma

The comma is used on numerous occasions:

1. To separate the items in a list, as in the sentence quoted above: *He was free, rich, happy, and very drunk.* Or: *The drinks available before lunch included white wine, gin and tonic, scotch and soda, orange juice, and spring water.* The question of whether there should be a comma before the last 'and' in such lists is a difficult one. If the final item needs to be stressed, or contrasts with the previous word (as in 'and very drunk'), or if the final item is a group of words which represents a single object but in which 'and' appears, (as in 'gin and tonic' or 'scotch and soda', if they had come at the end of the sentence), or if there is likely to be ambiguity (if you omit the comma after 'orange juice' do you mean that 'orange juice' and 'spring water' are alternatives, or form one drink?), it is better to include the comma before the final 'and'; indeed you will never be wrong to do so. It is, however, possible and usual to omit it in such a list as: *The jewellery consisted of diamonds, rubies, emeralds, sapphires and pearls.* The list can also consist of a series of phrases: *He was aware of the brilliant sunlight, the dark shadows of the trees, the lack of a wind, and the stillness of the village.* Or a series of clauses: *She was the kind of woman who never complained, who thought only of his welfare, who would follow him anywhere, and who was happy however badly he treated her.* Or: *She hurried down the street, ran into the baker's, and bought a loaf, two macaroons and a cherry cake. Then she went to the take-away, waited in the queue, and eventually emerged with packets of fried chicken, individual steak-and-kidney pies, and fish and chips.*

2. To separate two or more descriptions appearing in sequence of the same thing: *the ripe, golden sheaves of corn.* Or: *the happiest, funniest, most exciting show in town.* Or: *My wife,*

Rosetta, will accompany me. But note that the comma is not always necessary. We write, for example: *the little black dog.* Or: *the well-known English author.* You can usually tell when the comma is necessary and when it can be omitted if you say the words aloud. You would not pause after 'little' when saying 'the little black dog', so no comma is needed; on the other hand, you would almost certainly make a very slight break between 'ripe' and 'golden' so a comma is required in that case.

3. Before or after the name of someone to whom a line of dialogue is addressed (and both before and after the name if it comes in the middle of the sentence): *'What's the matter, Kevin? Darling, please be reasonable.' 'All I wanted, Carol, was for you to be happy.'*

4. Before or after (and, if necessary, both before and after) direct speech which is attributed to a person: *He said, 'I don't understand.' 'You wouldn't,' she replied.* Or: *'All I wanted,' he began, 'was for you to be happy,' and he laughed bitterly.* Note that the comma which comes before the attribution (that is, 'he said' or 'he began' or 'she replied'), or before the continuation of the sentence (as in 'and he laughed bitterly'), appears inside the quotation marks.

5. To separate a phrase or clause which is subsidiary to the main sentence: *In her haste, she had forgotten to get anything to drink.* Or: *It was a forlorn hope, which she was foolish to cherish.* Note that while the comma is virtually mandatory if the subsidiary clause or phrase comes at the beginning of a sentence, it may sometimes be omitted when the clause or phrase appears in the middle of the sentence: *Somewhat despairingly, she hoped that he would not notice,* but *She hoped somewhat despairingly that he would not notice.* If you do separate such a phrase by placing a comma in front of it, then you must also insert one at the end of the phrase: *She hoped, somewhat despairingly, that he would not notice.* The same applies if it is a clause appearing in the middle of the sentence: *The take-away food, which was still hot, would be on the table in a moment.* Equally, it would be wrong to insert the comma at the end of the phrase or clause in such cases without putting one in before it. The commas are acting rather like brackets, and must be opened and closed, as it were. As a special point, it is worth noting that 'however' almost always needs the comma wherever it occurs in the sentence: *However, he saw it at once,* or *He saw it, however, at once.*

6. To separate sentences joined by the conjunctions 'and' or 'but', particularly when the sentences have different subjects. *They*

attacked again, but our defence was strong. Or: *She looked at him defiantly, but he did not notice.* On the other hand, when a sentence has a single subject controlling two verbs, the comma after 'and' may be omitted: *Emma put down her book and sipped thoughtfully at her cup of tea.* Or: *He grabbed the bag and ran off down the street.*

Commas are not 'strong' enough to separate sentences which are not joined by conjunctions. So it is incorrect to write, for example: *She shut the door, he turned towards her.* The two sentences in that example need to be separated by a full stop or a semi-colon. On the other hand, commas can be used if what you are writing is, in effect, a list, especially if you are aiming at a special effect. For instance: *She shut the door, the cat ran towards him, he grabbed at it and missed, and Grandma, sitting in the corner, gave a little scream.* By running those sentences together and using commas instead of full stops, you have added a sense of everything happening at once, which would not have been so apparent if you had used full stops.

Note also the difference between *He picked up the card which was by his hand,* and *He picked up the card, which was by his hand.* The first sentence, without the comma, suggests that he picked up the nearest of several cards; the insertion of the comma in the second sentence implies that there was only one card, which was by his hand.

Correct use of the comma is very difficult, and the tendency among most writers is to use too many. If your work is spotted all over with commas, there are three tests you might try: firstly, are the commas there to separate items in a list, before or after the attributions in dialogue, before or after the name of persons addressed in dialogue? If so, they will probably have to stay, for such commas are virtually mandatory. Secondly, looking at the remaining commas, will the meaning remain clear and as you intend if you take out the commas? If so, you can probably remove some or all of them. Thirdly, try reading the work aloud; where you pause (unless you have stopped simply because you have run out of breath), you will probably need a punctuation mark – a full stop (or possibly a semi-colon, a colon, or the appropriate signs if it is a question or an exclamation), but a comma if the pause is a slight one.

The Semi-Colon

The semi-colon is used to separate two or more sentences which are usually related by subject matter. It often, therefore, takes the place of 'and' or 'but'. For example: *The pause indicated by a semi-colon is considerably longer than that suggested by a comma; on the other hand, it is less weighty than a full stop; by linking sentences, it can sometimes give a smoother effect than a series of full stops.* Or: *He had forgotten to turn out the light; the door should have been closed, too.* The four short sentences quoted in the section on the full stop above could also have been written as: *The cat sat on the mat; the dog watched it; the cat purred; the dog growled.*

Many writers forget or hesitate to use the semi-colon, perhaps because they feel that it is unusual nowadays and therefore draws unwanted attention to itself. It is true that a conscious effort is needed to insert a semi-colon; before many years have passed it may even be considered archaic. This is a pity, because it is an extremely useful punctuation mark. It is rarely seen in dialogue, where the full stop seems more natural, but in prose it has a genuine function to perform and can add variety and a change of rhythm to your work.

The Colon

The colon is used:

1. To introduce a list or an example. For instance: *The ingredients for Pineapple Surprise are: ½ fresh pineapple, 1–2 tablespoons water, 50g icing sugar. Method: Scoop out the pineapple ...*

2. To introduce dialogue. For example: *He shouted: 'What's the matter?'* (But note that the comma is more usual in such cases.) The colon is particularly useful if introducing a quotation which would not normally follow such a word as 'said' or 'wrote'. For example: *There is a proverb which seems apt at this time: 'Many a true word is spoken in jest.'*

3. To introduce an explanation or amplification of a statement. For example: *She gave her recipe for a prosperous Britain: freedom from unnecessary controls.* Or: *He realised at once where she had gone: to her mother's.*

It is quite common to use a dash after a colon, the two marks being joined together, but the only virtue in this usage is at the end of a paragraph to draw particular attention to the fact that a list follows. Even then, it is not really necessary.

The Question Mark

The question mark comes at the end of a direct question. For example: *Why?* Or: *How do you do?* (It must be admitted, however, that if we are old-fashioned enough to say 'How do you do?' when introduced, we do not expect a direct reply, other than perhaps a 'How do you do?' in return, and the question has turned into a formal way of saying 'Hello'. It could be argued, therefore, that a full stop would be more appropriate, but it is in fact a question and should be shown as such.)

The question mark also transforms into a question a group of words which would otherwise appear to be a statement. For example: the question mark in *He said he was coming?* tells us to read it as a question.

Two problems arise with question marks. The first is the matter of indirect speech. Question marks should not be used. For example: *He asked if we had seen it.* Or: *Uppermost in his mind was the question of whether they should go.* But if you say, *Uppermost in his mind was the question: should they go?* the question mark goes in.

The second difficulty arises with a long and complex sentence which begins with a question, but ends with a statement. For example, if you were to write, *May I ask whether this is really so, since it is contrary to all previous advice that I have received, and until you convince me that you are right, I shall continue to withhold payment,* you should put a question mark at the end however out of place it may seem. (It might be preferable to rephrase the sentence to read: *May I ask whether this is really so? It is contrary to all previous advice ...*)

The Exclamation Mark

The exclamation mark is used after exclamations like *Oh!*, or *Oh dear!*, or *Hell's bells!*, and to add emphasis to commands or statements such as *Go away!* or *I didn't!*.

It is also used to express the idea that something is extraordinary or surprising. For example, at the end of a story about someone who believed that she had heard burglars in the house: *It was only a mouse!* Or: *Shakespeare's vocabulary contained no fewer than thirty thousand words!*

While the use of exclamation marks is legitimate, and often essential, in dialogue, in order to convey the sound, the expression, the emotion which the author intends the reader to understand, their appearance in other circumstances is largely to be avoided. No one minds if, in a letter to a friend, you use exclamation marks, even in threes (*My dear, I was flabbergasted!!!*), and there may be some place for them in an article written in a popular style. In a book or in any piece of more serious writing, however, an exclamation mark appearing other than in dialogue can often seem to be an intrusion. It is as though the author were saying, 'Isn't that strange?', 'Wasn't that funny?' Readers are quite capable of making such judgments for themselves, and usually prefer to do so.

The Dash

The dash is an interesting punctuation mark. In some instances its use is entirely legitimate, but in others, many purists consider it to be a lazy way of punctuating which should be confined, like triple exclamation marks, to informal correspondence. It is, in fact, not to be sneered at, for even at its sloppiest, it can add certain qualities to your writing which no other punctuation mark can exactly provide.

It is used in dialogue, entirely in its own right, as it were, to indicate a speech which has been interrupted. For example: '*I heard it yesterday,*' he said. '*I was in the office, and Jeremy –*' He broke off as the door opened. Or: '*Let me explain. I was –*' '*I don't want to hear your explanations!*' The dash is sometimes used to indicate a speech which is not completed, rather than one which is actually interrupted, but I prefer to use three full stops (see below) in such cases, as I also do to indicate hesitancy in a speaker.

Another use of the dash (or sometimes a series of dashes) is to indicate a word which has been censored, and it is quite usual to substitute a dash for each letter of the offending word. For example: '– – – – *you!*' he said. The Victorians often used dashes in words like *d*—— (for 'damn') or *d*——*d* (for 'damned'). Nowadays, since the so-called 'four-letter words' are freely used, the device is rarely seen. Similarly, while writers fifty or more years ago would often refer to a character in a story as, for instance, *Dr F——*, or *a lady whom I shall call M——*, we tend now to be less coy, and even if, for some reason, we wish not to give a character his or her full name, we would probably write 'M.', rather than 'M——'.

It is when the dash replaces other punctuation marks that some people disapprove. It can be used, for instance:

1. In place of commas. *He took the suitcase, the bunch of*

flowers – and my umbrella – when he left. An additional emphasis has been placed on the umbrella by the use of the dashes. Note that there is a dash both before and after the interpolation. It would be wrong, or at least would give a different sense to the sentence to write, *He took the suitcase, the bunch of flowers – and my umbrella when he left.*

2. In place of brackets. *The use of dashes – whether you like them or not – is widely accepted.* The difference here is a subtle one. If 'whether you like them or not' had been placed in brackets, the effect would have been something like an 'aside' in the theatre; it would have isolated the words from the rest of the sentence rather more strongly than the dashes do. Again, don't forget to put in the closing dash after the interpolation, or parenthesis.

3. In place of a semi-colon or full stop. *Her head was swimming – the whole room was going round.* This adds an immediacy to the linked sentences which would not be achieved by either a semi-colon or a full stop.

4. In place of a colon. For example: *The decoration of the Christmas tree, the stuffing of the turkey, the sudden recollection that he had forgotten the wine, and the run to the off-licence to buy it – all these tasks filled his Christmas eve.* Or: *Everything he needed was there – wig, make-up, dark glasses and even a white walking-stick.* These seem to me entirely acceptable usages.

When typing your work, you can indicate a dash in several ways. If you use a single dash you must put a space before it and after it (for example: *flowers – and*), for otherwise it could be confused with a hyphen. If you use a double dash, you can do so either with spaces either side or without (for example: *flowers — and* or *flowers—and*). There is no need to put a comma in front of a dash.

Brackets

Brackets are sometimes called 'parentheses'. A 'parenthesis' is an interpolation – something which is often enclosed in brackets (although it can also be within dashes or commas) – and the plural of the term has come to be applied to the brackets themselves.

Brackets are used to surround an interpolation in a sentence which demands to be marked as such. There have been many instances of their use already in this chapter. The essential character of material placed in brackets is that, although it is relevant to what is being said, and, indeed, may be very important, it can be removed from the sentence without altering the sense. As already suggested in the section on the dash above, the use of brackets tends to separate their contents rather more strongly from the surrounding material than dashes would do.

Brackets are frequently used for 'asides', often with comic effect: *He said that he was young (which was true) and innocent (which was not).*

Three Full Stops

Three full stops in a row form a useful device to indicate an unfinished sentence, particularly in dialogue. For example: *'I have been wondering about ....'* *Lost in thought, he did not finish the sentence.* The three dots always suggest to me a trailing off, rather than an abruptly interrupted speech.

Three full stops can also be effective in conveying hesitancy in dialogue. For example: *'I ... I don't know.'* Or: *'The ... er ... the fact ... is ... well ... I hesitate to ... er ... say exactly.'*

These usages are not properly examples of an ellipsis, which is the term given to three full stops when they indicate the omission of a word or words, often in reporting a speech. For example: *The Chancellor stated that 'in view of the state of the economy ... the pound will have to be devalued.'* The missing words might be *which has performed less well than expected.* An ellipsis can also sometimes be used at the end of a sentence. For example: *It was an unworthy thought, but ....* The reader will understand the rest of the sentence, which might be *he could not prevent himself from thinking it.* Or it is used at the end of a list. For example: *The circus arrived with the swings, the hoop-la stalls, the caravans, the blaring music, the fairground people ...* The unwritten words in this case are *and all the rest of the elements which make up a travelling circus.*

The observant reader will have noticed that in some of the examples above the three full stops have turned into four. It is conventional, when the ellipsis falls at the end of a sentence, to add the full stop which would have been there anyway, if you see what I mean. When you are typing your work, there is no need ever to put more than three full stops in a row, or four if they come at the end of a sentence. They will do the work just as efficiently as a dozen.

Be careful not to use three full stops too often. Their frequent repetition can be irritating.

The Apostrophe

The best-known use of the apostrophe is to indicate possession: *John's bike, the cat's saucer, Wednesday's child.* In fact, it always signifies the omission of a letter or letters. The original form of the possessive was 'John, his bike'. This was contracted to the ''s', which then became applied indiscriminately whether the person or thing concerned was masculine, feminine or neuter. A frequent mistake is the omission of the apostrophe in such phrases as *a year's work* and *a fortnight's holiday.* On the other hand, although strictly we should say, *the baker's* or *Sainsbury's*, because the expressions are short for 'the baker's shop' or 'Sainsbury's shop', there is an increasing tendency to drop the apostrophe in such cases.

Some confusion arises with the possessives of singular words ending in s. They should also take 's: *the Cross's significance, the morass's appearance.* But we usually get round the awkward sound of such possessives by saying, for instance, *the significance of the Cross,* or *the appearance of the morass.* Please note that proper names ending in s also take 's to indicate the possessive case: *Mr Williams's dog, St James's Square, Dickens's books.*

When we want to express the possessive of a plural word ending in s, the apostrophe goes at the end of the word without the addition of an extra s: *Several girls' clothes were lost,* or *the politicians' pay rise.* If the plural ends in -es, it is quite correct to put an apostrophe by itself at the end of the word to indicate the possessive, but again we usually get round the problem by saying, for instance, *the gardens of the houses* rather than *the houses' gardens.* Plurals which do not end in s are given 's: *the women's protest,* or *the mice's tails.*

Apart from possessives, the other main use of the apostrophe is, as already stated, to show that a letter or letters have been dropped. For example: *don't, didn't, wouldn't.* Please note, the form is not *did'nt* or *would'nt*, because in all of those cases the apostrophe stands for the letter o, which has been dropped from 'do not', 'did not', 'would not'. In contractions such as *we'd* or *you'll* or *fo'castle* more than one letter has been dropped, the full form being 'we would' (or 'we had') or 'you will' or 'forecastle'. There are also some rather extraordinary words like *shan't*, which should really appear as *sha'n't* since there have been two separate contractions (of 'shall' and of 'not'), but which is accepted with the single apostrophe, and *won't*, which we say instead of 'will not'.

The dropped letter is of course the reason for the apostrophe in *it's*, meaning 'it is'. *It's* should not be confused with *its*, which is the possessive form of 'it'.

Apostrophes can appear in many places as well as in the middle of words: at the end, for instance, in *huntin', shootin' and fishin'*, or at the beginning, as seen particularly in the reproduction of Cockney speech – *'Ave yer seen 'em?* Or: *'is 'orrible 'ound*. Many new long words that come into the language inevitably get shortened – we say *phone*, for instance, instead of *telephone*, and *bus* for *omnibus*. When such contractions first appear, it is usual to put an apostrophe in front of them, so people used to write *'phone* and *'bus*, but after a while the contractions become so generally used that the apostrophe is dropped.

A further use of the apostrophe is to indicate the plurals of single letters: *Mind your p's and q's*. It used also to be inserted when using the plurals of numbers and abbreviations: *the 1980's, There are three 4's in 12, B.A.'s, G.P.'s*, but nowadays the practice is more often to write, *the 1980s, 4s* and, since it is acceptable also to omit the full stops, *BAs, GPs*.

Quotation Marks

Quotation marks, or inverted commas, indicate direct speech. For example: *'Were you there?' she asked. 'Yes,' he replied. 'Then you must have seen it,' she said*. They are also used to enclose a quotation, or to show that you are using a word with a special, usually popular, meaning: *He pleaded that 'the quality of mercy' might be shown to his client*. Or: *If you like the 'classics', you will probably admire Jane Austen*.

A further use of quotation marks is to enclose a title or name: *The action of 'Hamlet' takes place in Denmark*. Or: *the 'City' class of locomotive*. Or: *Rodin's 'The Kiss'*. It is almost always preferable to use italics in such cases (see below).

Quotation marks normally come in pairs – that is to say, at the beginning of the direct speech or quotation and at its end. However, if a speech by one character or a single quotation consists of more than one paragraph, the convention is to open the quotation marks at the beginning of each paragraph, and to close them only at the end of the last paragraph.

There are two main problems with quotation marks. The first is whether to use single or double quotation marks in your typescript. There is no definite rule. Both are acceptable, but the tendency to choose single inverted commas is increasing. Many publishers have their own 'house rules' on this and other subjects (such as whether the Deity must always be given a capital letter), and will correct your typescript accordingly, or give instructions to the printer to do so. I must say that I prefer to use double quotes in a typescript, because the single quote on a typewriter looks exactly the same as an apostrophe, and that can cause confusion.

When, in dialogue, the speaker quotes the exact words of some other person, or includes a quotation or a word with a special meaning in his speech, the convention is to use single inverted commas for the quoted material if you are normally using double inverted commas, and vice versa. For example: *"Gary said, 'I am going to the shops,' and that was the last I saw of him," he told her.* Or: *'I plead that "the quality of mercy" should be shown to my client.'* Or: *"If you like the 'classics'," he said, "you will probably admire Jane Austen."*

The second difficulty concerns the placing of other punctuation marks when quotation marks are used. Generally speaking, the rule is to put them inside the inverted commas. For instance: *'Where are you going?' she asked.* Not: *'Where are you going'? she asked.* Or: *'I don't know,' he said.* Not: *'I don't know', he said.* (By the way, no extra full stop outside the quotation marks is required when the attribution precedes the line of dialogue: *He turned to her and said, 'I love you.'* Not: *He turned to her and said, 'I love you.'.*) On the other hand, if you are quoting a single word or short phrase, it is often legitimate to put the punctuation outside the inverted commas: *If you admire the 'classics', you will probably admire Jane Austen.* Or: *Invoking 'the quality of mercy', he pleaded for his client.*

The Hyphen

The main function of hyphens is to link together words which have a special meaning when so joined. For instance: *first-night, dog-like, best-seller, dry-clean, sweet-shop.* Other words are traditionally hyphenated, although the meaning is not necessarily at all obscure if there is a space between them, instead of a hyphen, or if they are written as a single word. For example: *first-born, top-class, semi-colon.* Indeed, the modern tendency is to omit the hyphen and put the two words together: *firstnight, doglike, bestseller, semicolon,* and usages like *to-morrow* and *to-day* have virtually disappeared in favour of *tomorrow* and *today.* If you want to use hyphens, you can usually tell whether or not they are necessary by trying the experiment of writing the two words as one. If, for example, you wanted to say *The first night it happened,* it would not be reasonable to write *The firstnight it happened*; on the other hand, if you were referring to *a first-night audience,* it would be possible to use the form *firstnight,* and that is therefore a case in which you have a choice between using a hyphen and running the two words together. There are still some cases where hyphens are essential – *four-year-old houses,* for instance, has an entirely different meaning if the first hyphen is omitted.

Hyphens are also needed in certain phrases which are used almost as single words, but which would look very odd with spaces between their elements, or if run together. For example: *will-o'-the-wisp, devil-may-care, love-in-the-mist* (the flower).

The hyphen is also the conventional sign for a break in a word at the end of a line when there has not been room to complete it. The art of hyphenation in such cases is to break the word in an appropriate place. For instance, if the word 'conventional' were needed to be broken at the end of a line, the best place for the hyphen would be before the t – *conven-tional,* rather than *convent-ional* or, even worse, *conve-ntional.*

Although the hyphen is usually a linking device, in some cases it is used to separate. Thus we write *co-adjudicator,* because *coadjudicator,* by the juxtaposition of the two vowels, makes the word difficult to understand at first sight. *Strap-hanger* is a less obvious example; if you saw it printed as *straphanger,* you would probably have no difficulty with it, but it would nevertheless be possible, at first glance, to pronounce it to yourself as *straffanger.* The hyphen may also be used as a separating device if you want to indicate perhaps that someone saying a long word has deliberately split it into syllables for emphasis: '*It is fund-a-mental!*', or, of course, in an expression such as *abso-bloody-lutely.*

Italics

There are two principal uses of italics: to emphasize a word or words, and to indicate a title (such as that of a literary work, or even, if rarely, that of a public house), or a foreign word (unless, like 'apartheid' or 'aide-de-camp' it has become anglicized). For example: 'He said that when he even *thought* of *the King's Head* he experienced a *frisson,* since it was there that he had first read *The Turn of the Screw.*' Or: 'The direction for the first movement of Mendelssohn's *Italian Symphony* is *allegro vivace*; the conductor took it so slowly that it lasted almost *twice* as long as usual.'

Italics may also be used for a quotation, instead of surrounding the words with inverted commas. For example: 'Hamlet, in the famous soliloquy beginning *To be or not to be*, reveals the indecision in his mind.' They are also a convenient way of separating a specific part of a text from the rest of it, as in the examples of various usages given in this book.

When we are writing by hand, or on a typewriter, we underline any material which, when printed, will appear in italics. If you have a typewriter or a word processor which can produce italics, don't use the facility – underlining will indicate more clearly to the typesetter that he is to set the words concerned in italics.

It is perhaps worth noting that if you wish to emphasize words or show titles in a text the rest of which is in italics, those words will appear in roman (upright) type – for example: *It may be claimed that* Hamlet *is the greatest of Shakespeare's tragedies* – so in your typescript you would leave them without underlining.

Capital Letters

It goes without saying that you need a capital letter at the beginning of a sentence, and this includes the beginning of dialogue, even if it has been preceded by an attribution. For example: *He asked,* 'Where are we going?' A capital is not needed if the attribution comes in the middle of the speech. For example: '*I believe,*' *he said,* '*that it is true.*' Capitals are also used for the names of people, places, organizations, the months and the days of the week, and for titles (for example: *the Prince of Wales*, or *the Leader of the Opposition*). They are also used in certain abbreviations – *UNESCO, MP* – when capitals would be given to the words for which the letters stand (but not in such abbreviations as *a.m.* or *i.e.*). Capitals should also be given to the adjectives derived from the names of countries, such as *English, French*, and *German*.

Don't use capital letters unnecessarily. 'Archbishop', for instance, is a title and is given a capital if you write, say, *the Archbishop conducted the wedding ceremony*. But it is also a common noun, and no capital is needed for it in such a sentence as *the function of an archbishop is to lead the clergy*.

2 Spelling

Spelling used to be taught in schools, and tuition was greatly needed because English spelling is undoubtedly difficult to master. From Victorian times right through to the 1930s 'spelling bees' were popular, in which teams competed against each other in trying to spell correctly anything from the slightly tricky 'separate' (not 'seperate') to real stinkers like 'eschscholtzia'. Nowadays, however, the ability to spell well is often regarded as a mild eccentricity, and many teachers feel that it is far more important to encourage children to express themselves in an interesting way than to bother about whether the words they use are properly spelt or not (and let us face the fact that several of the younger generation of teachers, brought up under the same system, are not so hot at it themselves).

I think this lack of attention to spelling is a pity, and while I agree that a facility with words should be a target for every pupil, I don't see why the children should not be taught simultaneously to get their spelling right.

It is particularly regrettable that so many authors cannot spell. Spelling, punctuation, grammar, and indeed everything to do with words, are the tools of the author's trade, and just as a carpenter will keep his chisels sharpened and his saw slightly greased to prevent rust, so an author should take every possible care with the tools he uses. There is in fact some excuse for those of us who use English. Our grammar is fairly simple, and we have done away with most inflexive endings to words, but we have what is probably the world's most extraordinary spelling, which frequently bears little relation to pronunciation. What other language, for instance, can boast of such confusion as ten different ways of pronouncing that infamous group of four letters, 'ough'?

No one demands perfection. Even the most literate authors sometimes slip up on certain 'bogey' words. I count myself a good speller, but was rightly reprimanded by some reviewers when, in a previous book, after going on about the importance of spelling, I used the word 'miniscule' (it should, of course, have been 'minuscule'). But let your spelling mistakes be few and far between, the exception rather than the rule. A good dictionary is an essential for any writer, and you should never look upon it as a waste of time to check the spelling of any word when you are not absolutely certain of it.

'Why bother at all,' you may ask, 'when publishers employ editors who will correct my spelling?' Partly because a well-presented, well-spelt, well-punctuated typescript really does give you a slight edge when it is considered for publication – the editor thinks, Ah, this is someone who really cares about writing, someone who is taking a more professional approach than most. But you should also take trouble as a matter of your own pride. Why rely on someone else to put you right when you could, with a little trouble, do it for yourself?

It may help you to make your own list of words which you find difficult, so that you can check them quickly. Some of those words may appear in the list which begins on the next page. (Incidentally, a separate note of certain words included not so much for their spelling but for the style in which you are going to use them may also prove worthwhile. Are you, for instance, going to use the form 'bestseller', or will you hyphenate it as 'best-seller'? Are you going to write 'the village hall' or 'the Village Hall'? It is easy to forget which particular mode you have used earlier in your book, and a list will help you to be consistent.)

It really is possible to learn to spell, and it's never too late to start. If you use your list regularly, you will probably find, after a time, that you have learnt the correct spellings and will never again have difficulty with them. That really is the best way of all to learn.

Another way is to read with care and attention. In her excellent book *Becoming a Writer*, Dorothea Brande suggests that you should read a book twice in quick succession: the first time simply to enjoy the story, and the re-reading so as to try to discover how the author tells it, the techniques used, the successes and failures of the narrative. During that second reading, you might also pay attention to the spelling, and attempt to learn from it. (Don't, by the way, rely on newspapers for correct spelling; it is not that journalists can't spell, but that all too often printing errors creep into their columns.)

It is helpful, too, to be careful in your pronunciation, which can often give a guide to the spelling. For instance, if you say the word properly, you will know that it should be 'implicate', not 'implacate' or 'implecate', and you will not write 'refrence' if you say it, correctly, as 'reference'. Of course, this does not always help: we make no difference in the sounds of many words, and not only simple ones like 'made' and 'maid', but also in longer and more easily confused words such as 'complement' and 'compliment'. There is also danger, for example, in the false belief that 'disastrous' should really be pronounced, and spelt, 'disasterous'.

Some Correct Spellings

accelerate (two c's)
accommodation (two c's and two m's)
accordion (not accordeon)
acknowledgment, acknowledgement (either is acceptable)
acoustic (not accoustic)
acquaintance (note the first c)
acquire (note the c)
aerated (not aereated)
affair (no need to add a final e when writing of a romantic liaison)
aggravate (two g's)
agreeable (one g)
align, alignment (not aline, alinement)
allege (not alledge)
all right (preferable to alright)
almighty (only one l)
alms (not arms, in the sense of offerings to the needy)
Alsatian (not Alsation)
aluminium (aluminum is the American spelling)
ambidextrous (not ambidexterous)
appalling (two p's and two l's)
aubrietia
auxiliary (not auxilary)

bachelor (not batchelor)
banister (only one n)
benefited (only one f and one t)
biased (preferable to biassed)
bizarre
bony (not boney)

camellia (two l's)
canvass (the usual spelling when the meaning is to seek political opinions)
capsize (always '-ize', not '-ise')
chaperon (without a final e)
charisma, charismatic
chauffeur (two f's)
cheque (not check, except in America, for a bank draft).
chequer (as in 'chequered flag')
chilblain (one l)
chord (not cord when the meaning is a musical sound)
chronic
clientele

coconut (not cocoanut)
coiffeur (meaning a hairdresser)
coiffure (meaning hairstyle)
colander (only one l, but cullender is also acceptable)
committee (two m's, two t's, two e's)
conscience (note the second c)
conscious (note the second c)
consummate (two m's)
controversy (not contraversy)

delirious (not delerious)
dependant (the noun)
dependent (the adjective)
desiccated (one s, two c's)
deteriorate (note the i)
developed (one p)
diarrhea (or diarrhoea)
dilapidated (not delapidated)
diphtheria (not diptheria)
diphthong (not dipthong)
disappear (one s, two p's)
disappoint (one s, two p's)
disastrous (not disasterous)
discomfit (discomfort is rarely used as a verb)
dullness (two l's)

ecstasy (not ecstacy)
eerie
embarrass (two r's)
excite
exercise (not excercise)
existence (not existance)

fascinate
focusing (only one s)
forbade (pronounced 'forbad')
forgivable (no e after the v)
fulfil, fulfilment (one l)
fulfilled (two l's)
fulsome (one l)

gladioli (not gladiolae – the singular is gladiolus)
gramophone (not gramaphone)
granddaughter (two d's)
grey (gray is the American spelling)
gypsy (preferable to gipsy)

haemorrhage
hallo, hello, hullo (all acceptable, but hillo looks affected)
handful (only one l)

harass (one r)
hereditary (not hereditry)
hiccup (preferable to hiccough)
hirsute (not hersute)
honorary (not honourary or honoury)
humorous (no u after the first o)
hypocrisy (not hypocricy)
hysterical

idiosyncrasy
imaginary (not imaginery)
independent (not independant)
instal, instalment (or install, installment)
installation (two l's)
intercede (not interceed)
irascible
irrelevant (not irelevant or irrevelant)
itinerary (not itinery)

jewellery (preferable to jewelry, which is the American spelling)
judgment, judgement (either is acceptable)

ketchup (preferable to catsup)
kidnapped (two p's – kidnaped is the American spelling)

lachrymose
lacquer
lightning (as in 'thunder and lightning', not lightening)
liquefy (not liquify)
liqueur (not licqueur)
liquor (not licquor)
liquorice (not licquorice or liquorish)

macabre
mackintosh (don't forget the k)
maintenance (not maintainance)
manoeuvre (maneuver is the American spelling)
mantelpiece (not mantlepiece)
matt (meaning dull in finish, not mat)
mediaeval, medieval (either is acceptable)
mien
millepede (preferable to millipede)
minuscule (not miniscule)
mischievous (not mischievious)
mistakable (not mistakeable)
monstrous (not monsterous)
mouth (not mouthe when used as a verb as in 'to mouth the words')

naphtha (not naptha)
necessary (one c, two s's)
noticeable (not noticable)

nuclear (not neuclear)

obeisance
obscene
opportunity (not oppertunity)
orang-utan (or, less usually, orang-outang)

pallor (not pallour)
paraffin (two f's)
parallel (not paralell or paralel)
parliament (note the second a)
persistent (not persistant)
phenomenon (not phenomenom)
possess ('possess possesses many esses')
prejudice (not predjudice)
privilege (not priviledge or privelege)
proffer (two f's)
putrefy (not putrify)

questionnaire (two n's)

racquet (as in 'tennis racquet')
reconnoitre (one c, two n's)
recuperate (not recouperate)
relevant (not revelant)
renege (not renaig, but renegue is also used)
rhetorical
rhyme
rhythm
rigor (as in *'rigor mortis'*)
rigour (meaning 'severity')

saccharin (the sweetener)
saccharine (meaning 'over-sweet')
sacrilegious (not sacreligious)
sceptic, sceptical (not skeptic, skeptical, which is American usage)
sceptre (note the c)
schedule (not shedule or skedule)
secateurs (one c)
secretary (not secertary)
separate (not seperate)
sepulchre
silhouette
sillabub (or syllabub)
skilful (single l's both times)
slyly (not slily)
sobriquet (not soubriquet)
somersault (not somersalt)
speciality (specialty is an American usage)
spectator (not spectater)

spurt (spirt is also acceptable)
squalor (not squalour)
storey, storeyed (referring to the floors of a building)
strait-jacket (not straight-jacket)
stupefy (not stupify)
success (two c's and two s's at the end)
sumptuous (not sumptious)
supersede (not supercede)
surprise (not surprize)
surveillance
susceptible
synchronize (not sinchronise)
synthetic (not sinthetic)

temporary (not tempory)
titillate (two l's)
tranquil (one l)
tranquillity (two l's)
tremor (not tremour)
tyro (tiro is also acceptable)

umbrella (not umberella)
unconscious
unnecessary (two n's as well as two s's)

vermilion (one l)
veterinary (not vetinary)
vigorous (not vigourous)

waiver (the relinquishing of a right)
waver (meaning 'one who waves' or 'to hesitate' or 'to flicker')
whiskey (the Irish form)
whisky (Scotch)
wilful (not willful)
wistaria (not wisteria)
withhold (two h's)
woollen (not woolen)
wryly (not wrily)

It should be noted that some of the spellings above may vary in American usage. Reference should also be made to the list of common problem words on pages 69-88.

Rules for Spelling

English, as I have said, is not an easy language to spell correctly, and although certain basic rules exist, they are often complex and riddled with exceptions. Take, for instance, the familiar saying, 'i before e, except after c'. It sounds very simple, but the first thing to remember is that it applies principally when the syllable concerned has an 'ee' sound, as in 'deceive' or 'receipt' (after c), or 'yield' or 'hygienic' (following a letter other than c). It is not an entirely reliable rule, because of such exceptions as 'species' and 'seize', 'seizure', 'counterfeit', 'weir', 'weird' and certain chemical words like 'caffeine' or 'codeine', despite the fact that all of these have the 'ee' sound. When the sound is not 'ee', the e usually comes before the i, as in 'deign', 'reign', 'heir' or 'leisure' (you may,by the way, get thoroughly mixed up about 'leisure' if you use the American pronunication 'leesure'). And again there are exceptions, such as 'friend'. It is all very confusing. Nevertheless, if you follow the rule 'i before e, except after c (when the sound is ee)', you will be right more often than wrong.

All the rules of English spelling, together with lists of exceptions, can be found in any good English Grammar, or in such a useful book as *The Oxford Guide to the English Language*, which also includes a dictionary containing some 30,000 words. Another extremely valuable book is *Hart's Rules for Compositors and Readers at the University Press, Oxford*. First produced in 1893 by Harold Hart, who was Printer to the University, and originally intended solely for the use of printers, it has been revised and updated since, and has become indispensable to many authors as well as to printers. It gives a great deal of information on spelling (and on a variety of other subjects), including, for instance: lists of those words which end in -able and those which end in -ible (such as 'excitable' and 'extendible' – it is an interesting fact, by the way, that -able is a far more common ending than -ible); difficult and unusual plurals (such as 'ghettos', 'mottoes', 'poets laureate'); words which double their final letter when a suffix like -ing is added (for instance, 'refer' and 'referring'), etc.

Anyone who has difficulty with spelling will find it worth while to buy the *Oxford Guide* or *Hart's Rules*. However, one word of caution should be added: there are a few cases when the spelling which they recommend may be regarded as something of a personal choice of the Oxford University Press. For instance, both books suggest strongly that you should always use -ize rather than -ise in such words as 'realize', 'criticize', 'civilize' (but not in certain others including 'televise', 'exercise', 'surprise'). However, the use of the -ise ending is becoming far more acceptable than the Oxford books would suggest, and you will not be wrong if you use them. In any case, you may find that your publisher has strong feelings on this particular question (and on such matters as the use of capital letters, and whether or not there should always be a full stop after Dr, Mr,

Mrs and Ms). If the publisher has such firm house rules, he will not condemn you for not following them, but will make suitable alterations in your typescript before it is sent to the printer.

The Really Hopeless Speller

I recognize, of course, that there are some writers who have a block about spelling, amounting to near dyslexia. If you are such an author, don't rely on the publisher to correct your work. There are two possible courses of action open to you. The first is to look up in a dictionary every word you write; this is a laborious process, made worse since you will probably be looking the word up the way you think it's spelt and may not be able to find it as a result; all you can do in that case is to check every possible spelling until you find the right one.

The following list of sounds which may have confusing spellings may help:

A Phonetic Guide

Sound	*Possible unexpected spellings*	
a (as in 'day')	a–e	(male, militate)
	ae	(Gaelic)
	ai	(bait, laid)
	ao	(gaol)
	au	(gauge)
	ay	(day, stray)
	e or é	(usually in foreign words, such as auto-da-fé, fiancé)
	ea	(break, steak)
	ei	(deign, weight)
	ey	(prey, they)
a (as in 'mat')	ai	(plaid)
a (as in 'father')	ae	(heart)
	al	(calf, half)
	au	(laugh)
	er	(clerk, sergeant)
b	bb	(bubble, stubble)
c (as in 'cat')	cc	(accuse, occupy)
	ch	(cholera, chronicle)
	ck	(sack, tickle)
	k	(kaleidoscope, king)
	kh	(khaki)
	qu	(liquor)
	que	(physique, unique)
ch	t	(future, question)

Sound		Possible unexpected spellings
	tch	(match, ratchet)
cw	ch	(choir)
	qu	(question, quick)
d	dd	(griddle, muddle)
	ld	(could, would)
e (as in 'see')	ae	(aesthete)
	ay	(quay)
	ea	(leak, pea)
	e–e	(sere, theme)
	ee	(committee, see)
	ei	(seize, weir)
	eo	(people)
	ey	(key)
	i	(police)
	ie	(families, wield)
e (as in 'bed')	a	(any, many)
	ae	(anaesthetic)
	ai	(said)
	ay	(sàys)
	ea	(dead, treasure)
	ei	(leisure)
	eo	(jeopardy)
	ie	(friend)
f	ff	(sniffle, suffer)
	ft	(soften)
	gh	(laugh, rough)
	ph	(philanthrophy, physical)
g (as in 'girl')	gg	(giggle, struggle)
	gh	(ghastly, ghetto)
	gu	(guess, guide)
g (as in 'gentle')	dg	(ledge, midget)
	dj	(adjoin, adjutant)
	gg	(exaggerate)
	j	(jewel, jury)
h	wh	(who)
i (as in 'like')	ai	(aisle)
	ei	(height)
	ie	(fie, lied)
	i–e	(file, rite)
	y	(fry, spy)
i (as in 'bit')	ie	(sieve)
	o	(women)
	u	(business)
	y	(rhythm, sympathy)
j	dg	(edgy, lodge)
	dj	(adjudicator, adjust)
	g	(gesture, gin)
	gg	(exaggerate)
k	c	(cataract, comic)

Sound	Possible unexpected spellings	
	cc	(acclaim, ecclesiastic)
k	ch	(chromium, scholar)
	ck	(pocket, track)
	kh	(khaki)
	qu	(liquorice)
	que	(pique, toque)
kw	ch	(choir)
	qu	(quantity, quota)
l	ll	(llama, pull)
m	mb	(comb, dumb)
	mm	(dimmer, summer)
	mn	(hymn, solemn)
n	gn	(gnome, gnu)
	kn	(knife, knowledge)
	nn	(running, winner)
	pn	(pneumatic)
o (as in 'low')	au	(mauve)
	eau	(bureau, trousseau)
	eo	(yeoman)
	ew	(sew)
	oa	(broach, load)
	oe	(ice-floe, potatoes)
	oo	(brooch)
	ou	(dough, soul)
	ow	(crow, follow)
o (as in 'top')	a	(quantity, watch)
	ou	(cough)
o (as in 'or')	au	(maul, taut)
	aw	(flaw, saw)
	oo	(floor)
	ou	(ought, thought)
ow	ou	(our, plough)
p	pp	(copper, ripple)
r	rh	(rheumatism, rhododendron)
	rr	(curry, mirror)
	wr	(wretch, writer)
s	c	(centre, cistern)
	ce	(ice, licence)
	ps	(psalm, psychology)
	sc	(ascend, science)
	ss	(asset, bass)
	st	(castle, fastened)
	sw	(sword)
sh	c	(ocean, special)
	ch	(chaperon, machine)
	s	(mansion, sugar)
	sc	(conscious)
	ss	(fission, session)

Sound	Possible unexpected spellings	
	t	(action, conventional)
	x	(anxious)
t	bt	(debt, redoubt)
	ct	(indict)
	ed	(forked, talked)
	pt	(ptomaine, receipt)
	th	(thyme)
	tt	(battle, sitting)
u (as in 'mud')	o	(done, ton)
	oo	(bloody)
	ou	(double, younger)
u (as in 'cute')	eau	(beauty)
	eu	(pneumonia, pseudo)
	ew	(lewd, new)
	o–e	(move, prove)
	oe	(shoe)
	oo	(food, too)
	ou	(soup, through)
	ue	(flue, true)
	ui	(fruit)
u (as in 'curt')	ea	(heard)
	e	(herd, infer)
	eu	(coiffeur, restaurateur)
	i	(firmament, sir)
	o	(word)
	ou	(journal)
	y	(myrrh)
x	cs	(ecstasy, tocsin)
	ct	(fiction, section)
z	s	(cosy, freesia)
	ss	(scissors)
	x	(xylophone)
	zz	(dazzle, jazz)
zh	s	(casual, treasure)

In the above list there are some examples of silent letters, such as the p in 'ptomaine'. Other silent letters which often occur are h, in words like 'heir' and 'hour', and s in 'isle' and 'island'.

It will always help you to find words in a dictionary if you pronounce them carefully, sounding the d in 'soldier', for instance, as a d rather than 'dg'.

The easier alternative to looking up everything in a dictionary is to seek help from a friend who can spell. You must surely know *someone* who is good at spelling and who would be willing – indeed, may be flattered to be asked – to correct your work before you type out the fair copy.

3   Grammar

Grammar is concerned with the parts of speech and the formation of sentences and clauses. It is a subject which can occupy whole books and to which teachers used to devote many hours of instruction. For the average person it is not a subject of immense interest, but anyone who wants to write well is, or should be, a lover of words and everything to do with them, and grammar is the basis on which we put words together for the purposes of communication.

I once asked a class to write a short piece without using adjectives or adverbs, and one of my pupils had to confess that she did not know what an adverb was. If you are like that lady, this chapter is essential reading for you, and if you want to know more than the rudiments, there are many good books easily available. If you already have a good grounding in grammar, you will probably not mind reading about it again.

Parts of Speech

Parts of speech are the names we give to words when they are performing various functions – as names, perhaps, or action words, or to describe or modify other words, or to define their relationships to each other. It is often impossible to know in which function a particular word is operating until it appears in a sentence. The word *love*, for instance, can be a noun (*my love of books*), a verb (*I love you*) or an adjective (as in *love story*); *like* can be a verb (*he likes strawberries*), an adjective (*the falcon, and like predators*), an adverb (*she moved like lightning*) or even a noun (*roses, dahlias and the like*); while the present participle of a verb can be a noun (*parting is such sweet sorrow*), an adverb (*he came running*) or an adjective (*typing paper*).

THE NOUN

A noun is the name of something, and the majority are known as 'common' nouns (for example: *dog, table, grain, office, rubbish,* etc.). A 'proper' noun (always given a capital letter, unless you are a disciple of the American writer e.e.cummings) is the name of a person, a town, a country, etc. (for example: *Jennifer, Middlesbrough, France, Monday, the Iron Duke*).

Nouns can be singular (*song, bird, keg*) or plural (*songs, birds, kegs*). The plural form is usually indicated simply by adding an s, but there are many, mostly familiar, irregular plurals, such as *mouse* and *mice, ox* and *oxen, knife* and *knives,* while nouns which end in -ch, -s, -sh and -x take -es (*match* and *matches, mass* and *masses, sash* and *sashes, box* and *boxes*). Other exceptions are nouns ending in a consonant followed by y, which change the -y into -ies (*ruby* and *rubies, caddy* and *caddies*); but note that if the y is preceded by a vowel, the plural is formed simply by adding s, (*boy* and *boys, ray* and *rays*), a point which would hardly be worth making if it were not for the mistake commonly made with *money,* the plural of which is *moneys,* not *monies.*

The formation and use of plurals is simple enough to most of us until we come to 'collective' nouns – words such as *crowd, police, school, people.* Although made up of several elements, a crowd or a school is a single entity and should therefore take a singular verb and a singular pronoun – *The crowd is hostile, and it looks quite frightening.* Or: *The whole school gathers in its main hall each morning.* But some collective nouns, like *police* and *people* always take plural verbs – *The police want to question him in the course of their enquiries.* Or: *The people demand an answer; they are in no mood for shilly-shallying.* Most of us know without thinking whether to use a singular or a plural verb or pronoun, but a problem arises with a phrase like *a crowd of hooligans,* or *a school of porpoises. Crowd* and *school* are the governing words in those cases, and we should really say *A crowd of hooligans is coming this way,* or *A school of porpoises frolics in the water*; it seems much more natural, however, because the plural noun intervenes before the verb, to say *A crowd of hooligans are coming this way,* or *A school of porpoises frolic in the water.* Either is acceptable nowadays, at least in speech, but it is preferable to use the correct verb in writing. And always beware of mixing plurals and singulars in one sentence, like a news broadcast heard recently: *The government have announced its plans* ... *Government* is a collective noun, when used in this way, and can take either a singular or a plural verb and pronoun, but not both in one sentence.

Although, except for genitives, the form of the word does not change, nouns have four cases:

The nominative, when the noun is the subject of a sentence (*The river runs swiftly, The bibliophile smiled* – *The river* and *The bibliophile* being the subjects).

The accusative, when the noun is the direct object in a sentence (*The boy reads the book, The woman washed the dress* – *The boy* and *The woman* being the subjects, and *the book* and *the dress* being the objects).

The dative, when the noun is the indirect object in a sentence (*John gave the present to Julia, The foreman told the workmen what he had said* – *John* and *The foreman* being the subjects, *the present* and *what he had said* being the direct objects, and *Julia* and *the workmen* being the indirect objects).

The genitive, which indicates that the noun or pronoun owns or is the source of something (*That ball is the dog's, the boys' uniforms, the countryside of England, Jesus's teachings* – *dog's, boys', of England* and *Jesus's* are all genitives). The genitive is usually indicated by an apostrophe (with or without an s) or by 'of'.

THE PRONOUN

Pronouns are words which takes the place of a noun or nouns, and there are many varieties of them.

First, there are the personal pronouns, which take five different forms:

The nominative – *I, thou, he, she, it, we, you, they.*

The accusative (also used for the dative) – *me, thee, him, her, it, us, you, them.*

The possessive (or genitive) – *mine, thine, his, hers, its* (N.B. not *it's*, which is short for *it is*), *ours, yours, theirs.* (Please note that *ours, yours* and *theirs* do not use apostrophes.) These pronouns are not to be confused with *my, thy, his, her, our, your, their*, which are adjectives rather than pronouns.

The reflexive and emphatic, which both use the same words – *myself, thyself, ourselves*, etc. The difference between reflexive and emphatic can be seen in such sentences as *He killed himself* (reflexive), or *I myself was there* (emphatic).

The principal problem with personal pronouns arises in such a phrase as *you and I*. Because people are aware that it is wrong to say, for example, *You and me will go*, instead of *You and I will go*, they tend always to use the nominative pronouns when often they should not. *Between you and I and the gate-post*, or *He wanted you and I to go* are incorrect. *Between* and *wanted* both take the accusative form, and you should therefore say *Between you and me and the gate-post*, or *He wanted you and me to go*. If you leave out the *you and* in such phrases, you will usually see that *I* is wrong: you would probably not say *Between I and the gate-post* or *He told I to go*. (Incidentally, it is worth noting that the real reason for the confusion is that *you* can be either nominative or accusative or dative.)

Next, there are the demonstrative pronouns: *this, that, these, those*, which are pronouns in such sentences as *That is my house, This is Your Life*, or *Those who are about to die salute you*. If, on the other hand, you say *That book belongs to him*, or *These ducklings are two days old*, you are using *that* or *these* as adjectives.

We come next to interrogative and relative pronouns: *who, whom, whose, what, which, that*. They are interrogative when used in direct or indirect questions – *Who is that?* or *She asked which it was* – and relative in such examples as *the sun whose rays are all ablaze* or *the man to whom she spoke* or *What I said was …* The most confusing of these is *whom*. It is correct to say, for example, *The man whom the Police accused of the crime*, but *whom* is wrong in such a sentence as *The man whom it is said is already known to the Police was arrested*. If we put in the necessary commas – *The man, whom, it is said, is known to the Police, was arrested*, we can see that *it is said* is an interpolation in the clause which at present reads *whom is known to the police*. Leave out the interpolation, and it becomes clear that the clause should be *who is known to the police*.

Finally, there is a large group of indefinite pronouns, which include:

The impersonal pronouns – *one, you, they* – as in such usages as *One does one's best, You always hurt the one you love, They say a stitch in time saves nine*.

The distributive pronouns (when these words are used by themselves rather than as adjectives) – *some, all, any, many, none, several, both, much, each, either, neither, few* (and *fewer* and *fewest*), *more* (and *most*), *former, latter, such*, and the words formed by the addition of *-one, -body*, and *-thing* to *any, every, no* and *some*, such as *anyone, everybody, nothing, someone*.

THE VERB
Verbs are action words, the words which indicate what the subject of a sentence is doing. They have five basic forms: the infinitive (*to go*), the present (*I go, he goes, we go*), the past (*she went, you went*), the present participle (*going*), the past participle (*gone*).

Two verbs, *to be* and *to have*, although they have their own specific meanings of *to exist* and *to possess*, are also known as 'auxiliary verbs' because they are used in conjunction with certain other verbs to form tenses (see below). Other auxiliaries are *shall, will, may, should, would* and *might* (but only when they are used to form tenses or moods – not when they are 'modals', as indicated below). The verb *to do* is also used in a similar way in such questions or statements as *Do you like reading?* or *I did tell the truth*. The verbs used in conjunction with auxiliaries (*like* and *tell* in the examples just given) are in the infinitive form, although they usually omit the *to*.

Most verbs can stand on their own, but there are some which are used only in combination with other verbs, and are called 'modals': *can, may, might, must, ought, will, shall, would, should, could, let*. These verbs all express the ability or the wish or the obligation to do something, rather than being used as auxiliaries to indicate tenses. Other modals are *dare, need* and *used to*.

Verbs have tenses, which indicate the time at which the action is taking place or has taken place or will take place. The tenses are the present (*I write*), the present imperfect (*I am writing* – formed by the present of the auxiliary *to be* and the present participle of the main verb), the past (*I wrote*), the past imperfect (*I was writing* – formed by the past of the auxiliary *to be* and the past participle), the past perfect (*I have written* – formed by the present of the auxiliary *to have* and the past participle), the pluperfect (*I had written* – formed by the past of the auxiliary *to have* and the past participle), the future (*I shall write, you will write* – formed with the auxiliaries *shall* or *will*), the future-in-the-past (*we should have written, they would have written* – formed with the auxiliaries *should* or *would*). Note that the future takes *shall* for the first person (*I shall write, we shall write*) and *will* for the second and third persons (*you will write, they will write*); if *will* is used for the first person, and *shall* for the second and third persons, they become modals and the sense changes from the simple future of the verb to one of determination or obligation.

There are other ways of expressing the future or the future-in-the-past: by the use of the auxiliary *to be* and *going* (*I am going to write, you were going to write*); by the use of the auxiliary *to be* with the infinitive of the verb (*We are to write to him tomorrow*) or with the present participle of the verb (*They are writing to him tomorrow*); by the use of the present tense together with a word or phrase which in itself expresses the future (*I write to him next week*).

Verbs have two voices: active (*Sue drove the car*) and passive (*The car was driven by Sue*).

Verbs have four moods: the indicative, used in straightforward statements or questions (*The sky is blue, Who goes home?*); the imperative, used in commands (*Go away, Don't do that*); the subjunctive, used in the expression of possibility, uncertainty or hope (*if I were you, He suggested that the meeting be adjourned, May you be very happy, had he known the outcome, They would join in, if they could*); and the infinitive, often preceded by *to*, in which form it may be simple (*to make, to sing*), or modified by forms of the verbs *to be* or *to have* (*to be going, to have gone*).

Verbs can be transitive or intransitive. Transitive verbs are those which take a direct object (*He chopped the wood, Jan gave up smoking*). Intransitive verbs do not take a direct object, and are frequently concerned with movement (*to come, to go, to appear*). Some normally intransitive verbs are sometimes forced into becoming transitive; the verb *to smile*, for instance, is usually intransitive, but it is possible to say something like, *The leprechaun smiled a funny, mocking smile*, and in that sentence the verb has become transitive.

THE ADVERB
An adverb is a word which is attached to a verb, an adjective, a preposition or another adverb to indicate manner, degree, time or place. For example: *She smiled sadly. The monster was undoubtedly dead. He told her later. He parked close by Rupert's two-seater..*

Adverbs can consist of single words (*sadly, undoubtedly, later, close* in the above examples are all adverbs) or of phrases. For example: *She smiled in a sad way. The monster was without question dead. He told her at two o'clock. He parked with inches to spare by Rupert's two-seater.*

A special kind of adverb is the 'conjunctive adverb', used to link two sentences. These include words and phrases such as *however, on the other hand, especially, in conclusion.*

Many adverbs are formed by adding -ly or -ally to an adjective (*slowly, beautifully, prosaically*), but others, such as *hard, fast, late* and *early* (and their comparative forms, *harder, hardest*, etc.) do not change the adjectival form. *Deep* can be used either as an adjective or an adverb, but one can also add -ly to make the adverb *deeply*.

THE ADJECTIVE
An adjective is a descriptive word applied to a noun. Such words as *quick, brown, lazy, descriptive* are adjectives plain and simple.

Other forms are the possessive adjectives (*my, thy, his, her, its, our, your, their*), the demonstrative adjectives (*this, that, these, those*), the interrogative adjectives (*what, whose, which*) and the distributive adjectives (*some, all, any, many, no, several, both, much, each, either, neither, few, fewer, fewest, more, most, former, latter*). You will note that most of these words have already been listed under pronouns. If you say *His won the prize* or *Those were the alternatives* or *Few agreed* or *Either is acceptable* or *Such was the burden of his speech,* you are using *his, those, few, either* and *such* as pronouns; if you say *His essay won the prize* or *Those proposals were the alternatives* or *Few people agreed* or *Either solution is acceptable* or *Such nonsense was the burden of his speech,* you are using them as adjectives.

THE ARTICLE

The, a and *an* are articles, *the* being the definite article and *a* and *an* indefinite articles.

THE PREPOSITION

Prepositions are words such as *to, from, by, with, in, on,* which link a noun with another part of speech to indicate a relationship between them. Some combinations of prepositions have become single words, such as *upon* and *into,* but others remain separated even when used together – *on to* and *up to,* for example.

Prepositions are sometimes used in combination with verbs to form 'phrasal verbs', which have their own special meanings. For example: *break in, get on with, climb down.*

THE CONJUNCTION

Conjunctions are words which link two words, phrases, sentences or clauses. *And, but, either ... or* and *neither ... nor* are co-ordinating conjunctions since they join words or groups of words of equal importance. The subordinating conjunctions, *unless, as, since, because, if, provided, in order to* and many similar words and phrases are used only to join sentences or clauses of lesser importance to the main statement.

THE INTERJECTION

Interjections are words or short phrases, usually used only in dialogue, indicating an emotional reaction. For example: *Oh, Heavens above, Never, Well, Good Lord, My God* and such splendid old-fashioned expressions as *Pshaw, Ugh* or *'Zounds.* They often stand on their own, with an exclamation mark to emphasize them or a question mark to indicate a querying expression, but can also appear, less emphatically, as the introduction to a sentence or phrase – *Well, I did so. Oh, I don't think so. Good heavens, no.*

Sentence Structure

A basic sentence is made up of a subject and a predicate (which must include a verb). The subject is the person or thing which performs the action described in the predicate (or, in the passive voice, to whom or on whom the action is performed). The sentence can be as short as two words: we could, for instance, take the pronoun *she* as the subject and the verb *sang* as the predicate, and put them together to produce a complete sentence – *She sang.* Or we can write a much more lengthy sentence, such as the first one in this paragraph, in which *a basic sentence* is the subject, and all the rest is the predicate.

A more elaborate form is to join two sentences into one by the use of a conjunction. For example: *She sang, and the audience applauded.* Or: *A basic sentence is made up of a subject and a predicate, and the latter must always include a verb.*

In addition to the verb, a simple predicate may include a direct object (*She sang the song* – *the song* being the direct object), or an indirect object (*She sang to me* – *to me* being an indirect object), or both a direct and an indirect object (*She sang me the song* – *me* being the indirect object and the song the direct object), and an adverb (*She sang me the song softly* – *softly* being the adverb). Or the predicate may include a complement, the term given to words which follow verbs concerned with existence, such as *to be, to appear, to feel*, and with creation, such as *to make, to appoint*. In the sentences *She is angry* and *He made her angry, angry* is a complement.

CLAUSES
Sentences may also include clauses, in which case they become known as 'complex'. A clause is, in effect, a subordinate sentence, and always includes a verb. It can be adjectival or adverbial – *The cat, which had grown fat since I last saw it, or so it seemed, was sitting by the fire as I entered the room I remembered so well.* That sentence has a long and involved predicate containing five clauses: *which had grown fat* is adjectival, describing the cat; *since I last saw it* is adverbial, qualifying *grown fat*; *or so it seemed* is adverbial, linked to the previous clause by the subordinating conjunction *or*, and further qualifying *grown fat; as I entered the*

room is adverbial, indicating when the cat was sitting by the fire; *I remembered so well* (*which*, having been omitted at the beginning of the clause, is nevertheless to be understood) is adjectival, describing the room.

Clauses may be generally distinguished from phrases by the fact that they contain verbs, whereas phrases do not. In *The cat, old and fat, sat by the fire*, the words *old and fat* form an adjectival phrase, although it would turn into a clause if we inserted the understood words *which was*. Some groups of words which contain verbs may still be categorized as phrases – *so to speak*, for example.

Figures of Speech

Certain literary devices are known as 'figures of speech'. We frequently use them in everyday life, without necessarily realizing that we are doing so, and probably in ignorance of the names for them, many of which are unfamiliar and often derived from Greek or Latin. It is certainly not essential for any writer to know those names and to be able to say, 'Ah, that's *zeugma*,' or 'He's used *litotes*.' Nevertheless, in case you do want to use them, or are faced with a creative-writing tutor who talks about them to your bafflement, here is a list of the commoner figures of speech:

ALLEGORY
An allegory is a work which the reader is intended to understand as referring to persons or events other than those directly described. It has similarities with a parable. The author of an allegory usually desires to instruct or to criticize, and uses this device to add to the reader's entertainment and to point his moral more sharply. George Orwell's *Animal Farm* is an allegory which attacks the Stalinist form of Communism.

ALLITERATION
In alliteration two or more words beginning with the same letter are placed next to each other or so close that the similarity of sound is apparent, as in *Round and round the rugged rock the ragged rascal ran*. Alliteration was much used in Old and Middle English poetry.

ANTITHESIS
Antithesis is the setting against each other of contrasting words or ideas. *Two's company, three's a crowd. To lose one parent, Mr Worthing, may be regarded as a misfortune; to lose both looks like carelessness.*

APOSTROPHE

Apostrophe as a figure of speech (not to be confused with the punctuation mark) is seen when a writer or speaker breaks off from what he is saying or writing to address directly a person or thing. For example: *... and then the soldiers came – O God, have mercy on us! – and the looting and the raping and the killings began.* Or, *I loved the view from my bedroom window. O, you meadows and hills, have you now vanished beneath some soulless housing estate?*

BATHOS

Bathos is an anti-climax. Often used for humorous purposes, it usually consists of ending a list of some kind with a triviality, as in *The burglar got away with two thousand pounds in cash, several pieces of valuable jewellery and two packets of Corn Flakes.*

CLIMAX

The opposite of bathos, exemplified in a list in which the items are of ascending importance. *The evening began quietly, became rowdier and ended in a full-scale punch-up.*

EUPHEMISM

Euphemism is the use of a milder expression in place of something unpleasant or something which might appear indelicate. For example: *pass away* instead of *die, powder-room* in place of *lavatory, social disease* instead of *venereal disease.*

EUPHUISM

A name taken from *Euphues*, a book by John Lyly, and used to describe very elaborate, flowery language.

HYPALLAGE

In hypallage a description of one thing is transferred to another to which it does not really belong, as in *a cloudless moon* (it is the sky which is cloudless) or *He is always readable* (his writings are readable).

HYPERBOLE

Hyperbole is a deliberate exaggeration which is recognizable as such. *There are millions of reasons why I can't do it. She puts at least two pounds of grease on her face before she goes to bed. He's so fat that once round his waist is twice round the Albert Hall.*

IRONY

Irony is one of the most familiar figures of speech. It consists of the use of words to convey the very opposite of their natural meaning. *Charming!* we say ironically when someone has behaved outrageously towards us. *Of course, the Minister would never stoop to vote-catching*, says an opposition spokesman with heavy irony, when about to accuse the Minister of that and worse.

LITOTES

Litotes is an understatement. *You might call it slightly cold today* (when the temperature is well below freezing). It is often used with a negative, as in *He's not bad at maths* (meaning that he is pretty good at it).

MALAPROPISM

The absurd misuse of words. The word comes from Mrs Malaprop, a character in Sheridan's *The Rivals*, who was given to such phrases as *an allegory on the banks of the Nile* and *a nice derangement of epitaphs*. She meant, of course, *an alligator* and *arrangement of epithets*.

METAPHOR

In a metaphor the quality or appearance or properties of one thing are attributed to another with which the first has no direct similarity. Another way of explaining it might be to say that a metaphor expresses an idea which is not to be taken literally, but which, by association, paints a vivid picture of what is meant. If we say after a line of dialogue, *he thundered*, we do not mean that he brought about rumblings in the heavens, but that the sound of his voice was like thunder. A comparison is therefore made, but it is an indirect one. Many metaphors have become clichés, such as *a hive of industry* (the metaphor taken from bees) or *at death's door* (the metaphor representing Death as a house-owner).

METONYMY

Metonymy is the use of part of something, or something associated with it, to represent the thing itself. *He took to the bottle* (*the bottle* being substituted for *drinking*). *The way of the Cross* (*Cross* standing for *Christianity*).

ONOMATOPOEIA

The use of words which convey the sound of the object described. *Peewit* is an onomatopoeic name taken from the sound of the bird's call. *The ringing, clanging, jangling sound of the bells* is another example.

OXYMORON
In oxymoron two contrasting ideas are placed together for effect, as in *He said, with smiling despair, that he was never satisfied*, or *the painful pleasure of divorce*.

PARADOX
A statement which appears to be absurd, but which may contain a truth. For example: *Only in death is there life eternal*, or *If you want something done quickly, ask a busy person*.

PERSONIFICATION
Personification is the attribution of human qualities, feelings or actions to non-human objects. For example: *The tree lifts her leafy arms to pray*, or *The sun smiled down upon them*, or *Panic wrapped its icy fingers around her heart*.

PLEONASM
The use of unnecessary words to express an idea, as in *at this point in time* (meaning *now*). *As*, *as to*, and *of* are also often inserted without good reason, in phrases like *as yet, as to whether and inside of* – *yet*, *whether* and *inside* are all quite adequate by themselves. A pleonasm is often directly tautological (that is to say, it says the same thing twice in different words, as in *He ambled along, walking slowly*.

PUN
A pun is a play on words in which two different meanings suggest themselves. *His express wish was to come by fast train*. The poet Thomas Hood specialized in puns: *They went and told the sexton, and/The sexton toll'd the bell*.

SIMILE
A simile is a simple comparison, and almost always involves the use of either *as* or *like*. For example: *The ballet dancer seemed as light as thistledown. Like a diamond in the sky*. Many similes have become clichés: *As busy as a bee. He went like lightning. As good as gold*.

SYLLEPSIS
Syllepsis is a figure in which one word is used in two different

senses. *She took her leave and my umbrella*, or *He played the piano and the stock market*. See Zeugma below.

SYNECDOCHE
More or less the opposite of metonymy, synecdoche is the use of the whole to represent the part, as when we say, *The NUM threatened a strike*, when we mean, in fact, that the leaders of the NUM made the threat. Or *Australia won the Test Match*, meaning the Australian team.

ZEUGMA
Zeugma is often used as synonymous with syllepsis, that is to say, a device in which one word is used with two different meanings. Purists draw a distinction between the two figures, saying that in zeugma the word concerned is appropriate to only one of the objects concerned. For example: *Her eyes flashed and frowned her disapproval* (eyes can flash, but cannot frown).

4 Style

For some beginners style is a mystic word, signifying some mysterious quality which can only be achieved after years of practice. But every writer has a style as soon as he or she puts pen to paper, or taps out words on a typewriter or word processor. Style is simply the way you write. The question is, of course, whether you have what is called a good style. How do you decide whether or not your style is good? It may be a matter of personal taste, and it is difficult to make any more definite pronouncement than to say that it should be suitable for the work you want to do. In most cases, the less obtrusive the style, the better it is – if the reader is over-conscious of the way something is written, its style is probably getting in the way of the communication which the author wants to establish with that reader.

If you are fortunate, you will have a good natural style which is also flexible, changing according to the kind of writing you are engaged on. It will probably be unobtrusive, and the reader will be more interested in what you have to say than in the way you say it; he or she will not be distracted by poor syntax, or misused words, or clumsy constructions, or lack of clarity, and equally will not spend so much time admiring the 'beautiful' writing that the actual meaning becomes of secondary importance.

If you do not have this gift, there is no need for despair. It is quite possible to improve your style, provided that you are prepared to accept the idea that writing is a craft which needs to be learnt, practised and constantly looked at with an analytical and self-critical eye. The effort involved is really not over-demanding, and you should be spurred on by the knowledge that even those with an instinctive ability for expressing themselves will, if they are serious about writing, keep refining and polishing their style, trying to reach a higher standard. Only a genius can afford to rest on his or her laurels (and, in fact, few geniuses have ever been content to do so).

Let us look at some of the guidelines which you may find worth following.

Write As You Speak

The most common form of human communication is speech. Most of us can talk reasonably fluently, especially when we have something we want to tell other people about. The easiest way to write is to transcribe the words that you would use if you were telling the story or the facts orally, but, just as in a conversation you would try to avoid waffling on with a string of repetitions, hesitations and deviations, it is essential to work out in advance exactly what you want to say. If you know what you are aiming at, your spoken version will probably be direct and to the point; in other words, the style will be good. You may meet some problems. To begin with, our speech is often slovenly, filled with repetitions, unfinished sentences and other confusions. Moreover, when we speak, we frequently use the tone of our voice, pauses and variations in the speed, as well as the words themselves, to convey the desired meaning, and we add facial expressions and gestures to make it even clearer. If the person we are speaking to does not understand, he or she can ask questions, or demand additional information. The written word has to stand entirely on its own, and you will therefore have to make sure that you write down exactly what you mean to say, and that your reader is left in no doubt about how you intend the words to be read. You may be able to achieve the effect you want by the careful choice of your vocabulary, by the use of punctuation, and, where really necessary, by employing suitable adverbs.

On the other hand, although you must be aware of the dangers, you will almost certainly find that by writing as you speak you will have achieved that most desirable quality of simplicity.

Simplicity

Generally speaking, simple, straightforward writing is always best. Say what you want to say in direct terms, as briefly as possible, and you will achieve a far stronger effect than if you try to impress by using an inflated vocabulary and convoluted sentences. As a rule, short words of Anglo-Saxon origin are preferable to the long words which derive from Latin – so *chew*, for instance, should be more readily used than *masticate*, or *have* or *own* than *possess*. Of course, there are always exceptions to rules of this sort, and a longer, more formal-sounding word may sometimes be the right one, or indeed the only one, which will express exactly what you want to say. But always beware, unless you really know what you are doing, of using an outlandish word – the kind which is beyond a normal person's vocabulary – because it not only puzzles the reader, but draws attention to itself and away from the meaning of the passage in which it occurs. Simplicity is indeed a goal worth striving for.

Clarity

Make sure that you say what you mean to say. Take care with the words you use, and avoid malapropisms. Never allow ambiguities. If you are writing about two women, and use the pronoun 'she', you need to be certain that the reader will know which of the two women you are referring to. In the same way, ask yourself what the reader will understand if you write a sentence beginning: His report on the new regulation, which was highly controversial ... Is it the report or the new regulation which is controversial? Make it clear by rewriting. A couple of possibilities are: *His report, which was highly controversial, on the new regulation ...,* or *His report on the highly controversial new regulation ...* Make sure too that you have not created an ambiguity by placing a phrase in the wrong place, as in that celebrated advertisement, *For sale: large dog, will eat anything, fond of children.*

Similes and Metaphors, Adjectives and Adverbs

Poor writing is frequently overloaded with adjectives, metaphors and similes, which the author has included in an effort to achieve a richness of style. Such devices can help to provide an interesting texture in your prose, but they will not do so simply by being there in large numbers, or by any 'fancy' quality of their own; the richness comes when the writer has chosen them imaginatively and has used them only when they add essentially and effectively to the meaning; the more sparingly they appear, the more illuminating and powerful they will be.

Much the same can be said about adverbs. Mention has been made of the difficulty of conveying to the reader meanings which would be made obvious in speech by the tone of voice, and if you find yourself using a great many adverbs in an attempt to get such meanings across, see whether you can eliminate any of them, either because little doubt exists in fact about your intentions, or because it is possible to reword the sentence to clarify it.

In general, the more you restrict yourself to nouns and verbs, the more effective your writing is likely to seem.

Choosing Strong Words

We may call words weak or strong according to the sharpness of the images which they produce in our minds. Strong words conjure up pictures which are clear and well-defined, while those produced by weak words are fuzzy and indistinct. Taking nouns, for instance, those which may be called 'concrete', because they describe physical objects, such as *animal, tree, woman*, are much stronger than those we call 'abstract', which deal with concepts and emotions, such as *beauty, friendliness, cupidity*. The concrete nouns create definite pictures, but it is difficult to be sure exactly what constitutes *beauty, friendliness* or *cupidity*, especially in visual terms. If we then look at nouns with even more specific meanings we see that, for instance, *lion, oak* and *Mary* are all much stronger than *animal, tree* and *woman*, precisely because they produce more clearly defined images.

The same comments apply to many adjectives, adverbs, verbs, and indeed almost any word you can think of. Choose strong words when you can.

Avoid circumlocutions and hints in favour of definite descriptions – for instance, see how much stronger it is to say *It made him laugh*, rather than *He was greatly amused by it*, because, once again, the image is clearer.

Try not to use the passive voice of verbs, which usually results in a much more laboured and even pompous sound. *Mary Smith was presented with the prize by the mayor* sounds much more awkward than *The mayor presented the prize to Mary Smith* (although it must be admitted that in the latter instance the focus is less clearly on Mary Smith, which may not be the author's intention).

Clichés

We can barely open our mouths to speak without using a series of clichés, or hackneyed words and phrases. They come from many sources, including direct quotations or allusions to quotations, and similes and metaphors. Almost invariably, the words were striking when they were first used in that way, producing strong and splendid images, but they have been worn out by over-use. Too often we say or write a phrase such as *blissful ignorance* automatically – the words come naturally without a moment's thought. Or we describe a busy scene as *a hive of industry*, without bothering to see in our mind's eye the busyness of bees. These clichés have become weak, and their use makes an author sound tired and uncaring. You don't have to avoid them totally, but just make sure that if you do use clichés they are there because you can find no better way of saying what you mean.

Variety

Variety, if you will forgive a cliché after what I have just been saying, is the spice of life. It is also the spice of writing, and while all the points so far made in this chapter are, I believe, valid, a balance needs to be struck. If everything you write is 'strong', then the constant strength will somehow turn into weakness. You must have contrast and variety.

Repetitions

Occasionally, repetitions of words or phrases can be extremely effective, but it is a device to be used with the utmost care. The unintentional repetition usually sticks out like a sore thumb (another cliché) and is just as irritating to the reader. You must beware, on the other hand, of using too many alternatives in order to avoid repetition, which can be equally distracting. Many writers find it particularly necessary to substitute a whole series of words and phrases in place of, for instance, *John said* or *he said*. John (or he) becomes in quick succession *the former, the thickset man, the owner of the Jaguar, the financier, the proud husband*, and so on; while to avoid repeating *said*, the author comes up not only with *replied, answered, shouted* and the like, but also indulges in *gritted, gloomed, came the swift rejoinder* and similar absurdities, when the repetition of *John said* or *he said* would have been quite satisfactory.

Rhythm

One of the best bits of advice that any writer can be given is to read his or her work aloud, or, better still, have it read aloud to him or her, because the ear is so much better than the eye at picking up infelicities of phrasing, ambiguities and the like, and, especially, faulty rhythms. Any group of words has a rhythm, and it is something to which you must pay considerable attention if you want to improve your style. Beginners frequently produce a sequence of short sentences with the same construction, and therefore with jarring repetitive rhythms. Read the following passage aloud, and you will see what I mean:

> The man walked down the street, which was totally deserted. He paused by the jeweller's shop, glancing surreptitiously over his shoulder. The policeman stood on the opposite side of the road, and watched every movement. A sudden gust of wind swirled around the corner, snatching the man's hat away. It revealed the oddly dyed hair, so carefully concealed until then.

It would sound much better if rewritten to bring variety into the sentence lengths and their construction:

> The man walked down the totally deserted street, until he reached the jeweller's shop. There he glanced surreptitiously over his shoulder. The policemen stood on the opposite side of the street, watching every movement. A sudden gust of wind swirled round the corner, snatched off the man's hat and revealed the oddly dyed hair, which he had so carefully concealed until then.

Slang, Contractions, Dialect and Other Variations

Many would-be writers worry a great deal about the use of slang and of contractions such as *can't* or *wouldn't* or *I've*, feeling that informality is to be avoided at all costs. Well, yes, and again, no. It all depends on what effect you are trying to create, and on the sound or the rhythm of your sentences. In dialogue, informal contractions and slang are almost certainly not merely acceptable, but essential if you want to create a natural effect, though the usage will depend, at least to some extent, on the character of the person who is speaking. In straightforward narrative it is more usual to avoid slang and informality, but there is no rule against using them, and to do so occasionally may stop your work from sounding pompous. Let your ear be the judge.

Beware of using dialect or foreign words, or the jargon attached to a particular activity, such as a trade, unless you are sure that such words will be familiar to the average reader, or that their meaning is unmistakable from the context. To be presented with words which one does not understand is irritating, and the insertion of translations into the text, after the unfamiliar word, is as bad, if not worse.

Dialect can sometimes be validly presented in dialogue, but even then should be used sparingly. You can get as much effect from saying, *He spoke with a strong Cockney accent*, and then leaving your reader to supply the dropped aitches and strangulated vowels and glottal-stop t's, rather than splattering the text with apostrophes and attempting as Shaw did in *Pygmalion* to render the speech semi-phonetically – '*Wal, fewd dan y' de-ooty bawmz a mather should, eed now bettern to spawl a pore gel's flahrzn than ran awy athaht pyin.*'

Archaic words (*betimes, aught*, for example), vogue words (such as *parameters* or *yuppies*), poetic words (*ere* or *beauteous*) are best avoided unless they really belong to the period and the scene you are writing about, and even then best used with great discretion.

Tenses

Choose the appropriate tense for your writing. If you are producing a book similar to this one, you will probably use the present tense throughout, but although the present can be effectively used in fiction or biography or other forms, rather than the more usual past tense, you need to be a little wary of it, because in large doses it becomes rather obtrusive.

Do not mix the tenses in your narration. Stick to whichever tense you have chosen, at least for the main part, and if you change, for the sake of effect, keep the new tense going consistently and long enough for the reader to adjust to it and accept it. You might, for instance, wish to put an account of violent action in a thriller into the present tense for the sake of the immediacy it suggests, although the rest of the book is told in the past tense. But don't mix tenses within paragraphs.

The one exception to that rule is for flashbacks. Flashbacks often entail a great many pluperfect verbs – *He remembered the day he had first seen her. He had gone up to her, and had complimented her on her dress. She had smiled at him, and he had asked her to dine with him, and she had* ... Well, she had done this, and he had done that, and they had had a marvellous time, and all those 'hads' become very boring to read. It often works quite well in such cases simply to use the standard past imperfect: *He remembered the day he first saw her. He went up to her, and complimented her on her dress. She smiled at him, and he asked her to dine with him, and she* ... The introductory sentence in that example signals clearly enough that what follows is a flashback.

Grammatical Agreements

Try to make sure that everything you write is in agreement, in the grammatical sense. Verbs need to be singular or plural according to whether their subjects are singular or plural. The parts of speech in a list should be of the same kind – all nouns, or verbs, or adjectives. All sorts of words in a sentence need to agree with what has gone before – for instance, it is wrong to say *He played cricket, soccer, squash and swimming for his school*, because we do not 'play' swimming. It happens, by the way, to be a difficult sentence to get to sound right. If you say, *He played cricket, soccer and squash, and swam for his school*, it suggests that the only thing he did for the school was to swim. You could solve the problem by saying *For his school, he swam and played cricket, soccer and squash*, but the inversion (that is, putting *for his school* first in the sentence) makes it sound rather stilted, and you would probably have to end up by writing something much longer, such as *He played cricket, soccer and squash for his school, and also represented the school at swimming*. Perhaps a better solution would be *He was in the school teams for cricket, soccer, squash and swimming*. A problem such as that, incidentally, is a good example of the kind of difficulties which a writer often meets, the solution to which may take some time to find, and may involve several complete recastings of the sentence concerned before an acceptable version is found.

Keep Yourself Out of Your Writing

That may sound rather strange advice, especially since all writing must to some extent reflect its author. Obviously, you are in your work because the ideas and the words are yours, but, unless you are writing autobiographically, the reader should rarely be aware of you directly. This applies especially to fiction. You must not lecture your readers, and you must not explain to them things which are either obvious or better left for them to work out for themselves. You must not tell them that what follows is fascinating, or hilarious, or frightening, or anything like that – let them make up their own minds on such matters. Don't use exclamation marks (except perhaps in dialogue), because by doing so, you, the author, are saying to the reader, 'Isn't this funny ha-ha (or funny-peculiar, or whatever)?' If you are trying to write humorous material, don't be over-breezy, or lay on the irony too thickly – the best jokes are told in ordinary words which do not seek to be funny in themselves. The careful choice of words can be very important in creating atmosphere and effect, but the point is that the reader should never be aware that the author is trying to force the atmosphere and effect down his or her throat.

Revision

Unless you are a genius, your style will almost certainly be capable of improvement at the stage of revision. You should take endless pains over your revision – and it is something to be done not merely once, but as often as necessary to bring your work as near to perfection as you can. Look at every word you have written and ask yourself whether it is performing its intended and useful function, and whether it is the best possible word that you can put in that context. Check that you have written with clarity and simplicity, and with variety. Look out for and cut or alter unnecessary words, habit words (such as *of course, in fact, actually* – and I would add *you know*, if that boring, overworked phrase were not almost totally confined to the spoken word), repetitions (whether of individual words or of rhythms), and anything else which does not advance your story or your theme. Cut and cut and cut – the sparer your prose, the more sparkle it is likely to have.

Variations in Style

On the first page of this chapter I mentioned the need for flexibility in your style. The way you write must be influenced by the market for which you are aiming. While simplicity is always to be desired, however high the IQs of your potential readers may be and however complex your theme, there are degrees of simplicity. If writing a serious book for an adult market, or an article for such a paper as *The Times* you can use polysyllabic words and sentences with dependent clauses. On the other hand, if you are writing for small children, your style and vocabulary will probably be very basic (and far less demanding nowadays, incidentally, than those used by such writers as Beatrix Potter), and if your market is the tabloid press you will use short words, short sentences and short paragraphs.

Special Effects

The comments and suggestions made so far in this chapter are not rules, or if they are, they are rules which can be broken. If you know what you are doing, if you have an instinctive feeling for the use of words, you can break any number of rules. You can write a series of short staccato sentences or phrases without a verb in sight, or you can produce sentences of great complexity, which seem to go on for ever; you can write with a highly charged vocabulary or in dull and measured tones. If you have that special ability, your work can still be held up as an example of good and effective style.

Here is the first paragraph of *Judith*, a novel by that excellent Irish writer, Brian Cleeve:

> She stood listening. The wind battering at the house, the timbers creaking, cold whispers of air like the wind's spies, in the corridors, down chimneys, making the flame of her candle bend and darken, running the shadows on the kitchen floor, and cupboards. Her heart beating as she tried to listen, not to the huge buffets of the wind, the howling of it against roof and walls, the banging of loose shutters, the groaning of one of the great doors in the stable yard; not listening to any of those sounds, but trying to hear beyond them, under them, as if in such a gale she could hear their hoofbeats, men's footsteps, whispering.

It is basically a quite simple passage, but you could hardly say that the style is unobtrusive. Many of the sentences do not have proper verbs, and seem to be made up of lists. The whole paragraph is breathless, and possibly confusing, and yet the words have a very clear sense of having been chosen to present a series of the strongest possible images. The important thing is that it works. It is atmospheric and exciting, and it fulfils that essential purpose of an opening paragraph of making most readers want to know more.

Or take just half of the opening paragraph of *The Turn of the Screw* by Henry James:

> The story had held us, round the fire, sufficiently breathless, but except the obvious remark that it was gruesome, as, on Christmas eve in an old house, a strange tale should essentially be, I remember no comment till someone happened to say that it was the only case he had met in which such a visitation had fallen on a child. The case, I may mention, was that of an apparition in just such an old house as had gathered us for the occasion – an appearance of a dreadful kind, to a little boy sleeping in the room with his mother and waking her up in the terror of it; waking her not to dissipate his dread and soothe him to sleep again, but to encounter also, herself, before she had succeeded in doing so, the same sight that had shaken him.

It is hardly simple, with all those clauses and phrases enclosed in their pairs of commas; the language lacks excitement, and indeed has a certain heaviness; and the passage could be cut – oh, surely it could be cut! – to great effect. And yet to cut it would be to diminish its strength. Its structure is complex and its vocabulary is occasionally ponderous not merely because the novella was written nearly a hundred years ago, but because the author was intentionally creating an atmosphere of menace. Henry James is notorious for the convoluted quality of his prose, but he could also write extremely directly when he wanted to, and in this case the flat, deliberate approach is a preparation for the horror which is to follow, and a splendid example of an author not forcing his effects down his reader's throat by the use of emotive words.

In contrast to the two foregoing passages, here is a genuine extract from a letter received from a would-be author. The punctuation and spelling are both shown exactly as in the original.

> Notwithstanding after many Moons of tenacious struggle I finish what I consider to be a masterpiece,and yet not a single Publisher seems interested enough to as much as going beyond a brief synopsis,which does not reveal the unique novels true merits..A novel which I feel is abundant in literary merit-and with commercial possibilities -action, drama and

it's share of suspense,and what is more told in a true beleivabi-
lity style.

Perhaps the author is a foreigner (which is the only reasonable
explanation for such a strange jumble of words and the hopeless
punctuation). The reader of this book may like to try his or her
hand at amending the passage. In the meantime, I can only say that
if the synopsis of the 'masterpiece' was all in that style, it is hardly
surprising that no publisher was interested in reading more.

Some Do's and Don't's

AND/BUT
Teachers used to say that to begin a sentence with *and* or *but* was
unacceptable, and to use either of those little words at the very
beginning of a paragraph was considered even more deplorable.
While there is no reason at all why you should not defy the teachers
in this respect, you should be aware that you are placing an extra
emphasis on the *and* or the *but*, and probably also on the sentence
or paragraph which follows, if you do so.

AT THIS POINT IN TIME/IN THIS DAY AND AGE
Please, please say or write 'now' instead of these ugly, tautological
clichés.

DIFFERENT
For many years it has been argued that you must use 'from' after
'different', rather than 'to'. The justification for 'from' rests on the
fact that we say that something 'differs *from*' something, but recent
editions of Fowler's *Modern English Usage* say firmly that
'different *to*' is justifiable. In any case, 'to' is so frequently used that
many of us who still automatically say or write 'different *from*', do
so more out of habit than because we believe it is the only correct
form. What about 'different *than*', widely used in American
English? 'From' or 'to' is usually to be preferred, but 'than' is neater
in a construction such as *It is different than I thought it was*, when
otherwise we would have to say, *It is different from (or to) what I
thought it was*, or … *the way I thought it was*.

DOUBT
You do not need to add 'but' when you use 'doubt' as a verb. For
example: *I do not doubt that he will come*, not *I do not doubt but
that he will come*.

EACH AND EVERY ONE
This is another popular expression which contains unnecessary words. 'Each' is quite capable of conveying the meaning on its own, and so is 'every one'. You don't need both.

'FOUR-LETTER' WORDS
In a period when freedom of expression is widely accepted, there is no reason why you should not use the so-called four-letter words if you wish. It is worth remembering, however, that they still retain some shock value, and if you want to use them in that way, then it works only if they are used sparingly. In other words, one four-letter word can be shocking; many four-letter words are usually boring. You should also bear in mind the audience at whom your work is aimed – don't expect to sell a story larded with the more offensive swear-words to the typical women's magazine.

HE OR SHE
An author writing in general terms in the past could use 'he' and 'him', and the other masculine pronouns to cover both sexes. Feminism, with some justification, objected, and it is now necessary to say 'he or she' (and I suppose one should really vary it occasionally and put 'she or he'), 'him or her', and so on. It is a great pity that there is no easy way round this, for the 'he or she' construction is undeniably clumsy. One solution is to use plurals: if you say 'readers', for example, instead of 'the reader', you can then put something like *what readers want is something that they can understand,* rather than the awkward *something that he or she can understand* which would have to follow 'the reader'. However, to use the plural is not always the perfect answer.

Feminism has also been responsible for turning 'chairman' into 'chairperson' (which to many people has a faintly absurd sound) or 'chair' (which some find difficult to understand as anything but an inanimate object). Oh, dear. At least I do not find 'chairperson' and 'chair' quite so distressing as the 'ploughperson's lunch' which I have seen on some pub menus.

HELP
The use of 'but' in such a sentence as *I could not help but see what happened* is to be avoided. *I could not help seeing what happened* is simpler and better.

IF AND WHEN
Yet another example of unnecessary words. One or other will always do the job for you.

LITERALLY

The trouble with 'literally' is that we use it as an emphasis word, without stopping to think what we are saying. *It was literally raining cats and dogs*, we might say. Well, I doubt it. 'Literally' means that we should take what follows as being factually true, when we would normally look upon 'raining cats and dogs' as the sort of colourful and well-known idiom which is not to be taken at face value. If you write, *It was raining cats and dogs*, we know that it was really bucketing down; but if you say, *It was literally raining cats and dogs*, then you can only mean that cats and dogs were actually falling out of the sky, like rain. It is probably best to avoid using 'literally' as much as you can, and if you do use it, make sure that you mean it – literally.

This is perhaps an appropriate place to mention words like 'terribly' and 'awfully', which we also use, at least in speech, as emphasis words. If you say, *It is terribly cold today*, we know that you don't really mean that it is so cold as to terrify us, and if you tell us, *It's awfully funny*, you don't expect us to believe that you have been overcome by awe at the humour of whatever it was. By all means include such usages in dialogue if it seems natural to do so, but you should be aware that you are debasing the words if you use them elsewhere simply as an emphatic substitute for 'very' or 'extremely'.

NICE

Many people were taught as young children to avoid the word 'nice', meaning 'pleasant, agreeable', because, they were told, it is an over-used word, and weak into the bargain. Both accusations are valid, but there are many times when it is a useful word, and its very weakness can be a strength. It also has a number of other definitions, most of which are archaic, but it can still be used validly to mean 'precise', as in *a nice distinction*.

NONE

'None' is a singular word, a contraction of 'no one', in fact. Since it is so often followed by a plural – *none of them, none of the players* – there is a temptation to use a plural verb. The temptation should be resisted. For example: *None of them wants to come. None of the players is over twenty-five.* It has to be admitted, however, that many people will regard my insistence on a singular verb after 'none' as yet another piece of pedantic advice to be found in this book. The trouble is, of course, that one man's precision is another man's pedantry.

ONE

If you use 'one' as a pronoun (an indefinite pronoun), as in *One is aware of what is going on*, you must be careful not to follow it with a personal pronoun in any of their versions. So you must not say, *One is aware of himself*, but *One is aware of oneself*. (See also *They* below.)

ONLY

The pedantic insist that 'only' must be placed next to the word that it qualifies. *I only like milk chocolate*, they say, probably means that you like it, but you don't love it (because the 'only' is attached to the 'like'), and that if the sentence is to be given the meaning which the speaker probably intended, it has to be rearranged to *I like only milk chocolate* or *I like milk chocolate only*. The only thing you need to worry about is whether the sense is clear. In most cases it will be, because we are so used in ordinary speech to putting 'only' where it sounds right rather than where, perhaps, it ought to be. Just be careful with a sentence like *I only laughed*. Does that mean that you didn't do anything more than laugh, or that you were the only person to laugh? Probably the former, but it could mean the latter, and if that was your intention, you really ought to rephrase it to avoid any ambiguity.

PERSONALLY

'Personally' is often used unnecessarily in such sentences as *Personally, I am against it*. It may be argued that if the order of the words is changed to *I, personally, am against it*, an additional emphasis is added, but this is legitimate only if you are, for instance, contrasting a personal view with an official one, as in *I, personally, am against it, but in my capacity as a delegate to this meeting I have to vote in accordance with my members' views, and so have to say that I am in favour.*

PREPOSITIONS AT THE ENDS OF SENTENCES

There used to be a rule that prepositions should not be used at the end of sentences or clauses, but Winston Churchill pointed out the absurdity of rigid adherence to that convention in his ironic example, *up with which I will not put*. However, his mockery was a little unfair, since *to put up with* is a rather special case; like *jump at*, *stand for* and *face up to*, for example, it is a phrasal verb, and to separate the preposition from the verb sounds quite ridiculous, especially when, as in 'up with', two prepositions are involved. When a phrasal verb is not concerned, it may be better to avoid placing the preposition at the end of a sentence or clause. *It was her sister to whom he was particularly attracted* is probably preferable to *It was her sister he was particularly attracted to* and *The cupboard, in which he had stored the food, was bare* is smoother in sound than *The cupboard he had stored the food in was bare.* In dialogue the rule should be to use whatever construction sounds most natural for the character concerned.

SPLIT INFINITIVES
Grammarians have been teaching for years that it is wrong to split an infinitive verb ('to' and the verb itself, as in 'to make', 'to run', 'to sing') by the insertion of an adverb, and have shuddered, for instance. at the phrase used in the introduction to the television series "Star Trek", *to boldly go where no man has gone*, which they would prefer to hear as *to go boldly where no man has gone.* By convention, infinitives should never be split, but it has to be admitted that there are occasions when adherence to the rule results in a clumsiness or an ambiguity which could be avoided by breaking it. Fowler's *Modern English Usage* gives two examples which it says (even if a little doubtfully) are acceptable: *to further cement trade relations* (if you say *to cement further trade relations* it is unclear whether the word 'further' belongs to 'cement' or to 'trade relations'), and *to better equip successful candidates for careers in India* (in which 'better' cannot easily be moved to another position without making the phrase sound awkward). In most cases, however, the rule is still valid, and you should try not to split your infinitives, even though you may be right to believe that common usage will eventually force us 'to readily accept' the practice.

THEY
'They' should not be used after words like 'each', 'anyone', 'everybody', which may sound as though they are plurals, but are, in effect, singulars. So you should not say, *Everyone knows that they must obey the rules*, but *Everyone knows that he or she must obey the rules.* The 'he or she' in that sentence sounds very clumsy, and although William Strunk, jun. and E.B. White in their excellent book *The Elements of Style* advise you to use 'he' in all such cases, that will not please the feminists. The only answer is to avoid the construction if you can (*Everyone knows that the rules must be obeyed*), or to argue that common usage makes 'they' acceptable.

UNIQUE

'Unique' is what is known as an 'absolute' word. It means 'the only one of its kind,' and therefore cannot be qualified. If you say that something is 'more unique' than something else, you are saying that both are unique, although their degree may differ; but that is nonsense. 'Almost unique' is acceptable, but 'very unique' and 'most unique' are not. 'Quite unique' is equally liable to condemnation, although it can be argued that in this case 'quite' is an emphasizer (like 'indeed'), rather than a qualifier. Like 'unique', 'perfect' is also an absolute word, and should never be qualified.

5   The Right Words

English is a hybrid language. It has grown principally out of Anglo-Saxon, Latin and Norman French, giving it roots in both the Germanic and Romance languages, and it has also adopted many words of Celtic origin, together with others from a number of different sources, including Greece, many parts of the Commonwealth and, more recently, the United States. There has never been, as in France, any attempt to keep the language 'pure', and the result has been a richness which no other language can equal. We have a wide vocabulary, with a large number of alternatives at our disposal for almost any idea we wish to express.

Moreover, except for 's to indicate possession and, more often than not, s for plurals, we have done away with the majority of inflexions (the endings to words which show whether they are nominative, accusative, genitive or dative, singular or plural), we have adopted a singularly simple form of grammar, and we allow ourselves the flexibility of using nouns as verbs and verbs as nouns. Despite its unparalleled virtues, English also has its drawbacks – it has quite extraordinary pronunciations which often bear no relation to the spelling, and almost all the rules we have, for such matters as the formation of plurals, the declension of verbs, and, indeed, spelling, are full of exceptions. All in all, English is a complex language.

It is also, of course, a living language – or, as a friend of mine prefers to call it, a 'growing' language – and is subject to change. This means not only that we adopt new words to fit modern technology, but that old words change their meanings or become confused with each other. These alterations often have to be accepted. We may regret that we can rarely if ever use 'gay' nowadays to mean 'light-hearted' or 'merry', since it has become a common term for 'homosexual', but there is nothing that can be done about it – the English language has 'grown' to accept the new meaning.

The richness, the complexity and changing usages place a burden on the writer to choose words as carefully and accurately as possible. Growth can be accepted, and indeed welcomed, but not when it leads to a weakening rather than a strengthening of the language. There are many words which are losing their precision or are simply wrongly used, often through confusion with a similar-sounding word. We can and should do something about this – a loss of precision in a language is always to be regretted, and while it may be funny to give words their wrong meanings when Mrs Malaprop says them, for writers it is a sin.

If you are at all uncertain of the meaning of a word, look it up in a dictionary (or check it in the list below). You may also find it surprisingly useful to see what Fowler's *Modern English Usage* has to say. 'Fowler', as amended by Sir Ernest Gowers, is a fascinating book; it will not only offer guidance on such matters as split infinitives and which preposition should follow the word 'different', but if you look up 'jocose', for example, it will distinguish between a host of words with very similar meanings – 'arch', 'facetious', 'flippant', 'jesting', 'jocose', 'jocular', 'merry' and 'waggish'; it is also an amusing book – see, for instance, what it says about the pronunciation of 'margarine'.

Some of the Most Frequently Confused or Misused Pairs of Words

A/AN
Do you use 'a' or 'an' before a word beginning with h? Although *an hotel* is frequently seen, in fact the only words beginning with h where 'an' is needed are those in which the h is silent, such as 'heir' and 'hour'.

ACCEPT/EXCEPT
I would not have expected confusion between these two words – to 'accept' is to 'receive' or 'agree to', and 'except', as a verb, means 'leave out'. However, I recently saw a form for a local club which said, *When excepted for membership, your subscription will become due*, and I don't think they really meant that.

ACUTE/CHRONIC
When these two words are used in connection with illness, 'acute' means 'sharp', or 'sudden', and often 'dangerous' – *He has acute appendicitis* – while 'chronic' refers to a lasting or continuing condition – *She suffers from chronic indigestion*.

AFFECT/EFFECT

'Affect' is a verb, and means, in its most common usage, 'to have an effect upon', or 'to alter' or 'to change' in some way. For example: *The closing of the road will affect many people.* Or, *He was badly affected by the disease.* 'Affect' also has other meanings, including 'to assume ostentatiously' (*He affects the manners of an aristocrat*), but these uses are less likely to be confused with 'effect'. 'Affect' can also be a noun, referring to a mental state, but this is a comparatively rare medical usage. 'Effect' is usually a noun, meaning 'result', but can also be used as a verb, when it means 'to carry out'. For example: *The effect of the road closure will be disastrous. The closure of the road will be effected on Monday.*

ALLUDE/ELUDE

'Elude' means 'escape from (a pursuer)', whereas 'allude' means 'refer to indirectly' (see *Allusion* below).

ALLUSION/ILLUSION

'Allusion' is widely used to mean a direct reference to someone or something, but strictly speaking should be an indirect reference in which the person or object alluded to is not named. For example: *He said that Britain had similar troubles, and although he did not mention Northern Ireland, the allusion to the troubles there was clear.* 'Illusion' means something false or deceptive. For example: *The belief that all writers can spell correctly is an illusion.*

ALTERNATELY/ALTERNATIVELY

'Alternately' means 'in turn' or 'one after the other'. For example: *He hit him with his right and left hands alternately.* 'Alternatively' suggests a choice. For example: *You can go to London by private car; alternatively, you can use public transport.*

AMEND/EMEND

Both these words mean 'alter', but 'emend' is specifically concerned with the correction of errors.

ANTICIPATE/EXPECT

These two words can be used synonymously, but 'anticipate' has the additional meaning of 'act in advance', and may therefore be ambiguous. For example: *She anticipated the outcome* could mean that she expected it, or that she took some action before it was known.

ANXIOUS/EAGER

'Anxious' is widely used when 'eager' would be preferable. *I am anxious to see you*, we say, but really mean that we are eager to do so. 'Anxious' should only be used when you wish to imply anxiety (and one is usually anxious *about* something). You could perhaps say, *I am anxious to see my dentist.* Even that, however, would probably be better phrased as *I am eager to see my dentist, but anxious about what he will do to me.*

APPRAISE/APPRISE

'Appraise' means 'judge', whereas 'apprise' means 'notify' or 'make aware of'. It is therefore wrong to say, *She appraised me of the situation, which she had apprised.* Tell her to go away and appraise the situation, and then come back to apprise you of it.

AS/LIKE

There is a rule for deciding when you should use 'as' or 'as if' and when you should use 'like'; 'like', it says, is never followed by a verb, whereas 'as' or 'as if' must be. So it is correct to say, *Fiona writes like a professional*, but wrong to say, *Fiona writes like she had studied with a professional.* However, there are some occasions when common usage allows 'like' before a verb, especially if the 'like' comes after 'feel' or 'feeling' – *I feel like abandoning the attempt to clarify this problem.* To overcome the difficulty, try substituting 'as' or 'as if' for 'like'. If the sentence still makes the same sense, you should probably not be using 'like'. If in those two sentences above you substitute 'as' or 'as if', you will get: *Fiona writes as a professional*, and *Fiona writes as if she had studied with a professional.* In the first of these, the sense has been changed so that the sentence now means that Fiona is, in fact, a professional writer, and you will need to return to 'like' to preserve the idea that she is not a professional, but writes with a pro's ability. In the second sentence, on the other hand, the original meaning is retained, and you will probably be well advised to leave the substitution in place.

AURAL/ORAL

'Aural' is to do with the ear and hearing, and 'oral' with the mouth and, especially, speech.

BALMY/BARMY

Both these words can mean 'fragrant', as when describing the pleasant air of a warm evening, but it is preferable to use 'balmy' in that context. Equally, both can mean 'soft in the head', but, in that sense, 'barmy' is more usual.

BERTH/BIRTH
'Berth' means 'the place where a ship lies' or 'position' or 'sleeping-place'. 'Birth' is, of course, to do with being born.

BORN/BORNE
These are both past participles of the verb 'to bear'. 'Born' is used exclusively intransitively (i.e. does not take a direct object) in the case of birth – *I was born in March*. But when the verb is used transitively, the correct form is borne – *She has borne several children*. 'Borne' is also used in reference to putting up with something or carrying a burden.

BROACH/BROOCH
'Broach' means 'introduce', when first talking about a subject. 'Brooch' is an ornament worn on the dress.

BUSINESS/BUSYNESS
'Business' means 'occupation, work, a commercial concern', whereas 'busyness' is the act of being busy.

CALLOUS/CALLUS
A 'callus' is usually a patch of hardened skin. For example: *The constant digging had left calluses on his hands*. 'Callous' can also be used as an adjective to describe such patches, but is more often given the meaning of 'insensitive'. For example: *His attitude towards her suffering can only be described as callous*.

CAN/MAY
It is when they are used in questions that these two words are often confused, 'can' frequently taking the place of the correct 'may'. *Can I do something?* means *Am I able to do it?*, whereas *May I do something?* means *Am I allowed to do it?* Many readers will have discovered the difference while in school: *Can I leave the room, sir, please, sir?* And the teacher replied (at least, some of mine did), *You certainly can. The question is whether you may!*

CENSER/CENSOR/CENSURE
A 'censer' is the utensil in which incense is burnt, while a 'censor' is a noun meaning someone who inspects documents, films, etc. in a search for offensive material, or a verb indicating the removal of

such material. 'Censure' is similarly both a noun meaning 'blame, criticism', and a verb meaning 'to blame, to criticise'.

CHRONIC/ACUTE (see ACUTE)

COMMON/MUTUAL
These words both have to do with sharing. 'Mutual' is, strictly speaking, a sharing which refers to something which two (or more) people feel about each other. For example: *My wife and I have a deep mutual affection*. For anything else which two or more people share, but which is outside or apart from themselves, the proper adjective is 'common'. Therefore, *We share a common birthday*. The trouble, of course, is that 'common' has another, and unpleasant, meaning. That, presumably is why Charles Dickens called one of his novels *Our Mutual Friend*, when he really meant either *Our Common Friend* (which sounds as if the friend were vulgar) or *The Friend We Have in Common* (which is clumsy). In any case, *a mutual friend* is such a commonplace usage that we all know what is meant, even if it is not strictly correct.

COMPARED TO/COMPARED WITH
'Compared to' should be used in pointing out similarities between the things compared, and 'compared with' in pointing out their differences.

COMPLACENT/COMPLAISANT
These two words are very similar in meaning, and can both be used in the sense of 'obliging', but 'complacent' has the primary sense of 'self-satisfied', while 'complaisant' is often used, for instance, to describe a husband who does not object to his wife having a lover.

COMPLEMENT/COMPLIMENT
'Complement', as a noun, means something complete. For example: *The complement of a team in 'University Challenge' is four students*. As a verb, 'complement' means 'make complete or perfect'. For example: *The team was complemented by the addition of Joe Bloggs*. A 'compliment', on the other hand, is what someone pays you when they praise you. The word can also be used as a verb. For example: *He complimented her on her appearance*.

CONFIDANT/CONFIDENT
A 'confidant' (with a final e if female) is someone in whom someone else confides. 'Confident' is an adjective meaning 'sure'.

CONTINUAL/CONTINUOUS
These two words are so close in meaning as to be frequently confused. 'Continual' means 'very frequent', while 'continuous' means 'without a break'.

COUNCIL/COUNSEL
A 'council' is an assembly, as in *the town council*. 'Counsel', on the other hand is used as a noun to mean 'advice' or 'someone who advises', and as a verb to mean 'give advice to'.

CROCHET/CROTCHET
'Crochet' is a kind of needlework. A 'crotchet' is a hooked instrument or a short musical note, and from it we get the word 'crotchety'.

CROTCH/CRUTCH
All too often 'crutch' is used where 'crotch' is meant. A 'crotch' is a fork, and 'the crotch' usually means 'the fork of the body'. A 'crutch', on the other hand, is some kind of support, such as the implements that people use when they have damaged a leg. If you say, *He kicked him in the crutch*, it is unlikely to have hurt him very much, since the crutch was probably made of wood or metal. A kick in the crotch would be much more painful.

DEFINITE/DEFINITIVE
'Definite' means 'certain' or 'fixed'. It can also mean 'final', which is confusing, since the element which is always present in 'definitive' is finality – *a definitive book*, for instance, is one which covers its subject once and for all.

DEPENDANT/DEPENDENT
These words are interchangeable, but 'dependant' is usually used as a noun, referring to someone – a child, for instance – who is maintained by someone else, and 'dependent' is the favoured form for the adjective. You could say, for example: *His dependants are dependent on him.*

DEPRECATE/DEPRECIATE
The prime meaning of 'deprecate' is 'to pray against (something which is wrong or evil)', but it is more often used nowadays in the sense of 'disapprove of'. 'Depreciate' means 'to reduce or fall in value'.

DERISIVE/DERISORY

The difference between these two words is a subtle one. 'Derisive' is something which *shows* derision or mockery, whereas 'derisory' is applied to something which *deserves* derision or mockery.

DESERT/DESSERT

'Desert' is a noun meaning 'wasteland' or a verb meaning 'abandon'. 'Dessert' is fruit or a sweet served as the last course of a meal.

DISCREET/DISCRETE

The word which we usually want is 'discreet', meaning 'capable of keeping one's own counsel'. 'Discrete' is a comparative rarity, and means 'separate, distinct'.

DISINTERESTED/UNINTERESTED

'Disinterested' means 'impartial, without bias', while 'uninterested' means that the subject has no appeal to the person concerned. For example: *The referee for the League Cup is fair because he is a disinterested party; on the other hand, John does not care who wins, because he is uninterested in football.*

DUE TO/OWING TO

These two phrases are almost interchangeable. Use 'owing to' when you could equally well say 'because of', and 'due to' when you could replace it with 'as a result of'.

EAGER/ANXIOUS (see ANXIOUS)

EERIE/EYRIE

'Eerie' is an adjective which means 'strange and frightening', whereas 'eyrie' is the nest of a bird of prey.

EFFECT/AFFECT (see AFFECT)

ELUDE/ALLUDE (see ALLUDE)

EMEND/AMEND (see AMEND)

EMINENT/IMMINENT

'Eminent' means 'distinguished', while something which is 'imminent' is about to happen.

EXCEPT/ACCEPT (see ACCEPT)

EXCEPTIONABLE/EXCEPTIONAL
Something which is 'exceptionable' is something to which exception can be taken, something disliked. 'Exceptional' means 'out of the ordinary'.

EXPECT/ANTICIPATE (see ANTICIPATE)

FARTHER/FURTHER
'Farther' is the comparative form of 'far', and therefore refers to a matter of distance, whereas 'further' means 'additional'. It is wrong to say, for instance, *John went further than Mary* – he went farther than Mary – but correct to say, *John continued for a further three miles after Mary had stopped.* However, 'further' is nowadays so widely used when 'farther' would be more correct that only those who really care about the precision of the language will notice if you get it wrong.

FLAMMABLE/INFLAMMABLE
These two words mean exactly the same thing, 'capable of burning'. But because the 'in-' part of 'inflammable' sounds like a negative, 'flammable' is gaining some ground in manufacturers' warnings about the goods they produce, so that nobody shall be in doubt that something so labelled is not fire-resistant. 'Inflammable' is still, however, the preferred term in other contexts.

FLAUNT/FLOUT
'Flaunt' means 'display in an ostentatious way', but is sometimes mistakenly used nowadays where 'flout' is intended, with the meaning of 'disobey'. It is correct to say, *He flaunted his punk hairstyle,* but wrong to say, *He flaunted the law of the land* (when you mean that he disobeyed it). In any case, 'flout' is not simply a synonym for 'disobey'. It implies mockery, and means, when it is correctly used, 'act with contempt for', which is subtly, and importantly, different from 'disobey'.

FOREGO/FORGO
The verb 'forego' is used comparatively rarely, except in the forms 'foregoing' and 'foregone' – *the foregoing conditions* or *a foregone conclusion* – referring to something which has gone before, or has been said or written previously, or has been predetermined. 'Forgo' means 'do without'.

FOREWORD/FORWARD

'Foreword' is another term for an introduction or preface in a book. It is not spelt 'forward', which, whether used as an adverb, an adjective, a noun or a verb, has to do with being in front or in advance or going farther. You might think that a 'foreword', since it goes in the front of a book could be spelt 'forward'; it does, but it can't be.

FORMALLY/FORMERLY

'Formally' means 'in a formal manner', whereas 'formerly' refers to a former period, and can often be replaced by 'previously'.

GOURMAND/GOURMET

You will greatly offend a 'gourmet', who is a connoisseur of food and drink, if you call him a 'gourmand', for you will be saying that he is a glutton.

GRISLY/GRIZZLY

'Grisly' is an adjective for which we might substitute 'spine-chilling'. 'Grizzly' means 'grey-haired'.

HANGED/HUNG

'Hung' and 'hanged' are both past participles of the verb 'to hang'. 'Hung' is always used, except when you are referring to execution by hanging. So you say *The gold medal was hung around her neck,* or *The picture was hung in the Royal Academy,* but *The man was hanged.*

HOARD/HORDE

If you 'hoard' something, you collect it or store it, often secretly, or hide it, and what you have collected or stored is your 'hoard'. 'Horde' means 'crowd', and usually suggests that those who make up the crowd are unruly.

I/ME

The problem with 'I' and 'me' comes when they are used with other pronouns and linked by 'and'. People often say, *You and me will be there,* when the correct form should be, *You and I will be there.* And others, because they are aware that, in the first of those sentences, 'you and me' is wrong, then persist in saying or writing 'you and I' on every occasion, as in *He will talk to you and I tomorrow.* 'I' is the nominative case of a personal pronoun (and so are 'thou', 'he', 'she', 'we' and 'they'), and is used as the subject of a sentence. 'Me' is in the accusative or the dative case (and so are 'thee', 'him', 'her', 'us' and 'them') and is used as the direct or indirect object of a sentence. ('You' and 'it' can be nominative, accusative or dative, so no confusion arises with their use.) Therefore, in these combinations, 'I' is used when the combination is the subject of the sentence, and 'me' when it is the direct or indirect object. For example: *He said that you and I should go*, but *He told you and me to go*, and *He gave the order to go to you and me*. You can usually tell whether you have got it right by dropping the 'you and' part of the sentence. You would not say, *He said that me should go*, nor *He told I to go*, nor *He gave the order to go to I*. You can use the same test if the pronouns concerned are any of those which have different forms in the nominative or the accusative.

Some people try to avoid the whole problem by using 'myself'. *My wife and myself are going to the theatre. You are coming to the theatre with my wife and myself.* Well, it's one way out, but you can tell just how silly it really is by dropping 'my wife' from those sentences. It would be much more natural to say, *You are coming to the theatre with me*, and you would surely never perpetrate such a line as *Myself is going to the theatre*. An additional difficulty comes in the answer to such a question as *Who's that? It's only me*, we reply, although we should, of course, say, *It's only I*. It has to be admitted, however, that in ordinary speech (and therefore in written dialogue) the correct form often sounds pedantic.

It has been suggested, incidentally, that the best way of getting 'I' and 'me' right is to follow the rule: use 'me' whenever you think you shouldn't, and use 'I' whenever you know you should.

Yet another difficulty arises with the question of whether you should use 'we' or 'us' in such phrases as 'we women' or 'we voters'. You would probably not say, *He told we voters to consider the matter carefully*, (it should be 'us voters', because in this case 'us' is the object in the sentence), but you might be tempted to say, wrongly, *Us women have got to stick together*.

ILLUSION/ALLUSION (see ALLUSION)

IMMINENT/EMINENT (see EMINENT)

IMPLY/INFER
'Imply' is much the same as 'suggest'. 'Infer' is similar to 'understand'. For example: *He implied that the situation would change. She inferred from what he said that the situation would change.*

INFLAMMABLE/FLAMMABLE (see FLAMMABLE)

INGENIOUS/INGENUOUS
'Ingenious' means 'clever' or 'imaginative', usually with the sense of the skill involved being unusual. For example: *He arrived at an ingenious solution to the problem* almost certainly means that he solved it in an unexpected way. 'Ingenuous' is much the same as 'naive'.

ITS/IT'S
Some time ago I was a judge for a short story competition. At one stage I considered the possibility of giving a prize to any competitor who knew the difference between 'its' and 'it's' – at least forty per cent of the entrants apparently didn't. 'Its' is the possessive version of 'it'. In other words, 'its' means something belonging to 'it', just as 'his' is the possessive version of 'he'. For example: *The outer skin of a tree is known as its bark.* 'It's', on the other hand, is simply a short way of saying 'it is', and the apostrophe stands (as it usually does) for a missing letter, which in this case is i. For example: *A tree has an outer skin; it's known as the bark.* Since 'it's' is usually something that we say, it is more likely to occur in dialogue than in other parts of your work, where you will probably use the full form, 'it is'.

LAY/LIE
The confusion between these two verbs is largely due to the fact that the past tense of 'lie' is 'lay'. It is therefore correct to say *I lay upon the bed*, provided that you are writing in the past tense, but wrong if you mean to use the present tense, when it should be *I lie upon the bed*. In the same way, *I'll go for a lay-down* is wrong; it should be 'a lie-down.' 'Lie' is an intransitive verb, whereas 'lay' is transitive and therefore always has an object. When you 'lay' something you are putting it down (or, if you are a hen, producing an egg, or, if it is a table, putting things down on it). So, if you insist on using 'lay' in the present tense when you are talking about reclining, you must say, for instance, *I lay myself down*. The past tense of 'lay' is 'laid'. For example: *I laid my arm on her shoulder.*

LEAD/LED
The problem here is that these two words can both be given the same pronunciation. 'Led' is the past tense of 'lead' (to rhyme with 'heed'), meaning 'conduct' or 'go before', but when 'lead' rhymes with 'head' it is the name of a metal. Therefore *She led me into the room* is correct.

LIBEL/SLANDER
Both these words are to do with something which destroys or
severely damages someone's reputation. The principal difference
between them is that 'libel' refers to the written word, while a
'slander' is spoken.

LICENCE/LICENSE
'Licence' is a noun, and 'license' a verb, so you might say, *The
landlord has a licence to sell spirits. He is licensed to do so.*

LIE/LAY (see LAY)

LIGHTENING/LIGHTNING
'Lightening' is a reduction in weight. 'Lightning' is the electrical
phenomenon which accompanies thunder.

LIKE/AS (see AS)

LOATH and LOATHE
'Loath' (which can also be spelt 'loth') means 'reluctant'. For
example: *I am loath to punish you for so small an offence.* 'Loathe'
is a verb meaning 'to hate, or find repugnant'.

LUXURIANT/LUXURIOUS
The word 'luxuriant' is used to describe something which is
abundant and prolific. 'Luxurious', on the other hand, is usually
used in the sense of 'with all the trappings of luxury, expensive and
comfortable'. It can also mean 'lecherous', but this use is rare
nowadays.

MANNEQUIN/MANIKIN
Both these words can mean 'model', but a 'mannequin' is alive and
usually female and is employed to show off clothes. A 'manikin' is
an artist's lay figure, or a figure used for demonstrations in medical
schools, apart, of course, from its meaning of 'little man' or 'dwarf'.

MAY/CAN (see CAN)

ME/I (see I)

MENDACITY/MENDICITY
If you accuse someone of 'mendacity' you are saying that he is a
liar. 'Mendicity', on the other hand, is the state or the act of being a
beggar.

MILITATE/MITIGATE

As well as meaning 'serving as a soldier' or 'taking part in warfare', which are not the more common definitions of the word, 'militate' means 'conflict with' or 'be directed against', and is, indeed, usually followed by 'with' or 'against'. For example: *The actions of highjackers militate against one's confidence in the safety of air travel.* 'Mitigate', on the other hand, means 'make milder' or 'appease'. For example: *Her distress was mitigated by the fact that others were similarly affected.*

MUTUAL/COMMON (see COMMON)

NAUGHT/NOUGHT

Both words mean 'nothing'. 'Naught' usually appears in somewhat archaic sounding sentences such as *Naught availed him.* 'Nought' is the spelling we usually prefer when we mean the figure zero.

OF/'VE

One sometimes comes across 'of' wrongly used in dialogue in such a sentence as *I said I would of gone,* or *He'd of seen it if he'd looked properly.* What has happened is that the author has listened to the words in his head, but has not heard them accurately. He should have written *I said I would've gone,* or *He'd've seen it if he'd looked properly.* The confusion exists because in ordinary speech we often pronounce 'of' with exactly the same vowel sound (like the u in 'hut') as we use for ''ve'.

ORAL/AURAL (see AURAL)

ORALLY/VERBALLY

He said it verbally, we say. Of course he did – in that sentence 'verbally' is not needed. But what if we say, *He expressed it verbally?* All we are in fact saying is that he used words. 'Verbal' refers to words, whether they are in speech or writing. If you want to make it clear that the statement was spoken rather than written, you need to say, *He expressed it orally.* All contracts are 'verbal' – those which are not written down are 'oral contracts'.

OWING TO/DUE TO (see DUE TO)

PALATE/PALETTE/PALLET

The 'palate' is part of the mouth, and can also be used to describe a gourmet's sense of taste. A 'palette' is used by an artist to mix his colours. A 'pallet' is a straw bed or a wooden stand on which goods are stacked.

PASSED/PAST
It is perhaps not surprising that there should be some confusion between these two words when you consider the similarity in such sentences as *She passed by my window*, or *She had passed by my window*, and *She went past my window*. 'Passed' is the past tense or past participle of the verb 'to pass', and means 'went by' or 'gone by' in the sense of movement, or signifies a successful result in a test. 'Past', on the other hand, can be a noun or an adjective, referring to a previous time or period, or an adverb, meaning 'beyond' or 'from one side to the other'.

PIDGIN/PIGEON
'Pidgin' is the usual spelling for the special variety of broken English spoken in the Orient and the Pacific. 'Pigeon' is a bird.

PORE/POUR
I recently read a typescript in which the author had written at one point, *He was pouring over his book*. I wondered what he was pouring. Was it so hot that he himself had melted? Or was he pouring water over the book to quench its inflammatory ideas? Of course, the writer meant to say, *He was poring over his book*. 'Pore', as a verb, means 'study' or 'look at with close attention', while 'pour' is something which is done by or to liquids or by or to a stream of solids falling from one place to another or by people coming out in large numbers from, for instance, a theatre.

PRACTICABLE/PRACTICAL
'Practicable' means that the word it describes is capable of being put into practice. 'Practical' usually means 'sensible, helpful'.

PRACTICE/PRACTISE
'Practice' is a noun, and 'practise' is a verb. So, *The doctor practises medicine; his practice is in Birmingham.* Or, *It was her practice to practise the piano every day.*

PRINCIPAL/PRINCIPLE
One of the ways of distinguishing between these two words is to remember that 'principal' is the one which contains an a for 'adjective'. It is a rather solemn and impressive way of saying 'chief' or 'main'. 'Ah, yes,' you may say, 'but principal' is also a noun – as

in 'the principal of a college'.' Well, up to a point, Lord Copper. It is really still an adjective, because in such a case it is an abbreviation for 'principal teacher' (or some such term). 'Principle', on the other hand, means 'origin' or 'fundamental truth' or 'moral belief'.

PRISE/PRIZE
'Prise' is the spelling usually used when referring to leverage. For example: *He prised up the lid of the chest.* 'Prize' is, of course, a reward, or booty, or can be used as a verb to mean 'value'. For example: *His most prized possession was the cup he won as the prize in the tournament.*

PROPHECY/PROPHESY
'Prophecy' is the noun, and 'prophesy' the verb. Most people get the latter right, but some try to spell the noun with an s.

RAISE/RAZE
'Raise' means 'lift up'. It is often wrongly used, by the way, in such a sentence as *He gave her a raise in salary* – it should be *a rise in salary*. 'Raze' means 'demolish'.

RESPECTFULLY/RESPECTIVELY
It is not surprising that these two words are sometimes confused, since they can both mean 'in a respectful, or careful manner', but 'respectively' is rarely used in this sense nowadays. More often, it has the sense of 'separately' or 'one by one'. For example: you could say, *He treated her respectively*, but you would be more likely to use 'respectfully' in that sentence. On the other hand, you would be wrong to use 'respectfully' in a sentence like *Messrs Smith, Jones and Brown are respectively Chairman, Secretary and Treasurer of the Club.*

RETCH/WRETCH
'Retch' (which can be pronounced either to rhyme with 'fetch' or to rhyme with 'each') is what you do when you are about to be sick, or feel like vomiting. A 'wretch' is an unhappy or unfortunate person.

SENSUAL/SENSUOUS
Both these words are adjectives concerning the senses, but 'sensual' is usually used with reference to sexual activities. So you might refer to *the sensual delight of copulation*, but to *the sensuous delight of swimming in a warm sea*.

SCEPTIC/SEPTIC
'Sceptic' (always pronounced as if it were spelt 'skeptic', as indeed it is in America) is a noun meaning 'someone who is unbelieving, or doubtful about something'. For example: *He is a sceptic when it comes to religion.* 'Septic' is an adjective referring to putrefaction. For example: *I have a septic toe.*

SHALL/WILL
There is a rule about these two words: if you simply want to express something in the future tense, you use 'shall' with 'I' and 'we', and 'will' in all other cases. For example: *I shall be there. The Government will take action.* But a determination to do something is expressed by using 'will' with 'I' and 'we', and 'shall' in all other cases – *We will make sure of it. You shall do as I say.* However, as these examples prove, the meanings can easily be confused, and the distinction between them is increasingly blurred. Much the same applies to 'should' and 'would', but of course 'would' also has the meaning of 'was in the habit of'.

SLANDER/LIBEL (see LIBEL)

STATIONARY/STATIONERY
Something which is capable of moving, but is not doing so, is 'stationary'. 'Stationery', on the other hand, is paper, ink, pens, paperclips, and all the other things that you would buy at a stationer's shop.

STRAIGHT/STRAIT
'Straight' means 'without bends' or 'honest' or 'direct'. 'Strait' means 'narrow' (hence 'straits', the geographical term referring to a narrow stretch of water). Apart from 'straits', it is normally used only in such combination words as 'strait-jacket' and 'strait-minded'.

THEIR/THERE/THEY'RE
'Their' is the possessive adjective pertaining to the pronoun 'they'. 'There' is an adverb of place. 'They're' is short for 'they are'.

TORTUROUS/TORTUOUS
'Tortuous' means 'winding, twisted', whereas 'torturous' is more closely allied to 'torture', and should refer to something painful.

TURBID/TURGID

People often talk about *turgid prose*, when they mean that what they have been reading is full of long words and complex sentences, and is generally hard to follow. The word they should probably be using is 'turbid'. 'Turgid' means 'swollen', and in respect of the written word is used to describe grandiloquent or bombastic work.

UNINTERESTED/DISINTERESTED (see DISINTERESTED)

'VE/OF (see OF)

VENAL/VENIAL

'Venal' means 'capable of being bought' in the sense of being bribed. For example: *He is thoroughly venal – he will abandon every principle if you pay him enough.* 'Venial', a word which is often applied to sins, means 'pardonable' or 'of minor importance as a fault'.

VERBAL/ORAL (see ORAL)

WAIVE/WAVE

In its commonest usage 'waive' means 'to give up a right'. The noun derived from it is 'waiver', used to indicate a statement relinquishing a right. 'Wave', as a verb, means a movement to and fro or up and down, and the noun indicates the shape which results from waving in the sea or the hair or in material, or the action of waving with the hand. 'Waver' can either mean 'hesitate', if it is a verb, or 'someone who waves', if it is a noun.

WHO/WHOM

'Who' should be used when it is the subject of a sentence. For example: *Who is going to be the next Prime Minister?* 'Whom' is used when it follows a preposition, or is the object in the sentence. For example: *To whom it may concern. It will be the person whom the Queen appoints.* ('Whom', in the second case, is the object of the verb 'appoints'.) Confusion arises when it is not entirely clear which word in the sentence is governing the 'who' or 'whom'. For example, it is easy to be misled into writing, *The Prime Minister, whom it is said is an autocrat, denied the charge.* In that sentence the pronoun is not the object of 'it is said', but of the second 'is', and the correct version would be: *The Prime Minister, who it is said is an autocrat, denied the charge.* On the other hand, it would also be correct to say, *The Prime Minister, whom his opponents have charged with being an autocrat, denied the allegation.* In that case, 'whom' is the object of 'charged'.

WHO'S/WHOSE
These two are very like 'it's' and 'its'. 'Who's' is a contraction of 'who is' or 'who has'. For example: *Who's the man who's got the ball?* 'Whose' is the possessive version of 'who' or 'which', and therefore means 'of whom' or 'of which'. For example: *The man into whose hands the ball has fallen. The rose whose scent perfumed the room.*

WILL/SHALL (see SHALL)

WRETCH/RETCH (see RETCH)

YOUR/YOU'RE
'Your' is the possessive adjective pertaining to 'you'. 'You're' is short for 'You are'.

Single Problem Words

The following list includes some of the single words and usages which often cause difficulty, or the use of which is regrettable:

COMPRISE
This word means something like 'contain' or 'include' or 'be made up of'. So *A university comprises many faculties, but the faculties do not comprise the university.*

CRESCENDO
This is a musical term, indicating that the music should be played with gradually increasing volume. It is widely, and often wrongly, used in other contexts. If you say, *Her performance was greeted by a crescendo of applause,* you probably do not intend to say that the applause got louder and louder. Equally, you might write, *The crescendo of his career came with this appointment,* when you really mean 'the pinnacle' or 'the highspot'.

DILEMMA
A 'dilemma' is not any old problem, but means a situation in which there is more than one solution to a difficulty, neither or none of which is possible or will produce the desired result.

ENORMITY
'Enormity', though clearly connected with 'enormous', should always have the sense of wrongdoing rather than of mere largeness. For example: *The enormity of the drug trade*, but not *The enormity of Windsor Park*.

FORTUITOUS
'Fortuitous' means something which happens by chance, and is not a synonym for 'fortunate'.

GUESSTIMATE
This dreadful word has been formed on what I think of as the German habit of putting nouns together to make portmanteau words. (One of the most splendid, indeed, almost unbelievable, German examples is the 50-letter *Gesundheitswiederherstellungs-mittelzusammenmischer,* which means literally 'mixer-together-of-a-means-of-restoring-health', or, more simply and in a single word, 'dispenser'.) 'Motel' has been constructed on the same principle, but it is a useful word, combining elements of 'motor' and 'hotel' to produce a word for something which, when the name was first coined, was not easily and briefly described. 'Guesstimate', on the other hand, is a silly word, combining two elements which are already so similar that the new hybrid adds little to either. An estimate usually is a guess. I suppose that 'guesstimate' does suggest that the estimate is a very rough one, but my preference would always be, if a qualification is needed, for this to be effected by a suitable adjective ('careful', 'informed', 'rough', 'quick').

GRATUITOUS
'Gratuitous' can mean quite simply 'free', but is frequently used with the sense of 'uncalled-for, undeserved' (and therefore 'offensive'), as in *a gratuitous insult.*

HOPEFULLY
Those who care about language are, alas, fighting a losing battle over 'hopefully'. It should mean only 'in a manner full of hope'. For example: *She looked at him hopefully.* It is used nowadays so widely instead of 'It is hoped' or simply 'I hope', that such usage must soon become entirely accepted.

IRREGARDLESS
There is no such word as 'irregardless', although it is so often used nowadays, possibly because it seems to have an affinity with its

synonym 'irrespective', that it may come to be accepted. It adds nothing in meaning to 'regardless' (which is simpler, and has two fewer letters if you are typing it).

LEADING QUESTION
A 'leading question' is not, as many believe, a particularly searching question, nor one which raises the most important point in a discussion. Most people know that the term comes to us from the legal profession, and that judges disapprove of it. In fact, it means a question which, by the way it is phrased, leads the witness towards the reply which the lawyer wants to hear. It might be difficult to answer if you were asked, *Who is the finest contemporary American novelist?*, but it is not a leading question. If, on the other hand, your inquisitor changed the wording, and said, *You would agree that Saul Bellow is one of the finest contemporary American novelists, wouldn't you?*, that is a leading question, because it was put in such a way as to show that the expected answer was 'Yes'.

NOISOME
This word has little, if anything, to do with noise. It means 'offensive' and is often used in connection with ill-smelling odours.

PRAGMATIC
'Pragmatic' can be used as a synonym for 'practical' or 'down-to-earth', but it is worth remembering that it also means 'officious' and 'opinionated', and overtones of those meanings may attach themselves to it.

PRISTINE
'Pristine' means 'pertaining to the earliest, or original, condition' of whatever you are talking about, or even simply 'ancient' or 'primitive'. So it does not necessarily mean 'clean and shining'.

TRANSPIRE
Do you feel at all uneasy when you use the word 'transpire' to mean 'happen' or 'come to pass'? Probably not, because it is commonly used in that sense. Purists will tell you, however, that strictly it means 'breathe through, or across', and that the only other sense in which it can properly be used is 'become known'.

6 The Right Length

Beginners often seem to be troubled by the questions of how long a sentence should be, of when to start a new paragraph or a new chapter, and of the desirable extent of a book. As with so many writing problems, there are no rules, and it all depends on what you are writing about, and on the market at which you are aiming.

Sentences

A sentence can be very short, consisting of one word only (although, technically, since it would have no subject, verb and predicate, it could not really be called a sentence), or very long, with a whole succession of dependent clauses. Normally, however, it consists of one thought or statement, expressed quite simply in a conventional form such as, for instance, *The old man sat in the chair by the fire*, or, a little more elaborately, qualified by additional clauses, as in *The old man sat in the chair by the fire, which was, as the regulars knew, reserved for his exclusive use because he had sat there every evening for the past twenty years.*

In general, it is wiser to avoid the extremes. One word 'sentences' can be very effective, but you need to be sure of your technique, and use them with discretion, so that the style does not become obtrusive. The kind of complex sentence which goes on for half a page can also work very well, but you need to be as good a writer as Henry James or Bernard Levin to get away with it, and you have to be sure that you are making sense to the reader and that he or she will not have forgotten by the end of the sentence what its beginning was. It is also important, as has already been pointed out earlier in this book, to have a variety in the length of your sentences, so that you avoid a monotony of style.

Make sure that your punctuation is adequate. Read the chapter on punctuation – especially the sections on the full stop and the comma – and follow the advice given there. It is worth repeating the suggestion that you should read your work aloud, slowly, listening carefully to the pauses that you make. Read the following sentence aloud: *If there is a longish pause, you have probably come to the end of a sentence, you need to break the piece there with a full stop.* Of the two commas in that sentence, the first, after *pause*, is adequate, but the second, after *sentence*, is not strong enough, and should be replaced by a full stop. Alternatively, you could use a conjunction: *If there is a longish pause, you have probably come to the end of a sentence, and can join the next sentence on by using a conjunction.*

Paragraphs

Like a sentence, a paragraph can consist of one word – *Silence*, for example, might easily stand on its own as a complete paragraph. More usually, the paragraph will be made up of a number of sentences, but they will be connected in that they will be concerned with one basic thought or group of thoughts. So if you move to a new point, or take a new subject, then you begin a new paragraph. Look at the three paragraphs under the heading Sentences above. Each contains a number of sentences connected by the basic subject of the paragraph: the first is a definition of a sentence, the second is about short and long sentences, and the third is concerned with the punctuation of a sentence.

Think of paragraphs, if you will, as Christmas parcels sent to various families. Within the parcel are individually wrapped presents – these are the sentences. The presents inside the parcel are all linked by being destined for one group of people, just as the sentences in the paragraph hang together because they are all concerned with the same theme.

As with sentences, it is advisable to avoid very long paragraphs, less because you are likely to confuse your reader than because a too solid chunk of type has a somewhat formidable appearance, and may be off-putting. It does depend to some extent, however, on the total length of the piece you are writing. If you are producing a full-length book you can afford to have fewer and longer paragraphs than if you are writing a short article. Even more influential in this matter is the audience for whom you are writing: if your work is intended for small children or for the tabloid press, your paragraphs will rarely contain more than two fairly simple sentences (indeed, in these cases you may need to break the work into very short paragraphs even if the sense does not demand it), while much longer paragraphs would be acceptable in a serious article or a book intended for a reader who will be prepared to give more concentrated and lengthy attention. Even then, however, and if only for cosmetic reasons, it may be wise to look at any paragraph which extends for a whole page or more and consider whether it can be broken at some point. It usually can be so broken. The paragraph we are in at the moment is not exceptionally long, but it is getting near the desirable limit, and if it were really necessary, could be broken after the words 'a short article' without destroying the sense, and without it being too obvious that a break was not originally intended at that point.

For dialogue, while it should be remembered that, once again, there are no inviolable rules, it is customary nowadays to start a new paragraph for each different speaker. The paragraph will, however, include not only the attribution (*he said, she replied*, etc.), but also actions or other material relevant to that speaker. For example:

> 'Are you going to the meeting?' Anne asked.
> 'Yes.' Malcolm walked over to the window. 'I'm not looking forward to it.' His voice was a mere whisper. 'Everything is bound to come out.'
> There was a brief silence, broken only by the sound of a distant aeroplane.
> 'I don't think I can face it,' he said at last.
> The anguish in his voice was so plain that she went to him. 'You must, my dear. But try not to worry about it.'
> He laughed bitterly.
> 'Oh, I know it's easy for me to say that,' Anne said, 'but please try.'

Note that there are new paragraphs to describe the silence, which is not part of Malcolm's speech or actions, and for his laughter, which interrupts Anne's speeches. There is also, despite the fact that Malcolm has just been speaking, a new paragraph beginning with a mention of the anguish in his voice, because the point of view has changed and we see the anguish through Anne's eyes. Never change the viewpoint within one paragraph.

If a speech in dialogue is particularly long, it may be worth breaking into two or more paragraphs, in which case you will open the quotation marks at the beginning of each paragraph, and not close them until the end of the speech.

Chapters

In his largely excellent book, *Writing a Novel*, the late John Braine perpetrated one piece of nonsense, when he advised that every novel should consist of at least twenty chapters. You can have as many or as few chapters as you like, depending on the style of book you are writing, and they can be very long or very short, and do not necessarily have to be of similar lengths. Especially if you are writing fiction and building up your narrative by means of a series of short scenes, you can even do without chapters altogether, but you will probably want to indicate breaks in the story by means of blank lines. On the other hand, for certain types of novel, especially of the kind which publishers call 'category fiction' (romances, westerns, crime stories), you may need to conform to conventions regarding both the number and length of chapters.

In non-fiction, each chapter will almost certainly deal with a different aspect of the subject, or perhaps, if it is a biography or history, with a certain period or group of events. The author of non-fiction will usually have little trouble in deciding when a new chapter is needed, although some problems may still exist, as for instance in this book, in which I have had some difficulty in making up my mind how to place certain material which could have found a home in a number of different chapters. This discussion of sentences, paragraphs and chapters could, for instance, have been part of the chapter on punctuation or that on style, but in the end seemed to me happier as a short chapter on its own. In the same way, new chapters in fiction may begin because of a change of scene or of time or because the author is going to focus on a different character. After all, we speak of someone beginning 'a new chapter in his life', and if you think of what you are writing in those terms, you will perhaps have less difficulty in deciding when a new chapter is required. Alternatively, think of commercial television's 'natural breaks'; because of the needs of the advertisers, not all breaks in the programmes are as natural as they might be, but whenever possible, the programme breaks at a point when a new scene or development or argument is about to take place.

Something else which can be learnt from television is that those who decide when the breaks shall come try to place them at a point where the interest of viewers has been not only sufficiently aroused for them to want to go on watching, but preferably has reached a point when they cannot bear not to know what happens next. In other words, the break comes immediately following a 'hook', a 'cliffhanger'. The need for a hook was something else which Mr

Braine stressed, and this time with much more sense. So end your chapter, if you can, when a crisis of some description has been reached, and your hero or heroine is facing a dilemma or a major change in circumstances.

Chapter titles are almost always needed for non-fiction, but are rarely seen nowadays in novels.

Book Lengths

A question with which all teachers of creative writing are familiar is how long a book should be. The obvious answer is that any book should be long enough to cover its subject adequately, whether it is fiction or non-fiction. It should never be padded, and indeed there are very few books, even those which are extremely successful, which would not benefit from cutting, since most authors tend to overwrite rather than underwrite. But the would-be writers are really asking what length of book is acceptable to publishers.

Excluding books for children, which are almost always shorter than the general run of books for adults, the range is enormous. If you are writing romantic fiction a length of between 45,000 and 55,000 words is more or less standard, and much the same applies to the average western or crime book that you may see on the library shelves (check requirements with the publisher to whom you intend sending your work); family sagas and some historical novels tend to be longer, simply because they cover a wider canvas. But there are no rules; very short books get into print, and so do enormous tomes of 1,000 pages or more. All that can usefully be said is that, generally speaking, publishers are unlikely to be enthusiastic about submissions from unknown authors which are less than 40,000 or more than 120,000 words, and the reason for this is largely one of publishing economics. The length is perhaps less critical for non-fiction, partly because a publisher has greater freedom in the pricing of such books (fiction tends to appear at standardized prices).

Unless you are aiming at the library fiction market, it seems wiser to me not to start out with a specific word length in mind, or, at least, without more than a rough idea of how long the book will be. Let it decide its own length. If, when you are part way through, it becomes clear that it is going to be an extremely short book, you may need to ask yourself whether your material is substantial enough to form a book, or whether it might be more suited to a series of articles or a short story; equally, if the book looks like turning into a 1,000 page whopper, perhaps it is worth checking to see whether you are overwriting or whether the work could be split up to make more than one volume. Don't worry about it too much – no publisher is really daunted by the length of a book if it is of exceptional quality.

PART TWO
Getting Into Print

Almost anyone can be an author; the business is to collect money and fame from this state of being.

A.A. Milne

7   Presentation of Your Work

Is the way you present your work to a publisher important? Yes, it is – very important. You are working in a crowded market, and every editor receives and considers hundreds of submissions every year. Many are not publishable, because the author is without talent, or even illiterate, or because the work is grossly libellous, or for many other possible reasons. But if you and your work do not come in any of these categories, however wonderful your writing may be, if it looks a mess you are putting a barrier in the way of its publication. A neat, legible typescript, well set out, stands a much better chance, not only because it is easier to read (being human, editors do like something which is easy on their eyes), but also because it suggests that you have a professional attitude. If the editor senses, even before starting to read, that you care enough about your work to have presented it well, you have already chalked up a bonus point.

However badly you present your script, provided it is typed (see below), the publisher will undoubtedly give it some consideration, just in case it turns out to be a masterpiece. (It really is a myth that publishers do not even glance at everything that any author may send in; some material may, however, be given little more than a glance if, for various reasons, such as total illiteracy, or being on a subject which that particular firm never publishes, the submission is obviously unsuitable.) But if your work is no more than averagely good and is sloppily prepared, it may soon be abandoned in favour of one of the neater typescripts among the pile on the editor's desk.

Of course, the finest presentation will not help if your work is not up to the standards required, or if you have submitted something which is unsuited to the publisher's needs, but you will never help yourself by poor presentation.

General Matters of Presentation

TYPE YOUR WORK

Although a few magazines will occasionally accept handwritten articles (provided that your handwriting is consistently legible), almost all publishers expect work to be typed, especially if it is at all lengthy, and most book publishers will refuse to consider handwritten submissions.

What can you do if you don't type? You can take your work to a typing agency or to one of the many people, usually ex-secretaries, who do such work at home (you will find them in the small ads section of your local newspaper or of any magazine for writers). You may think that no one would be able to read your writing and cope with your crossings-out and insertions and so on, but those who undertake this work are usually used to pretty messy handwritten material. They will often correct your spelling and punctuation, if you ask them to do so. You will naturally need to go through the work when it comes back to you to check it for any mistakes, but in most cases you will have an accurate typescript with a professional appearance. Unfortunately, this method is going to cost a fair amount.

An alternative is to buy a second-hand typewriter, take an evening class course in typing, or even teach yourself to type, which is not as difficult as you might think. You will be slow at first, but although you may never approach the speed of a trained touch-typist, you can soon become reasonably proficient, even if you only use two fingers. Your script should be typed in double spacing. Never use single spacing (except for poetry and plays – see below), even for footnotes. If you are including a long extract from some other book, which in the printed form will probably appear in a smaller size of type than the rest of the text, it may be a good idea to indent each line in your typescript to distinguish it from the rest, but it is still better in double spacing. Double spacing is far easier to read, and also allows room for occasional corrections or insertions. Some authors use one-and-a-half spacing, presumably in order to save paper, but the saving is just not worthwhile. Type on one side of the paper only. Apart from the fact that if you use both sides, the typing on one side may show through on the other, again a typescript is physically easier to read if only one side is used.

Try to use the same typewriter throughout. 'Well, of course,' you may say. 'I've only got one, anyway.' But some authors submit books which have apparently been typed on half a dozen different machines, with different sizes and styles of type. It doesn't look good, and it makes the job of estimating the length of the book much more difficult.

Do make sure that you use a new, or reasonably new, black typewriter ribbon. Writing is not a wildly expensive occupation as far as the materials are concerned, but many authors seem to begrudge spending money on typewriter ribbons, and submit work which is typed in a faint shade of grey. You can't really blame an editor who looks at such a typescript and decides that it's just not worth straining his or her eyes to read it. If you are writing a book, it is a good idea to start off with a new ribbon, and, if the typescript is more than about two hundred pages long, to replace the ribbon halfway through. The same applies to word processors (see below). Don't, by the way, buy a two-coloured ribbon (unless you want the second colour for some other purpose than preparing a typescript for a publisher) – it is preferable that your work should be in black throughout.

CARBONS

You will need to make copies of your work. If it is accepted for publication, the publisher will almost certainly ask for a second copy, and sometimes wants a total of three. Additionally, you must have a copy for yourself (in case your original gets lost, or to refer to if necessary). If you are using carbons, again please do not economize on them. Many authors are even meaner about carbon paper than about typewriter ribbons. As soon as your carbons begin to give a grey and fuzzy impression, discard them and use new ones. In general, publishers like to see the top copy rather than a carbon, principally because the top copy is usually easier to read, but also because they suspect, if you send a carbon, that you have submitted the top copy elsewhere – which they don't like, unless you have told them that you are doing so and they have agreed to consider the work on that basis (see the section on multiple submissions on page 123). However, a photostat is usually acceptable, provided of course that the original which you have copied was good enough to give a clean, legible stat.

PAPER

The most acceptable size of paper nowadays is A4 (210 x 297 mm). Quarto is still used, but other sizes, including foolscap and most certainly anything smaller than quarto, are not to be recommended. If you are submitting your work in the United States, it is best to use their equivalent of quarto, which is slightly larger than the British variety (11″ x 8″). Use a 70 or 80 gramme bond paper for your top copy; bank paper (the flimsy kind) is usually acceptable for copies.

LAYOUT
Always leave good margins. I would suggest that these should be a minimum of an inch at the top and on either side, and an inch to an inch and a half at the foot of the page. There are three reasons for this: firstly, yet again the typescript in this form is easier to read; secondly, the margins leave room for an occasional insertion and for the publisher's instructions to the printer; thirdly, when the printer sets the book up in type, he clamps the page he is transcribing in a stand, and if there are inadequate margins, the clips will obscure part of the text.

Do not leave a blank line between paragraphs, unless it is your intention that a blank line should appear in the printed version to indicate a change of scene or of subject – in which case it may be wise to place an asterisk in the centre of the otherwise blank line to make sure that what you mean is clear.

EMPHASIZING WORDS
If you want a word to appear in italics, underline it. If you have a particularly clever typewriter or a word processor, don't use its facility for typing in italics, which may not always be clear. Underlining is always understood by the printer to mean that italics should be used. On the whole, you should not use capital letters for emphasis, unless you have already used italics and now want to indicate something even stronger, as for instance, in such a line of dialogue as: 'She didn't,' he said. 'She *didn't!*' His voice rose to a shriek. 'She DIDN'T!'

WORD PROCESSORS
More and more authors are turning to word processors for their work, especially now that capable machines are available at a low cost. If you buy a word processor, be prepared to spend some time learning how it works – it may be a few weeks before it becomes 'transparent' to you, which is to say that you can make it do what you want without having to consult the manual every time (and, incidentally, the manuals are notorious for being difficult to understand). It is worth persevering, however, for you will find that the word processor has two enormous advantages: it makes corrections and major alterations to the text simple to carry out (and many writers find that this facility actually improves the quality of their work), and it takes the drudgery out of producing

the final copy. It used to take me several weeks to type the final copy of a long novel, but with my word processor, I now print it in one or two days.

If your word processor has a daisy-wheel printer, you should have no problems with the appearance of your typescript as long as you don't use tired old ribbons. It will look like good, even typing. Dot-matrix printers, on the other hand, in which the letters are made up of tiny dots, produce work which is often less easy to read, especially if you have the kind which condenses the ascenders and descenders (the uprights on the letters b, d, h, etc., and the tails on the letters g, p, y, etc.). You may have the facility with a dot-matrix printer for using either draft or high quality printing, and you will probably want to choose the former. The high quality is obviously very much better, especially with punctuation, which is often very faint in the draft quality mode, but the problem is that high quality printing is so slow, and can take more than twice as long. If you use the draft quality, change the ribbon frequently so that you get as good an impression as you can. One possibility is to use high quality for the top copy and draft quality for the duplicates.

It may not be necessary for you to print your work at all if the publisher has word processors in the office, and the machines are compatible with yours. In such cases, you may be able simply to supply copies of your discs which the editor can then read on an office machine. However, you would need to check first whether the publisher would be willing to consider your work in this form. You should, of course, keep duplicates of the discs, and it is also advisable to have a print-out in case the discs should deteriorate, or part of the text should be wiped off by mistake.

CORRECTIONS

However desirable it may be, it is not absolutely necessary to present a perfect typescript. An occasional correction or insertion is permissible, provided that it is legible (unless your handwriting is always perfectly clear, it is better to use the kind of printing that small children learn, rather than 'joined-up' writing). Once a page starts looking messy, it is worth taking the trouble of re-typing it. If, after you have typed the whole of a long book, you have a lengthy insertion to make on, say, page 31, re-type the page to make pages 31 and 31a, and then add a note to say 'continue on page 32'.

MAKE SURE YOUR TYPESCRIPT LOOKS FRESH

If you have submitted the same work to several publishers, it is likely that the typescript will be looking rather battered. If you cannot afford the time or the cost of re-typing the whole thing (so easy on a word processor, of course), at least re-type the first page and any others which have become crumpled or have acquired coffee stains.

COPYRIGHT

Anything which you write is your copyright (unless you assign it to someone else), and it is therefore not necessary to put a statement to that effect on your typescript. It will do no harm, however. Such a copyright notice should be in the form 'Copyright © John Smith 19——'. Strictly speaking, you should use your full name ('John Brian Smith', for example, rather than 'John Smith' or 'J.B. Smith'), and it should be your real name and not the version of it which you use as an author or a pseudonym. However, this rule appears to be rarely honoured, and it is possible to copyright the work in virtually any name you like to use. The date will of course be the year in which the piece was written, but the publisher will change it to the date of publication when the work appears in print.

Titles are not copyright, but you should avoid using one which is already very well known. If you were to call your novel *The Day of the Jackal*, for instance, you could be sued for 'passing off' (that is to say, for misleading potential purchasers into believing that the book was the famous thriller by Frederick Forsyth – see page 131).

Ideas for books are not copyright either, and many authors fear that if they put up a project to a publisher, he may reject their work but then pinch the idea and give it to another author. It is not common practice among reputable publishers to behave in this way, but it does occasionally happen. If you believe you have been victimized, it is perhaps worth considering the possibility of legal action, but it may be difficult to prove that the theft of your idea was deliberate, rather than merely coincidental.

PERMISSIONS

Of course, just as your own work is copyright, so is that of other writers, at least, in most cases, until seventy years after their death. If you wish to quote more than a few words from someone else's book, or to use illustrations which are not your property (photographs of people, incidentally, are the copyright of the photographer, not of the subject, unless some prior arrangement has been made to vary this rule), you will have to obtain permission, and often pay a fee, in order to do so. There is no need, however, to seek such permissions before you are certain that the work is going to be published. At that stage, your publisher will be able to give you advice on how to proceed.

Now for some more specific points depending on the nature of your work:

Books – Fiction and Non-Fiction

LAYOUT
You should try to keep the same number of lines on every page. If you use a word processor which has a facility of rejecting 'widows and orphans' (a single line separated from the rest of the paragraph either at the top or the bottom of a page by a page break), you should override the command. If you do not do so, the number of lines may vary from page to page. Widows and, to a lesser degree, orphans are to be avoided in printed work, but do not greatly matter in a typescript.

Begin chapters on a new page. There is no need to start them halfway down the page, but it looks better to leave two or three blank lines at the top, then to have the chapter title (or 'Chapter One' or '1', for example) and then another blank line before the text begins.

Indent your paragraphs – five spaces at the beginning of the line are adequate to avoid any confusion, while anything more than ten spaces is unnecessary.

Be consistent in all these matters.

OVERLAP WORDS
Some authors put the first word of the next page at the foot of the page on the right, sometimes in brackets. This may help the reader to be sure that the pages are in the right order, but it is not necessary to use overlaps, and some editors find it positively irritating.

PAGE NUMBERING
Always number your pages. It does not matter whether you put the number at the top or at the foot, in the middle or at the right-hand side. But please number the typescript consecutively from the beginning to the end   that is to say from 1 to 237 (or whatever is the last page). Do not start again at 1 with each chapter. If you wish, you can also put the title, or a shortened version of it, or your name beside the page number (e.g. 'NUTS.1, NUTS.2 etc.' or

'Legat.1, Legat.2 etc.'), but this, though helpful if your typescript should get mixed up with someone else's, is not strictly necessary.

PRELIMINARY PAGES

The 'prelims' are the pages in a book before the text begins. In a printed book they usually include: a half-title page (on which only the book's title appears), on the reverse of which may be placed a list of other books by the same author, or volumes in the same series; a title page (which gives the title, author's name and publisher's name)́, and on its reverse an imprint page, sometimes called a biblio page (which gives the book's printing history, copyright notices and the printer's imprint). The prelims may also include a dedication, list of contents, list of illustrations, foreword, etc.

Your typescript does not need a half-title page or an imprint page. The publisher will prepare these if the book is accepted. He will also supply an ISBN. ISBN stands for International Standard Book Number. Each book, including different editions (but not straightforward reprints) of the book, has its own individual number, which also identifies its country of origin and its publisher. The publisher allocates ISBNs to the books when they are scheduled for publication.

The typescript should, however, have a title page, on which you should have typed (don't draw it in fancy lettering) the title, the author's name or pseudonym, and his or her name and address or agent's name and address. It is also helpful to show the approximate length of the typescript in the number of words. See example opposite.

Don't put 'First British Serial Rights' or 'F.B.S.R.' on the title page. That is something which goes on work submitted to magazines and newspapers, not on books sent to a book publisher (see page 111).

Whether you will have a list of previous books, a dedication, list of illustrations, a foreword, etc., depends on circumstances and your own wishes. Each should appear on a separate page in the typescript. If you have given titles to your chapters, or parts, you may wish to include a list of contents, but if you have simply called them 'Chapter 1, Chapter 2, etc.' it is probably not worth putting it in.

THE LAST PAGE

I would suggest that you should put your name and your address, or that of your agent, on the last page of the book. It is also quite a

THE NUTS AND BOLTS OF WRITING

Michael Legat

Approx. 60,000 words

Michael Legat
c/o Campbell Thomson & McLaughlin Ltd,
31 Newington Green,
London N16 9PU

good idea to put 'THE END' after the last words, especially if your book has the indeterminate kind of ending which is quite fashionable nowadays.

WORD COUNTS

You do not need to count every word in your book. Nor, if you have a word processor which counts the words for you, will the publisher wish to see the figure which it produces. The publisher wants a figure which takes account of short pages at the beginning and end of chapters, and of short lines. The way to calculate the wordage is therefore as follows:

Count the number of words in ten consecutive full lines on five different pages. You will then have counted fifty lines. Divide the total number of words in those fifty lines by fifty, to arrive at the average figure per line. If your total amounted to, say, 595, the average number of words per line would be 11·9. Next, count the number of lines on ten full pages; if you have been careful to keep the same number of lines on every page, you will obviously need to count one page only, but if the pages vary in length, then get to an average by dividing the total lines on the ten pages by ten. If your ten pages gave you a total of 275 lines, the average would be 27·5 lines per page. Now multiply the average number of words per line by the average number of lines per page. In the examples so far given the answer would be 327·25. Round the figure up or, in this case, down, and you get 327 words per page. Now multiply that figure by the number of pages in your typescript, ignoring the fact that some pages may be short. If, for example, your book has 219 pages, you would get a figure of 71,613. Round off the figure to the nearest thousand, and you would arrive at 72,000 as the wordage, and that is the figure which you would put on the front page.

This may sound very complicated, but it isn't really. If it totally baffles you, take heart – although many publishers like to see a word count, it is not absolutely essential to give one.

FASTENING THE TYPESCRIPT TOGETHER

There is considerable disagreement on this subject, although I believe most publishers are united in disliking the kind of typescript which is fastened together in one indissoluble lump – heavy to hold and clumsy to read. Even a ring binder can be awkward to work with. My own preference, in the days when I was a publisher, was always for separate sheets, held together only by being placed in the kind of box that typing paper comes in, or in a wallet-type folder, or by elastic bands round the whole thing. You could fasten your chapters or batches of pages together with paperclips or split pins, but I would not recommend either of these methods – paper clips have a nasty habit of picking up other papers accidentally, and split pins often have vicious points to them. If you insist on using some kind of fastening, perhaps the best way is to use staples – just one staple in the top left-hand corner is adequate, rather than a series of staples all the way down the side (and don't try to staple too many pages together).

ILLUSTRATIONS
Keep these separate from your typescript, especially if they are photographs. If they are diagrams, you should indicate where they are to go in the text. Photographs will probably be batched together by the publisher, but it is to be hoped that he will consult you about their presentation, so that important ones do not appear as miniatures while those of less account are given full pages. Just as you should keep a copy of your typescript, so you should have copies of your illustrations – any good camera shop will make copies of precious, irreplaceable photographs, and diagrams can be photostatted.

FOOTNOTES
Try to avoid them wherever possible by incorporating the material in the main body of the text. Publishers not only dislike them, because they add considerably to the cost of setting the book in type, but may insist, if there are many of them, that they should appear together at the end of a chapter or at the end of the whole book.

INDEX
If your book requires an index, and you are willing to prepare it yourself (and capable of doing so) – a matter which should be discussed with your publisher at contract stage – you clearly cannot carry out the work until the book has been set in print, so that you can include the right page references. You can, however, if you wish, make an index from your typescript for your own use, if you feel this will simplify your task when the proofs arrive. At submission stage, there is no need to supply this rough draft to the publisher, but it would be useful to indicate approximately how many entries there will be in it, or perhaps how many pages you would expect it to occupy.

Books for Children

In this section we are concerned basically with picture books. All the details given under Books – Fiction and Non-Fiction above apply equally to books for older children, which consist primarily of text.

LAYOUT
Follow the guidelines above as far as the text is concerned, typing it out separately, even if it consists of very few words (unless, of course, you are also providing the lettering, in which case text and illustrations will be integrated), and keeping the illustrations separate. Prepare a 'dummy', that is to say, blank sheets of paper made up like a book on which you indicate where the illustrations and the text will appear. Make sure that you use one of the standard page sizes for this kind of book (find out the usual sizes by looking at what is on offer in your local bookshop).

NUMBER OF PAGES
Books are printed in sections consisting of eight, sixteen or thirty-two pages (small sections of four pages can also be produced, and, on large machines, sixty-four and one hundred and twenty-eight pages can be printed on one sheet of paper). A picture book for children is likely to have a maximum of thirty-two pages, and quite often the figure is twelve, sixteen or twenty-four. Four of those pages are frequently used as endpapers, which means that nothing can appear on the first and last pages which will be pasted down to secure the binding. You will also need a title page and a biblio page, and your book cannot therefore really begin until page 5 and will have to end on page 14 or 15 if it is a sixteen page book, and on page 22 or 23 if it has twenty-four pages. If you find this difficult to understand, look at published picture books and work out for yourself how they have been physically made up.

Poetry

LAYOUT
It is usual practice not to type poetry in double spacing, but to put it on your page in exactly the form in which you would like to see it printed. Indentations of various lengths, blank lines – any variations you want – should be there for the printer to follow. This applies whether you are preparing a book of your poetry, or

submitting a single poem to a magazine or to one of the small poetry presses.

BOOKS OF POETRY

As explained in the section on illustrated books for children, books are printed in sections, usually of thirty-two pages. This is why you will find that most books you pick up have a total number of pages such as 160, 192, 224, 256 and so on. With a book which consists entirely or very largely of straightforward text, the publisher can juggle with different types and type sizes to make it fit into one of these lengths which is a multiple of thirty-two. The publisher's designer often has less scope with poetry, except, perhaps, by putting more than one poem on a page, which is rarely desirable, especially in recent times when the visual appearance of poems has become much more important. It is not essential to work out exactly how many pages your poems will occupy (if you have too few, the difference may be made up by a more generous allocation of pages to the prelims, or by leaving blank pages in certain places, and if you have too many, the publisher may ask you to drop one or two of them). But do make sure, if you are asking a hardcover publisher to bring out your poems, that there are sufficient to make a collection of reasonable size. If you have too few poems for that, then go to one of the little presses which publish booklets of poetry in paper bindings.

Plays

LAYOUT

Plays are usually presented with the dialogue in single spacing, but with a double space between speeches by different characters. The stage directions are in brackets and underlined, and are included within the speech if they apply only to the character speaking, but are on separate lines in other cases. The names of the characters speaking should be in capitals on the left-hand side, separated from all the dialogue.

These complicated directions will be made clearer by an example:

> (*Gwendolen and Cecily are at the window, looking out into the garden.*)

GWENDOLEN The fact that they did not follow us at once into the house, as any one else would have done,

seem to me to show that they have some sense of
shame left.

CECILY   They have been eating muffins. That looks like
repentance.

GWENDOLEN   (*After a pause.*) They don't seem to notice us at
all. Couldn't you cough?

CECILY   But I haven't got a cough.

GWENDOLEN   They're looking at us. What effrontery!

CECILY   They're approaching. That's very forward of
them.

GWENDOLEN   Let us preserve a dignified silence.

CECILY   Certainly. It's the only thing to do now.

(*Enter Jack followed by Algernon. They whistle
some dreadful popular air from a British
Opera.*)

If you are writing plays for television or radio, it is usual to number
each speech in the play, beginning with 1 and continuing all the way
through. The numbers are placed just before the names of the
characters who are speaking, on the left-hand side. *Writing for the
BBC* gives useful advice, and the BBC Radio Drama Department will
send you a specimen layout if you write to them, enclosing a large
stamped addressed envelope.

Articles and Short Stories

LAYOUT
You should use A4 and double spacing, but it is not necessary to
keep strictly to the same number of words per page, and indeed, if
there is a convenient paragraph break near the end of the page, stop
there and begin the next paragraph on a new page.

Do not put 'overlap words' at the foot of the page, but do put
'more', or 'more follows' or 'm.f.' at the bottom of the page on the
right-hand side, except, of course, on the last page, where you can
substitute 'ends'.

On the first page of the text you should put the title at the top or one or two spaces down (unless you are submitting your work to American magazines, when it is customary to begin halfway down the page). Do not use capital letters or underline the title – leave the sub-editor to indicate to the printer how it should appear.

PAGE NUMBERING
Number the pages as usual, but always include an identification too. For example: 'NUTS.1, NUTS.2, etc.' or 'Legat.1, Legat.2, etc.'.

TITLE PAGE
In addition to the title, your by-line (name or pseudonym) and your name and address (or agent's address), indicate whether the article is to be illustrated and whether the illustrations are supplied by you or not. A word count should appear, and this should be fairly accurate, without allowing for short lines. If, however, you use the technique described above for calculating wordage (that is, counting short lines as though they were full ones), round the figure up or down to the nearest fifty words.

You should also add 'First British Serial Rights' or 'F.B.S.R.' or 'Single Reproduction Only', to indicate that you are not selling the magazine or newspaper the copyright in your work (which you should never do). 'First British Serial Rights' means that you are offering the magazine or newspaper the opportunity to publish the article or story for the first time in Britain. You will be free to try to sell American or Australian or other overseas rights in the same piece of work, marking it 'First U.S. Serial Rights' or 'First South African Serial Rights' as appropriate. After its publication in Britain, if it is accepted, you may be able to sell 'Second Serial Rights' to other British magazines or newspapers, and the same applies in overseas markets. The term 'Second Serial Rights', incidentally, includes all uses of the article or story after the first one, whether it is being sold for the second, third, fifth or umpteenth time.

8   Selling Your Work

Market Research

One way of deciding where to try to sell your work is to get a copy
of *The Writers' and Artists' Yearbook* or of *The Writers'
Handbook*, turn to the appropriate section, and choose a publisher
because you like the sound of the firm's name, or by sticking a pin
in.

It is not the best way. Both the books mentioned are extremely
useful and, although they are available in your public library,
should be on every writer's bookshelf. They give details of book
publishers, magazines, newspapers, outlets for stage plays, radio,
television and films, agents, societies, etc., and include articles on
subjects of interest to authors. If you study them carefully you may
find invaluable advice on where to send your work. But you really
need to do more than that.

The idea of undertaking market research before making a
submission seems to fill some would-be writers with dismay. They
feel that it is very difficult and very time-consuming. The time that
it takes will be well spent, because it should prevent the writer from
sending work to a totally unsuitable outlet. As for being hard to do,
that belief stems simply from ignorance of how to set about it.

Market research is, in fact, extremely simple in essence. It
consists of looking (or, in the case of radio, listening) to see what
sort of things are accepted and by whom. So you do it in libraries,
bookshops, newsagents, the theatre or the cinema, or in your home
by listening to the radio or watching television.

MARKET RESEARCH BEFORE YOU BEGIN WRITING
It is often only after a piece is written that the author thinks about
market research, but it can also be done in advance and can, indeed,
actually inspire the writing. Many authors have achieved
considerable success by studying what was already available and
then deciding to fill a gap that they could perceive. 'I could write

such-and-such a book for such-and-such a market' – that is an approach which not only makes an acceptance more likely, but may result in a commission simply on the basis of the idea.

MARKET RESEARCH FOR BOOKS

Suppose you have written a biography of an historical figure (and I am assuming that you have the necessary qualifications to do so), and are wondering where to send it. Go to your local library and look on the shelves to see which publishers regularly bring out biographies of that type. Go to your local bookseller and talk to the owner or manager, who, unless you choose a particularly busy time in the shop, will probably be very willing to give you advice. You can also obtain more information about specific publishers by writing to them and asking for their catalogues. Exactly the same procedure applies whether your book is about gardening, or how to write, or any other kind of non-fiction, or whether it is a novel, whatever the genre, or whether it is intended for children.

You need to do this research with a certain amount of depth, so that you make sure that a given publishing house not only brings out books in the broad category in which you are interested, but that its publications are in the same specific mould as your work; you do not want to send a romance in the style of Barbara Cartland to a publisher whose fiction list is extremely highbrow, nor a right-wing political study to a left-wing house. Equally, you must avoid too close a match; a publisher who has just brought out a book on cooking for beginners is unlikely to want another on exactly the same theme, and if a particular house publishes, for instance, a well known author's series of historical novels featuring Charles II, you will only diminish your chances by sending to that publisher your own novel about Charles and Nell Gwyn.

Should you choose a large publisher or a small one? Both have advantages and disadvantages. The large publisher probably produces a wider spectrum of books, so you may stand a better chance of acceptance, but on the other hand the firm receives so many books for consideration that its editors can afford to be choosy; the small publisher is more likely to be hungry for new authors, but is likely to have a much more limited range. The large publisher may well be more efficient, and with a numerous sales force can be expected to achieve reasonably good sales; unless your book is a potential bestseller, however, it is possible that a small house will give you more attention. I remember expressing surprise to the successful novelist John Brophy when he moved from a large publisher to a medium-sized house; he said that he had not been one of the large publisher's top authors, but only in the middle rank, whereas with his new firm, he would be one of their leading writers – 'It's better to be a large fish in a medium-sized pond, than a medium-sized fish in a large pond.'

Make yourself a list of potential publishers for your work, and work your way through it until either you have an acceptance or you decide to give up. But don't give up too easily. Perseverance is a much needed quality for authors – perseverance in completing their work, and perseverance in their attempts to find a publisher for it.

Packagers

A packager is not a publisher. He or she produces books which are then sold in a finished state to a regular publisher, who then publishes and sells them. Most packaged books are lavishly illustrated, usually with a fair amount of colour printing, and they work principally because the packager sells editions in a number of countries and languages, and can therefore build up a substantial print run and produce the copies at a price which the individual publisher would not be able to match. To explain this further: a book illustrated in colour is usually printed in four colours – yellow, blue, red and black; the text usually appears in black; let us suppose that the British packager has sold 10,000 copies to a British publisher, 20,000 to an American house, 10,000 in France, 15,000 in Germany, and 10,000 in Italy, a total of 65,000; it is then possible to print 65,000 copies from the yellow, blue and red plates in one go, making the colour printing comparatively cheap, while the black plate will be a totally new one each time, to accommodate the change of language for the French, German and Italian editions, and will have some minor alterations for the American edition.

Obviously the books which are suitable for this kind of operation have an international appeal. They are mostly devised by the packagers, who approach and commission an author to write the text, usually supplying the accompanying illustrations themselves. However, if you have an idea which you think might interest a packager, it is certainly worth approaching one of those listed in *The Writers' and Artists' Yearbook*.

Articles

If you are hoping to place articles (and this is, incidentally, probably the easiest way to get into print for the first time), then your market research will have to be rather more precise. Whereas the majority of book publishers have a quite wide-ranging list and bring out books which vary in style, length, and the market at which they are aimed, newspapers and magazines tend to be much more limited in their requirements. You need to study the length of the articles they publish, their editorial policies, and, especially the kind of reader for which they cater. You will probably have to check several issues of a magazine to build up a reliable picture of its editorial policy. Do study the advertisements, by the way, for they can provide valuable clues about the age and interests of the readership.

Short Stories

The market for short stories is a diminishing one. It is generally useless to send a single story to a book publisher, and your chances of getting a collection of stories published are pretty small unless you are an established writer with a high literary reputation. Short stories do, however, still get published in magazines and occasionally in newspapers, and careful market research can tell you where your best chances lie. Be careful to get the length right. If you are writing for women's magazines, then not only will you need to have a woman as the central character, but she will have to be of the right age group for the magazine. Similarly, the age group is of prime importance if you are looking at the 'confessions' magazines.

Poetry

It is not easy to get a book of poetry published unless you have already established yourself in the field. If you keep your eyes open, however, you can find nowadays an increasing number of outlets for poetry. Large numbers of so-called 'little presses' have come into existence, primarily for the purpose of publishing new poets who would otherwise not be seen in print, and new literary magazines, which often publish several pages of poetry, constantly appear (and, regrettably, usually disappear again after a few issues). A useful address list of Small Presses and Little Magazines is published by Oriel, 54 Charles Street, Cardiff CF1 4ED.

There are also various less specialized magazines which will sometimes take a poem, especially if it is relevant to the main content of the publication, and local newspapers can sometimes be cajoled into filling a small empty space with a poem. None of the editors concerned will come knocking at your door, but there is nothing to stop you knocking on their doors, and you may well be invited inside, if you do your market research with care.

Radio and Television

Your market research for radio and television in Britain is necessarily restricted by the fact that you have the BBC on one hand, and the independents on the other, and that is all. The BBC publishes a booklet, *Writing for the BBC*, which tells you exactly what they want and how to set about selling it to them. Their requirements are very similar to those of the independent radio and television organizations. But yet again, the key to success in these fields depends on listening and watching to find out all you need to know about the requisite length of an item, what can and what can't be done effectively in these media, and what sort of content is likely to appeal. There is a strong belief that a kind of 'closed shop' exists for writers in television, and that it is therefore impossible for newcomers to break in. This is not so, but the belief survives partly because so many would-be writers are rejected not because they are newcomers, but because they have not done sufficient market research to ensure that their material is the kind of thing that contemporary television directors are looking for.

Stage Plays

If you want to be a successful dramatist you must study what is happening today in the theatre. Far too many amateur playwrights are producing plays which are old-fashioned in construction, in theme, in setting. Even among the amateurs, who, generally speaking, tend to lag behind the professional theatre in their acceptance of change, the 'well-made play', with its three acts, drawing-room setting and middle-class values, is less popular than it used to be. Nevertheless, it should be remembered that the amateur market is an important one, and not all the plays published by a number of firms (notably, of course, Samuel French Ltd) have previously received professional performances. This is particularly true of the one-act play, still very popular with amateurs, although rarely seen in the professional theatre. But if you want to write for the amateur market, then you must find out what the average local society wants to do and is capable of doing.

Overseas Markets

Market research in the USA, Australia, and other overseas territories may be very difficult for the British writer unless he or she is fortunate enough to travel to faraway places and thus to be able to conduct the necessary research on the ground. This is a pity, especially for the writer of articles or short stories, since there are many lucrative opportunities for this kind of material, especially in the United States. The American *Writer's Market*, available in the United Kingdom, may seem pricey, but is valuable in the detail it provides about American book and magazine publishers. *The Writers' and Artists' Yearbook* also gives useful information about English language markets overseas. Nothing, however, can replace direct study of any publications for which you hope to write, and it is well worth the trouble of getting hold of them if you possibly can.

The sale of overseas rights in books and, indeed, almost any literary form other than articles and short stories, is probably best left in the hands of an agent, if you have one, or the British publisher or other licensee of the rights in the material.

Agents

Although you will always need to do a certain amount of market research – at least to the extent of keeping yourself abreast of modern styles and trends – an agent can save you most of the chores which we have so far been discussing in this chapter. A substantial part of a literary agent's job is, in fact, market research. He or she must be constantly knowledgeable about where to send a client's work with the best chance of success, and will also always be looking for opportunities to bring publishers and authors together for the commissioning of new work. The same applies, of course, if the agent is one who specializes in work for the theatre, or radio or television.

Good agents have other extremely useful functions:

1. They will ensure that your contract is a fair one, and will often be able to get more money for your work than you would if you were negotiating on your own. This is not to say either that unless you have an agent most publishers will cheat you badly, or

that having an agent will transform you from a poor writer into a rich one. Some rogue publishers do exist, and if you have an agent, he or she will certainly save you from the clutches of such firms, but if you are on your own, you will be reasonably safe with any of the well-established companies (you can judge them, by the way, by the authors they already publish – if they have some well-known writers on the list you can be fairly sure that such people would not stay with a cheating publisher). As for becoming rich, all that an agent can normally do is to improve the terms of your contract to a comparatively small extent, and whether or not you become rich depends on whether or not you write the kind of books which have the qualities to become bestsellers.

2. An agent will be your watchdog, making sure that the publisher fulfils the terms of the contract (and that includes checking royalty statements for accuracy), and will also conduct any disputes that you may have with your publisher. This last can be very useful, because it saves you from having a personal row, which you may find embarrassing, and moreover the agent will know exactly how justified your complaint is and how far to go in the argument with the publisher without endangering the publisher's commitment to you.

3. An agent will try to retain most subsidiary rights in your work so that they remain in your control, and will then make all possible efforts to sell them on your behalf.

4. An agent will read your work with care, and will often be prepared to offer editorial advice.

5. One of the principal things that a good agent offers is friendship. Many authors regard their publishers as enemies, but even in those cases where author and publisher appear to be on good terms, there is usually some conflict of interest lurking beneath the surface, and a certain wariness behind the bonhomie. Of course the relationship between an author and his agent may not always be all sweetness and light – hence the story of the author whose will left instructions that he was to be cremated, and ten per cent of his ashes scattered over his agent – but in general the agent is on the author's side, and is a good, sympathetic friend and adviser, practised in the provision of a shoulder to cry on, ready to give encouragement, and always conscious that his or her client is a person, rather than an inhuman writing machine.

Most would-be authors, trying to get into print, have the impression that it is almost impossible to do so without an agent. That is not true. It certainly does not apply if you confine yourself to the writing of articles (with the sale of which most agents do not involve themselves) or of short stories (which most agents handle only for their established clients). Nevertheless, an agent is undoubtedly going to help you considerably – publishers do not buy only from agents, but they do look especially carefully at agented work, because they know that the agent would not be handling it if it did not have a modicum of merit, and would probably not have sent it to them if it were unsuitable for their list.

WHAT DOES AN AGENT COST?

Most agents charge ten per cent of any moneys earned from the literary work of their clients. The deduction may rise to nineteen or twenty per cent in respect of foreign sales, because two agents are involved – your own, and your agent's representative in the foreign country concerned. Agents do not normally take any fees until money has actually come in in respect of your work. Therefore, if their efforts to place it should fail, they will not charge you a fee to cover the expenses in which they have been involved. A few agents ask for fifteen per cent of earnings, and some charge a reading fee for unsolicited typescripts.

You also have some responsibilities towards an agent once you have been taken on as a client. Firstly, you should be prepared to give your agent your trust – it is his or her business to know what the going rates are, what is reasonable and what is not, how long to continue trying to place a typescript, and so on. The agent is a professional, and you should accept the advice you are given. Secondly, it is conventionally accepted that, unless it is agreed otherwise, you should involve your agent and pay the normal percentage on work which you have found for yourself as opposed to work which your agent has found for you.

Of course, you may come to the conclusion that, professional or not, the agent's advice and the effort made on your behalf are not what you had hoped for, or that you are obtaining all your work yourself, and therefore deriving no benefit from the agent. There is no contract between authors and agents, so you are free to leave at any time, either to find another agent or to work independently from that time on. Another convention dictates, however, that, unless specifically agreed otherwise, any work originally handled by an agent should remain in that agent's control, at least until the work goes out of print, and that he or she should continue to take the standard cut of moneys received in respect of the work.

HOW TO GET AN AGENT

Ay, there's the rub! It is even more difficult to find an agent than to find a publisher. To begin with, there are fewer agents – the listings for United Kingdom firms in *The Writers' and Artists' Yearbook* cover some dozen pages, whereas British book publishers take up four times as much space. Secondly, agents are involved in considerable expenses – they have staff to pay and offices to maintain, as well the cost of correspondence and the sending out of typescripts – and one agent has recently gone on record as saying that he can only make a profit out of clients who can be relied upon to make £20,000 a year from their writing (of which his cut would be £2,000). That is undoubtedly a high figure, but most agents would agree that when they take on a new client they are hoping for that author to be making, within a comparatively short period, a minimum of £5,000 a year from writing alone. Thirdly, since the relationship between an author and an agent is a very personal one, you need to find someone who is compatible with you (and if you do get an offer from an agent to take you on, the first thing to do is to arrange a meeting so that you can assure yourself that you have indeed found a friend as well as a business partner).

So it is difficult to get an agent. One possibility is to try some of the smaller, newer firms, who are more likely to be looking for clients. Another is to approach an agent once you have interested a publisher in your work – that is to say, when you have received the offer of a contract, but before you have actually signed it. An agent may be much more willing to take you on at that stage, with the guarantee of at least some income from your work.

If you cannot persuade an agent to represent you, do not despair. Very many authors work perfectly happily by direct contact with their publishers, and it has to be said that many publishers often prefer not to have an agent involved – not because they wish to cheat the author, but because if there is no agent, the publisher will usually control all the subsidiary rights, and that will mean not only that he receives some income from their sale but that he has those rights to offer, which gives him status and sometimes bargaining power with, for instance, foreign publishers.

Vanity Publishers

Vanity publishing is a technical term referring to a specific kind of publishing which is based on the author making a substantial contribution towards the production costs of the book, with the assurance that, when sufficient copies of the book have been sold, the money will come back to the author in the form of high royalties. In most cases, the 'contribution' consists of the entire costs, plus the vanity publisher's profit, and despite expansive promises, the book will not achieve a wide bookshop sale, and the author will never get any of his money back.

Vanity publishers are expert at flattering authors who have failed to get their books accepted by regular publishing houses, and at giving the impression that the success of the book in question is virtually guaranteed. They are also highly skilled in not saying anything which can later be held against them, and their contracts are usually watertight and contain no clauses which they do not fulfil. There is, in fact, nothing illegal about vanity publishing.

It has to be admitted that vanity publishers usually take considerable pains to ensure that the books which they produce are attractive in appearance. It is, however, an extremely expensive, and in the long run disappointing, way of getting into print, and you are strongly advised against it. There are some occasions when regular publishers accept contributions from an author towards production costs, but if you are ever offered a publishing contract which does include such a contribution, you should check carefully and take advice before signing.

If you have failed to interest a regular publisher in your work, and you have a little money which you wish to spend on putting the work into print, then the answer is to go to a printer (or even a printshop – at least make an enquiry there first) and pay the firm to produce copies for you. You should get an estimate first – preferably several estimates, from which you can make a choice. There are books available which will tell you exactly how to go about it, including such mysteries as the need for an ISBN and how you obtain one – *How to Publish Yourself* by Peter Finch is a helpful example. The point of doing it yourself in this way is that you will have all the expense, but you will also pocket all the receipts from sales of your book. However, it has to be said that comparatively few authors who publish their own work succeed in marketing it adequately – established publishers often experience difficulty in getting widespread distribution of their books, and it is obviously even harder for the author working on his or her own. But it can be done, and has been done – principally with books which really do supply a gap in the market.

Submissions

BOOKS

When you have decided where you are going to send your work it is advisable to write first to ask whether you may submit it for consideration. Apart from anything else, if your typescript is bulky it will save the cost of mailing it to a publisher or agent who might not be interested in it. It is worth phoning first to find out the name (and how it is spelt) of the chief editor or editorial director or the member of the agency who deals with that kind of work, so that you can write to him or her personally. Your letter should be brief and businesslike, describing the work in a few words which will give a clear indication of its scope, but without going into a long summary. If you have qualifications for writing it, mention them. There is no point in saying that your friends enjoyed the work, because the editor or agent does not know their critical abilities and will suspect that in any case they would not have dared to tell you if they didn't like it; on the other hand, if the typescript has been read and admired by a well-known personality or an authority in the field, you should certainly include that information. Enclose a stamped addressed envelope for the reply.

If you receive a favourable answer, mail or deliver the work, enclosing return postage. If you deliver by hand, do not expect to talk to the editor or agent – your work must speak for itself, and any essential information (such as the fact that you can supply additional illustrations if required) can be included in your covering letter.

Then be patient. Few publishers will give you a verdict in less than three weeks, and very often there is a much longer delay. If you have not heard after three months, you can send a polite inquiry; after six months without response, you are entitled to write a strongly worded letter, asking for your typescript to be returned. You will lose nothing by showing your anger at this stage – if you have heard nothing for that long, it is unlikely that the firm in question is interested in your work, and its behaviour will have been reprehensible.

SUBMITTING A SYNOPSIS

One way of cutting down on the time that publishers take to consider a typescript (and also of saving considerably on postage) is to send a synopsis of your work and a specimen chapter or two rather than the whole thing. This is quite a good idea for non-fiction (see the section on Commissions below), but may not work so well with fiction. Most, but not all, publishers prefer to see a complete novel, because it is often very difficult to decide from the sight of a single chapter, or even two, how effectively the story will be written. However, you will probably lose very little by trying. Before sending it off, it would certainly be worth asking your chosen publishers whether they would be prepared to consider your work in that form.

MULTIPLE SUBMISSIONS

Another possibility is to send your work to more than one house simultaneously. Is this allowed? Some publishers object to the practice, but many others are willing to tolerate it. You could ask in your preliminary letter whether the publisher would mind if you showed the typescript elsewhere at the same time.

POETRY

If you hope to get your poetry published in one of the little magazines, you can probably risk sending your work off without first seeking the magazine's permission, but you will of course enclose a short covering note and a stamped addressed envelope if you want your material returned. It is best to send no more than three of your poems for consideration. If the editor likes your work, he or she will probably ask to see more.

ARTICLES

If you have done your market research carefully and therefore have a good idea that your work will be of interest to a certain magazine or newspaper, you can submit your work 'on spec', without writing first. If, however, you make a preliminary enquiry and get a favourable response, you will at least have the certainty that your work will be looked at with interest. It is worth remembering, by the way, that most magazines work some way ahead, and if your article is intended, for instance, for a Christmas issue, it needs to be submitted in the previous August. If it is immediately topical, you will have very little chance of acceptance unless it is also a subject of continuing interest. For further information on the submission of articles, see *The Way to Write Magazine Articles* by John Hines, which is the best of the several good handbooks available.

SHORT STORIES

The remarks above on articles also apply to short stories, but since the outlets are comparatively few, market research is even more essential. Donna Baker's book, *How to Write Stories for Magazines* is very helpful.

PLAYS

Plays can be sent to theatre managements, or even to a leading actor for whom you have written a star part, but your best approach is probably through one of the agents who specialize in handling dramatic work. If your work is intended only for the amateur theatre, it can be submitted in the normal way to one of the publishing houses which caters for this market.

Commissions

Unless you are a well-established author you are unlikely to be commissioned to write a work of fiction. As already explained, if you send no more than a specimen chapter or two and a synopsis of a novel, most publishers will not go beyond an expression of interest in seeing the completed work in due course. There are, however, some exceptions to this rule, notably Mills & Boon.

With non-fiction, on the other hand, the submission of a detailed synopsis and specimen chapters stands much more chance of resulting in a commission and a contract. This is especially true if your work is of an original nature, if you can demonstrate that you have good qualifications for writing it, and if you have done your market research well and can show the publisher that no other book covering the same ground is already available. For more details on how to go about it, see *The Successful Author's Handbook* by Gordon Wells, which can be warmly recommended.

Rejections

Never despair if your work is rejected. There are dozens of reasons why a piece of writing is not accepted, and many of them have nothing to do with the quality of the piece. The person to whom you send it may just have taken on a very similar work, or may have so crowded a publication schedule that there is no room for additions, or, despite your careful market research, the editorial policy may have changed. Moreover, editors are human beings, with personal likes and dislikes, and good and bad moods, and it may be simply that your work has been looked at by someone who is out of sympathy with it, and that the next editor to see it will jump at it. Keep on trying. Remember the many stories of famous authors who have struggled for years before getting a book accepted, and have then immediately shot on to the bestseller list with it. Of course, if you receive a whole series of rejections, you should perhaps begin to wonder whether the quality of the writing is at fault, especially if you have not received any kind word from any of the editors who have seen it.

If you do receive a rejection which also contains some praise, and perhaps even a request to see anything else that you write, you can really feel encouraged. Publishers are not in the habit of writing in that vein unless they mean it.

Don't expect a rejection to include detailed criticism of your work. A few publishers will take the trouble to explain why they are turning something down, but most of them say that if they were to write lengthy, explanatory rejection letters, they would not have enough time to work on the books that they were accepting.

The Rights Offered

There is considerable confusion about 'First British Serial Rights', a phrase which many beginners believe they should type on the front of any work they produce. It should appear on work submitted to a magazine or newspaper (see p.111), but in the case of a book which you are offering directly to a publisher, what you are hoping to sell is 'Volume Rights', and indeed, the publisher will probably ask, if accepting the book, simply for 'World Rights'. The copyright will remain with you, but the publisher will have the right to grant licences for the use of the book in dozens of different ways, including U.S. and foreign rights, paperback, book club, film, radio, anthology and many other rights, sharing the proceeds with you in agreed proportions as laid down in the contract between you.

Keeping a Copy

Never ever send out your work without keeping a copy. The majority of publishers will take reasonable care of your typescript and return it, if it is rejected, but there are inevitable cases when the material is lost, and it is normal practice that work is submitted at the author's risk, so if your work does go walkabout, there will be no compensation. Parcels also sometimes go astray in the post. So always keep a copy. Some authors, when submitting articles, stories or poems will say in the covering letter that they do not expect the material to be returned if it is not accepted, but of course they can only do that if they are secure in the knowledge of being able to produce a second copy if need be. If you work on a word processor, you may feel that it is sufficient to keep your work filed on disc, but it is well worth printing out a second copy for yourself, because discs can occasionally become defective, quite apart from the hazard of accidental erasure.

9   Libel and Other Legal Problems

Before you send your work to a publisher, it is as well to feel easy in your mind as far as the legality of its content is concerned. If it is a book and it is accepted for publication you will almost certainly have to sign a warranty that it is free from unlawful material.

In the case of several of the offences listed in this chapter, such as obscene libel, blasphemous libel and sedition, the author will be fully aware of the risks he or she is taking. But many beginners worry over libel, which is probably the commonest cause for legal action as far as authors are concerned, and some appear to be quite unaware that plagiarism is a punishable sin.

Libel

If you publish something which damages someone's reputation in the eyes of other people you have perpetrated a libel, and may be sued.

The first thing to make clear is that you do not commit libel if you write in complimentary or even neutral terms about another person, unless your tone is so heavily ironic that you are clearly intending the opposite of the face value of the words. An essential quality of libel is that it is always damaging.

Secondly, you cannot libel the dead, although you must beware of making a statement about a dead person which might seriously affect the reputations of his or her descendants.

If you are writing non-fiction, the issues are usually clear-cut. A statement in a book or article which accuses a named person of criminal activity or of socially unacceptable behaviour can be very dangerous, unless you can prove that the facts you have presented are true (and preferably, widely known to be true).

'Justification' – that is to say that you have merely printed the truth – is the first and best defence against a threat of libel.

You may wonder how journalists get away with saying, for

instance, that the leader of a political party is an incompetent fool. The defence in this case would be that the statement is 'fair comment' – a matter of opinion, rather than of fact, stated in good faith and without malice. In any case, politicians, and indeed many public figures, are commonly treated in this way, and would spend their lives in litigation if they really believed that such comments were harmful to them. On the other hand, if you say that a politician has misappropriated moneys, for instance, you will be in trouble. Equally, your defence of 'fair comment' might be less easy to sustain if you had said in print that the managing director of a small firm was an incompetent fool. Although not necessarily nationally known, such a person would probably be very dependent on the good opinion of his customers, and might find your comment extremely damaging. To make matters worse, you could well have some difficulty in proving that your statement was true, in order to plead 'justification'.

A third defence against a libel action is 'privilege'. This applies chiefly to reports of judicial and parliamentary proceedings, and of public meetings, provided that the report is fair and accurate.

Before you include any potentially libellous material in your writing, do be certain that it is essential for your purposes. Even if you are sure that you would win any libel case brought against you, a court action is always extremely expensive, in time as well as in money. If you are doubtful about whether something you have written is libellous, always tell your publisher about it. He or she may take legal advice on the matter, but in any case it is your duty to make it clear that a risk exists.

The problems for fiction writers are considerable. You will no doubt have seen those notices which publishers often place at the beginning of novels – 'All of the characters in this book are fictitious, and any resemblance to actual persons, living or dead, is purely coincidental'. Such a notice may help to deter a frivolous litigant, but is basically worthless, and will not protect either the author or the publisher if the book does in fact contain libellous material.

It is always risky to portray characters from life if you are describing those persons and their actions as discreditable. You can give the characters different names, and it may help to change their physical appearance and circumstances. Nevertheless, if any of the persons concerned, and especially their friends and acquaintances, can recognize them as the originals of your characters, there will be the possibility of a case of libel.

You must also be careful in fiction to avoid using the real name of a professional person, such as a doctor or a lawyer, if you are going to ascribe unethical actions to the character concerned. If, for instance, you invent a doctor who is peddling illegal drugs, and you give him the name of a real-life doctor, you can be in serious trouble. A defence does exist on the grounds of 'innocence' – that is to say, you had no knowledge of the libelled person's existence, had no malicious intent, and used his or her name by accident, as it were. But that is a difficult defence to invoke, and in a situation like that it is worth consulting the BMA list of doctors to ensure that you choose a name which does not appear on it.

If a libel case is brought against something that you have written, the ultimate responsibility is yours. In theory, at least, you will have to pay all damages and costs awarded in the case, and the cost of the defence. In practice, your publishers may agree to share such costs, especially if you have warned them of the possibility of libel and they have agreed to take the risk of prosecution. It's far better to avoid the problem altogether, if you possibly can.

Plagiarism

Plagiarism is the deliberate copying of another author's work without either permission or even acknowledgment. You are permitted to quote small portions of someone else's published material under the convention of 'fair usage' – that is to say, the quoted material is used briefly, for instance, to support your own argument, or to illustrate a point. Such a quotation should always be acknowledged by the inclusion of the author's name, the title of the work from which it comes, and preferably its publisher too. If the passage to be quoted is at all lengthy, you should seek permission to use it, and pay any appropriate fee. By convention, however, you are free to quote a reasonable amount of material (say, up to 400 words) from a book in a review of it that you write.

But, apart from direct quotation, what about a more general use of another author's material? Supposing you are writing a non-fiction book on a certain subject; you will almost certainly read a large number of other books on the same subject. Can you be accused of plagiarism if your book contains similar material to those you have read? Generally speaking, no. Make sure, however, that everything you write is in your own words, and that you acknowledge the source of any specific material which is not a generally known fact. It is also advisable to avoid copying the exact arrangement of the material in a way which would suggest that you had taken someone else's work as a direct model.

What about plots in fiction? It is well known that the number of basic plots is limited to a handful, so can you be accused of plagiarism if your plot is similar to that of another author? It depends on the degree of similarity. If your story follows all the twists and turns of an existing work of fiction, with the same cast of characters, even if they have different names and perhaps a different setting, you would indeed be stealing (which is what plagiarism is). Your only defence would be to prove that you were totally unaware of the previously published book, and you might find it very difficult to do so.

Obscenity

You might think that nowadays there is no risk of prosecution for obscenity. It is certainly difficult to imagine any non-fiction being taken to court for this reason, as manuals on birth control were in the past, though perhaps in the field of autobiography it might be possible. Four-letter words and detailed descriptions of the sexual act are commonplace in published fiction, and there appear to be no limits. However, blatant pornography is still liable to prosecution, and the police still raid bookshops which deal in this trade (often including in their nets a number of books generally considered to be respectable).

The problem is that the borderline between pornographic writing and what is permissible is very vague – lawyers have struggled for years and in vain to produce a really satisfactory definition of pornography. Who can say with certainty that this piece of writing will 'deprave and corrupt' the average person, and who is the average person anyway? We all have our own standards in making this kind of judgment. Literary quality can be cited in evidence in obscenity trials, and it seems fair to say that the author's intention is of paramount importance – is the material in question an integral and essential part of the writing, placed there for serious literary reasons, or has it been inserted gratuitously, not merely to titillate, but indeed to deprave and corrupt? And that, of course, brings us back to the insoluble problem of deciding what is no more than acceptable titillation, and what is something a great deal worse.

Blasphemous Libel

Blasphemous libel, in Britain, is concerned with offensive material about the Christian religion, but in our multi-racial society, it is possible that a prosecution in respect of another religion might be successful, and, indeed, there is a move afoot to change the present law to protect the religious susceptibilities of non-Christians. As with obscene libel, it is difficult to define exactly what constitutes blasphemous libel. There is no illegality in any anti-religious writings which are serious in tone and moderate in language and approach. To be libellous in this sense the material must be of a truly outrageous nature, and will probably be obscene as well as blasphemous.

Racism

It is an offence to publish racially offensive material, for which you can be prosecuted under the Race Relations Act, especially if your aim is clearly to stir up racial hatred. Comparatively few writers will go that far, but it is as well to avoid any racist attitude which, even if not so blatant as to risk prosecution, could give offence. This is especially important for the writers of children's books (who have also, of course, to beware of sexism).

Sedition

Writings which aim to destroy the peace of the realm by violent means are subject to prosecution. Under this heading may also be included works which breach confidentiality, as instanced in the recent *Spycatcher* case, or remembering the furore which was caused some forty years ago when 'Crawfie', governess to the Princesses Elizabeth and Margaret Rose, published her memoirs. Prosecutions are rare, and the authors of such books frequently appear to benefit enormously from the publicity which is generated by attempts to ban their works. Presumably they are little troubled by conscience as they bank the proceeds.

Passing Off

There is no copyright in titles, and you are therefore free to call your work by any name you like. However, if you choose a title which is already a household word, you risk being prosecuted by the author or owner of the copyright of the original work for 'passing off' – that is to say, you will be accused of trying to persuade the public to buy your book under the impression that it is the famous one. Some titles appear quite often on different books, but should not be used if they have already been appropriated for a bestseller. So if you want to call your book *From Russia with Love* or *The Kon-Tiki Expedition* or *Gone with the Wind*, think again.

Equally, there is no copyright in authors' names, but however unfair it may seem, if your name happens to be the same as that of some famous contemporary writer, you will probably be well advised to use a pseudonym, if only to avoid confusion.

10 Payment For Your Work

The Publisher's First Offer

If a book publisher to whom you have sent your work decides to accept it for publication, you will almost certainly receive a letter containing an offer (unless the publisher wants you to do a considerable amount of revision before reaching that stage). The letter will not go into a great deal of detail, which will be left until contract stage, but will probably name a sum as the advance to be paid against the book's earnings, will specify the instalments in which that advance is to be paid, and will list the royalties payable on ordinary sales of the publisher's edition of the book in the domestic market and overseas.

The first thing to remember is that hardly any authors make enough from their writing to live on, so the amounts offered will not stagger you by their enormous size. Indeed, in certain fields, such as 'library fiction' (romantic novels, westerns and similar genre books which sell principally to libraries rather than in bookshops), the publisher is in a buyer's market, able to choose from dozens of submitted books of almost equal standard, and therefore the offer may indeed stagger you – but by its minuscule size.

The second point to remember is that the offer is not necessarily a final one. If the publisher has got as far as making an offer for the book, a fair amount of time has already been spent on it, and he or she actually wants to publish it, and may already have slotted it in tentatively to the publishing schedule. You are unlikely, therefore, to have the offer withdrawn if you dare to query its terms and ask for them to be improved. Don't, however, especially if this is your first book, expect more than a modest improvement, and be prepared for the publisher to refuse the request altogether.

You may be particularly ready to ask for an increase in the size of the advance. After all, it is guaranteed money, and you may feel too that the larger the advance, the more effort the publisher will put into the publication. The advances which publishers offer are calculated in rough proportion to the sales they envisage, including possibly the sale of subsidiary rights, and a book with a five figure advance carries greater expectations and is inevitably going to get more attention than one for which the publisher has put down, say, £500. But the difference in effort on a book for which the advance is £750 rather than £500 is minimal. Get an increase if you can, but since, if the publisher has offered a modest advance, you are unlikely to be able to pressure him or her into an astronomic figure, you will probably do better to try to increase the royalties. Royalties are, of course, birds in the bush, while the advance is a bird in the hand, but the higher the royalties the sooner the advance will be earned, and your long term benefits may be much greater if you secure an improvement in that field.

Copyright

Copyright exists in a work as soon as it is written, and normally extends, in respect of works published during the author's lifetime, for seventy years after his or her death.

You should always retain your copyright in your work. Most book publishers' contracts take the form of a licence, in which you give the publisher various rights in return for specified payments, but they do not usually entail the surrender of your copyright. Look askance at any offer, and especially any contract, which requires you to do so. It is not simply a matter of principle, but of hard commercial fact. If you abandon your copyright, the publisher who owns it may exploit your work in any way, possibly selling hundreds of thousands of copies of your work over a long period without paying you a single penny more.

There may, nevertheless, be certain extraordinary circumstances in which you could be tempted to sell your copyright, doing so with a fair amount of equanimity. One is if you are offered a really substantial sum of money for it, especially if you are in need of the immediate cash; but do think twice, for if the publisher is willing to lay out a big sum of money, the odds are that he expects to get it back tenfold, and you would do much better on a royalty. The only other reason I can think of for giving up your basic ownership of your work is if the publisher, when about to commission a book, threatens to give the job to someone else if you won't agree to surrender your copyright, and tells you, moreover, that he knows half a dozen competent authors who would be only too happy to sign a contract on those terms; it is very hard, for the sake of a principle, to give up a commission of that sort, and the certainty both of payment and publication. An author I know was commissioned to write a short book for a publisher who offered an outright fee for the copyright. When my friend protested, the publisher refused to alter his offer. The author, who was eighty-seven at the time, said to herself, 'If I insist on a royalty I may die before the book actually earns anything. The amount offered isn't bad, and if I take it now I shall have the benefit of it while I'm still able to enjoy it.' She took the money, and enjoyed it, and although she is still alive and might have earned a larger sum in royalties than she was paid, she does not regret her decision. If I live to be eighty-seven and am still writing, I might follow her example. Meanwhile, however, no.

Newspapers and magazines often attempt to purloin an author's copyright. In payment for the work some will send a cheque which requires to be receipted on the back, but the wording above the space for the author's signature grants the paper or magazine copyright in the piece. If you get a cheque like that, cross out the reference to copyright and initial the deletion before signing.

The Publisher's Contract

Following your acceptance of the basic terms offered by the publisher, a contract will, in due course, make its appearance. It is likely to be a document of formidable length and complexity, reflecting not only the many ramifications of the book business today, but also the modern need to specify in some detail the rights and duties of both parties. Many of those clauses and sub-clauses are there because neither publishers nor authors can always be relied on nowadays to behave in an honourable way without the constraint provided by a legal document. But in case you think I have in mind the 'good old days', when a handshake between publisher and author was sufficient to cover all eventualities to the satisfaction of both parties, let me hasten to add that there has never been such a time. Authors and publishers have always been in conflict, and always will be. To listen to or read articles by the more militant of today's authors, you might think that publishers have become much more villainous in recent times, and authors much more hard done by. Not so. What has changed is that the period following the Second World War has seen a previously unknown willingness of authors to air their mostly justified grievances against publishers and to campaign jointly for better terms. In fact, you are much better off with that long and complicated contract than you would have been in the days of nothing more than an apparently friendly handshake.

However, the document is indeed long and complex. Don't sign it without reading it carefully. Even if you have an agent whom you trust and the contract has been drawn up by him or her rather than by the publisher (most agents have their own agreement forms), you should still read it before signing.

If you do not have an agent, you will probably need to do more than read it. You will need advice. The book concerned could turn into a bestseller, or at least one which will continue to provide you with a substantial income for many years to come. Unlikely? Then think of a book such as *Jonathan Livingstone Seagull*, which was a failure when it first appeared, and then suddenly became a cult bestseller around the world. You should never count on miracles, but they do occasionally happen. So this contract could end up being more important to you than those you sign when you buy a house.

The cheapest advice you can get is probably from a friend who is a published author – perhaps someone you have met at a writers' circle. Such people can be knowledgeable and helpful, but quite often their experience of publishers' contracts is limited, so this cheap advice may not really be adequate.

You could go, as you would over the purchase of a house, to a solicitor. You do need, however, to engage the services of a firm which deals regularly with the book world and authors' contracts. Your local solicitor will understand the legal side of a publisher's contract, but is quite unlikely to appreciate fully how the book trade works, and will probably not know what is standard practice, nor see some of the implications of certain clauses. The problem is that, while expert legal advice is readily available, it is expensive.

The next possibility is to join the Society of Authors, which you are eligible to do as soon as you have a firm offer from a publisher. Or you could join the Writers' Guild of Great Britain. Both organizations are equipped to give their members free and reliable guidance on contracts.

Failing all else, you could do worse than to buy a copy of my book *An Author's Guide to Publishing*, and study the chapter on contracts. I say that without any lack of modesty simply because the chapter contains the full text of the Minimum Terms Agreement (see below), together with comments on it. The chapter will tell you a great deal about what you should expect to see in your contract, and what alterations to fight for.

The Minimum Terms Agreement

There is nothing standard about book publishers' contracts – each firm has its own form of contract, and so does each agent, and the terms and conditions vary very widely. In 1981 the Society of Authors and the Writers' Guild presented to the Publishers Association a document known as the Minimum Terms Agreement, which they had drawn up jointly. The MTA laid down the basic terms which, the Society and the Guild suggested, would be acceptable to their members, and the hope was that the substantial changes which it proposed should become standard throughout the industry.

The Publishers Association, on the grounds that it cannot make binding agreements on behalf of its members, refused to endorse the MTA; instead, it produced a bland Code of Practice to which its members may or may not adhere. The Society and the Guild were then forced to approach individual publishers, and try to persuade them to accept the agreement. Progress has been lamentably slow, and at the time of writing less than a dozen firms have signed. However, the pace of recruiting appears to have speeded up recently, and it can also be seen that the mere existence of the MTA has led some other publishers to make (mostly minor) improvements to the terms of their contracts. Many, however, still look upon the MTA as an arm of the Devil, designed to bring publishers to despair and ruin.

Since all publishers have their own little quirks, the MTAs which have been signed differ in certain clauses; additionally, since 1981 the MTA has been amended by the Society and the Guild to remove some of the points which they have been forced to admit were too contentious. Nevertheless, the two main principles remain: a reasonable sharing between author and publisher of the financial rewards, especially if the book is successful, and the recognition that the author should be regarded by the publisher as a partner, to be consulted and kept informed concerning the publication of the book. The present signatories of the MTA accepted these principles willingly, and it is to be hoped that more and more publishers will adopt them as time goes by.

Many authors feel that the second point is the more important; they are tired of being treated condescendingly by publishers, some of whom seem to feel that the author's part in the publication of a book should finish as soon as he or she has completed the typescript, and who take the attitude that any author is lucky to be published, and should, like small Victorian children, be seen and not heard (and preferably not seen either).

A few of the important points in the MTA are:

LICENCE

The majority of publishers will expect to have a licence for the full period of copyright, but it is becoming increasingly common to put a shorter term to the licence, such as ten or fifteen years, after which a new contract can be negotiated, or the rights may revert to the author. There should also be adequate provision for the reversion of rights to the author if the work becomes out of print or if the publisher fails in various respects to adhere to the terms of the contract.

ADVANCE

The advance which a publisher pays is normally non-returnable. It is set against all earnings, such as royalties and income from subsidiary rights, which means that you do not get any further payment until the advance has been earned.

The advance is usually paid either in two instalments (on signature of the agreement if the book has already been delivered, and on publication), or in three instalments (on signature of the agreement, on delivery of the typescript, and on publication). Publication should not normally be delayed for more than twelve months after delivery of the typescript, and you should ask for the final part of the advance to be paid 'on publication or one year after delivery of the typescript, whichever is the sooner'. If you have not delivered the typescript when the agreement is signed, do not accept a clause which says that the next instalment of the advance will be paid 'on acceptance' of the work by the publisher – that, in effect, means that all the publisher has agreed to do is to consider your completed work for publication, and it leaves him or her free to reject it at that stage.

ROYALTIES

Except in some cases, such as highly illustrated books for which the author does not supply the illustrations, the standard royalties are 10% of the retail price on sales in the domestic market, and 10% of the publisher's receipts on sales in the export market. Both rates should rise to 12½% after the sale of 2,500 copies in the respective markets, and to 15% after a further sale of 2,500 copies. You may have to be content with a less favourable rising scale, but always aim at these breaks.

ALTERATIONS
No alterations should be made to the typescript without the knowledge and approval of the author.

CONSULTATION
While the publisher retains control of the production of the book, the author should be consulted about the blurb, the jacket design, the review list and the date of publication.

AUTHOR'S COPIES
For years it has been standard for authors to receive six free copies of the published book. Ask for ten, or, if the book is a mass paperback, for twenty.

SUBSIDIARY RIGHTS
These include rights sold to a mass paperback house, to a book club, to U.S. and foreign publishers, serial, radio, television, tape, disc, dramatization, digest, merchandizing, anthology and quotation, and picture book rights. All other rights should be reserved by you.

As examples, you should look for the following shares of subsidiary rights income: mass paperbacks – 60%, rising to 70% after the first 50,000 copies; U.S. rights – 85%, or if the publisher sells copies of the book to an American publisher on a royalty-inclusive basis, 20% of receipts; first serial rights – 90%; second serial rights – 75%; translation rights – 80%; book club rights – 10% of the price received by the publisher on the first 10,000 copies, and 12½% thereafter, if the publisher sells copies to the book club at a price inclusive of royalties, but if the arrangement is subject to a royalty paid by the book club on its sales, the author's share of royalties should start at 60% and rise to 70% at a point to be agreed.

Although royalties on the publisher's own editions of the book are normally paid at six-monthly intervals, any moneys received by the publisher from sub-contractors, and amounting to £100 or more, should be paid to the author within one month of receipt by the publisher, provided that the advance has been earned.

ILLUSTRATIONS, QUOTATIONS, INDEX
The agreement should contain clear statements as to whether the author or the publisher is responsible for the provision of these and for any payment involved in the clearance of rights. In some cases payment may be shared between the author and the publisher.

OPTIONS

The MTA does not include an option clause giving the publisher the right to sign up the author's next work or works. You should not sign such a clause. If the publisher insists that you do so, at least never accept a wording to the effect that the publisher has the right to buy a subsequent work on the same terms as the contract you are signing – insist that it should be 'on terms to be agreed'.

The exclusion of an option clause does not mean that an author should not submit a new book to his existing publisher, but only that there is no legal commitment to do so. Publishers prize loyalty in their authors, and authors should be happy to demonstrate it – but only if they are satisfied with the treatment they have received.

Please note that the points above are not all those covered by the MTA, and let me emphasize again the value, if you do not have an agent, of joining one of the authors' organizations (see p.155) once an offer is made for your book, since you will be able to obtain detailed advice on the contract from those organizations.

It is also only fair to make it clear that an argument over a contract is a matter of haggling. The publisher is in business to make money; so are you. Both of you will get the best bargain that you can, and that may result in a compromise. Never be afraid to query anything in a publisher's contract before you sign it. As long as you do so courteously, and are prepared to listen to the arguments which the publisher puts forward, there is always the possibility that you will be able to improve the contract from your own point of view. Even if you don't succeed in persuading him or her to give you everything you ask for, you should not sign until you feel you have reached an agreement which is reasonably fair to both sides. To accept poor terms is a disservice not only to yourself, but to all authors.

It is also true that a publisher who presents an author with a manifestly unfair contract, and refuses to improve it, will probably not be a very good publisher anyway – however much you long to be in print, a rejection of the offered agreement may bring you less disappointment in the end. One word of warning, however: before you condemn an agreement as totally unfair, you do need to understand the market situation. Some publishers bring out small editions of books, produced as cheaply as possible, in order to fill a specific market requirement. Their contracts may not meet the requirements of the MTA, but those publishers would not find the books economically viable if they paid higher advances and royalties, and they would argue that their whole operation depends on keeping their overheads down and on their ability to process the books as quickly as possible, and that means that they have neither the staff nor the time to give their authors the personal treatment that they really should have. In other words, the terms those publishers offer are fair in the light of the particular publishing job which they are doing. And they would point out that no author is obliged to accept the terms, and that there are many who do.

Finally, it is worth trying to understand why a publisher may not agree to all the changes in the contract which you ask for. Some publishers may be reluctant, for instance, to give you the right to be consulted about the jacket design. Why? Perhaps because they have suffered in the past from authors who think 'consultation' means 'a right of veto' or 'the right to conduct endless time- and money-wasting arguments, and to make impractical demands'. You should try to persuade them that you will not behave in that way, and that you will respect their professionalism and demonstrate your own.

Packagers

The contract between a packager and an author will differ in many respects from a normal publishing contract. One of the principal differences concerns the royalties, which will almost certainly be at lower rates. However, there is a major compensation: the packager sells the books to publishers at a royalty-inclusive price, and therefore you will receive your percentage whether or not the publisher sells a single copy; moreover you will be paid at the time the books are delivered to the publisher, or shortly thereafter; the same system will apply if the book is reprinted. If you should be commissioned to write a book by a packager, it will almost certainly be advisable to place the negotiations in the hands of an agent.

Poetry

If you publish a volume of poetry with one of the major publishing houses, everything included in this chapter so far will apply to the book. If, however, your work is published by one of the so-called 'Little Presses', you may not be called upon to sign a formal contract, but there should at least be some correspondence on the matter, and you should always ensure that this covers the copyright, which must remain in your possession. You may also receive only a token payment, or none at all, other than free copies of your work. The little presses often act as a showcase, and you may feel that it is worth accepting a minimal reward for that reason.

Articles

Word for word (and payment is usually by the word) the writing of articles can be far more lucrative than most literary work. You can earn a reasonable sum for a published letter, or for a single paragraph used as a 'filler'. Unless you are writing regularly for a journal, in which case you may have a formal contract, acceptance of an article for publication will usually be in the form of correspondence. The letter from the paper or magazine may, however, have many inadequacies – it may not name the fee, it may make no commitment as to when the article will be published, and it may not specify what rights the journal will have in the article. It is obviously preferable to sort these matters out right from the beginning. You should always ask for full NUJ rates – it is possible to obtain them even if you are a beginner – but be prepared for the fact that small, specialist magazines may laugh at the very idea, especially if you are an unknown writer. Payment is normally on publication, but some journals do not send out their cheques automatically, putting an obligation on the author to watch for publication of his or her work and to send in an invoice when the article appears; try to overcome this difficulty by getting the journal to agree that you will receive the fee on a given date, whether or not the article has been published by then. Do make sure that you do not grant a newspaper or magazine more than First Serial Rights (see page 111) – always retain your copyright.

Plays and Films

The theatre has an equivalent of the MTA in a Minimum Terms Contract which has been accepted by the Theatre Managers Association. Make sure that any contract you sign for the production of your play adheres to this MTC. It will almost certainly be worth your while to employ an agent. If your play is published, the publisher will pay you a royalty on copies sold, and will also act as a licensing and collecting agency, usually taking between 20% and 50% of the performance fees it receives.

Contracts for screenplays are so complex and come in so many varieties that you will certainly need expert advice, and should use one of the agents specializing in this business.

Radio and Television

The BBC and the independent television and radio companies work on standard rates and contracts. If you are working regularly in these media, it will pay you to join the Writers' Guild, which has particular interest and expertise in these fields, and in the cinema business, and which will be able to guide you in all the relevant contractual matters.

11   Proof-Reading

Although some magazines and newspapers do not send out proofs to their contributors, many do, and if your work is published in book form, it is virtually certain that you will be sent proofs and expected to return them promptly with any necessary corrections clearly marked.

Proofs come in several forms, the most common of which are galley proofs and page proofs. Galleys are long strips of paper on which the text appears in a single column, not having yet been divided up into pages; galleys are often used when it is expected that the text will be subject to heavy alterations, or for illustrated books which will not have the same amount of text on every page. Page proofs are the most usual form; as the name suggests, the text has been divided into the pages in which it will finally appear, and the proofs have often been bound with a paper cover, so that they really do look quite like a book.

Before many years pass, both typescripts and proofs will no longer be necessary. Authors will submit their books on word processor discs, all corrections will be made on the discs, and they will then go to the printer who will use them to produce the printed books. In the meantime, however, you will probably receive proofs for correction.

Proof-reading is a skilled job, and although you need not be too concerned if you are not practised at it, since someone at the publishing house will almost certainly be reading the proofs too and you are therefore not solely responsible, the more efficiently you can do the work the better.

Although you will probably be limited by the short time available for proof correcting, it is advisable to read your proofs at least twice yourself, and if possible to get other people to read them too. It is surprising how a different pair of eyes will see things that others have missed, and even the same pair of eyes, on a second reading, will find errors which they passed over the first time.

Your main task should be to look out for 'literals' – that is to say, errors in spelling, spacing, style of printing, etc. Don't think that these will be 'printer's errors' only – some may result from mistakes in your typescript which were never corrected, and others may have originated in the publisher's office. To find the literals you need to put your mind into a special mode in which, as you read the text, the brain looks at each individual word on its own, checking that it is correctly spelt. It is inevitably a fairly slow and laborious process, and it is important to prevent yourself, if you can, from becoming caught up in the sense of what you are reading to such an extent that you stop examining each word separately; it is all too easy to fall into the trap of reading what you think *ought* to be there, rather than what *is* there, especially if you have been checking the proofs already for a couple of hours and your eyes and brain are tired.

And that leads to the advice to do your proof-reading in short bursts, rather than in long sessions.

Always have a copy of the typescript with you while you are proof-reading. Check back, when you find a literal error, to see whether it is really the typesetter's mistake, or whether the error existed in the typescript. This is important because it will affect both the way you mark the change on the proof (see below) and the cost of the alteration.

I said earlier that your main task is to look for literals. What about the opportunity of making improvements to your text? There is usually quite a gap between acceptance of your work and its appearance in proof form, and when you first see it in print, it will have become slightly unfamiliar (at least, more so than when you were working on it every day), and it may produce in you very mixed feelings; you will undoubtedly feel pleased and proud, but I can almost guarantee that you will also experience a keen sense of disappointment. You will realize that you have not expressed this or that point with the clarity you had hoped for, that the style over which you laboured so long reads leadenly rather than with elegance, that you have repeated the same word six times on page 43, and that (oh, dear!) your heroine's green eyes have later turned blue.

So, yes, of course, while your brain is examining each word for literals, another part of it is aware of the sense of the material, and its style, and is trying to keep tabs on accuracy and consistency, and the overall effect. You are certain to find things that you want to change.

Don't alter them unless they are really essential, *because corrections are extremely expensive to make.*

You will probably have seen in your contract a clause which

states that you will be responsible for the cost of proof corrections over a certain percentage (very often 10%) of the cost of composition of the whole book. You might think that that was fine – that you would be able to change completely one page in every ten without involving yourself in any financial penalty – but it doesn't work like that. The charges for corrections to proofs are very high, and indeed the cost will often seem out of all proportion in relationship to the initial cost of composition. The typesetter is responsible for any errors that he has made, so you don't need to worry about those, but every other correction will be charged for, and it is therefore essential to get your typescript into as perfect a state as you can before it goes to the typesetter, and then to keep your corrections to the absolute minimum.

One tip which can save a lot of expense is to make sure that any alterations you make affect as few lines of type as possible. So if you delete a word, a phrase, a sentence, or indeed a whole paragraph, try to replace the material with something of exactly the same length. Equally, if you insert new wording, try to cut something which will make the exact amount of room for it. Naturally, it is not always possible to do this, and it is less essential if the change comes at the very end of a chapter, or sometimes in the last line of a paragraph, where there is space available for a certain amount of new material, but the object of the exercise is to avoid any need for the typesetter to shift large chunks of text around, especially if the moves are going to involve several pages.

Of course, there are some occasions when you simply have to make substantial alterations at proof stage. It is advisable to consult your publisher in such cases to explain why the changes are essential and how best to carry them out.

When you find anything in your proofs which needs to be altered, you should use the conventional signs, the more common of which are printed on the following pages. *The Writers' and Artists' Yearbook* contains a longer list of these signs, extracted from a document called *BS 5261: Part 2: 1976* which may be obtained from the British Standards Institution, 2 Park Street, London W1A 2BS. While it is advisable to use the accepted markings, the most important thing is that your corrections should be legible and your intentions unmistakable.

You will probably be sent two sets of proofs, one of which may be stamped to indicate that it is the 'marked set', together with your original typescript. The marked set will probably contain some corrections and possibly some queries (to ask, perhaps, whether something in the typescript is really intended to appear in that form). These marks, which have been made by the typesetter, should be in green ink. When you come to mark the proofs yourself, use a red pen for typesetter's errors, and blue or black for your own alterations.

Having incorporated all your corrections into the marked set, you will be required to return it to the publisher. You may retain the second set of proofs, and if you mark in them all the necessary changes, you will be able to check that they have all been carried out when the finished books eventually arrive.

Proof Reader's Marks

The symbols for correcting proofs are taken from a British Standard BS 5261: PART 2 1976 *Copy preparation and proof correction – Specification of typographic requirements, marks for copy preparation and proof correction, proofing procedure.* Extracts from the new Standard are reproduced below with the permission of BSI. Complete copies can be obtained from them at Linford Wood, Milton Keynes, Bucks., MK14 6LE. All authors, printers and publishers are recommended to adopt the new correction symbols.

	Textual Mark	Marginal Mark
Correction is concluded	None	/
Leave unchanged	- - - - - - under character to remain	⟨√⟩
Push down risen spacing material	Encircle blemish	⊥
Insert in text the matter indicated in the margin	⋏	New matter followed by ⋏
Insert additional matter identified by a letter in a diamond	⋏	⋏ Followed by for example ⟨A⟩
Delete	/ through character(s) or ⊢———⊣ through word(s) to be deleted	↗

Instruction	Textual Mark	Marginal Mark
Delete and close up	ỉ through character or ⊢⟨⟩⊣ through character e.g. character characcter	⌒
Substitute character or substitute part of one or more word(s)	/ through character or ⊢————⊣ through word(s)	New character or new word(s)
Wrong fount. Replace by character(s) of correct fount	Encircle character(s) to be changed	⊗
Change damaged character(s)	Encircle character(s) to be changed	✕
Set in or change to italic	———— under character(s) to be set or changed	⊔
Set in or change to capital letters	≡≡≡ under character(s) to be set or changed	≡
Set in or change to small capital letters	══ under character(s) to be set or changed	═
Set in or change to capital letters for initial letters and small capital letters for the rest of the words	≡ under initial letters and ══ under rest of word(s)	═
Set in or change to bold type	∿∿∿∿ under character(s) to be set or changed	∿
Change capital letters to lower case letters	Encircle character(s) to be changed	≢
Change italic to upright type	Encircle character(s) to be changed	⊔

Instruction	Textual Mark	Marginal Mark
Invert type	Encircle character to be inverted	↺
Substitute or insert full stop or decimal point	/ through character or ⋏ where required	⊙
Substitute or insert semi-colon	/ through character or ⋏ where required	;
Substitute or insert comma	/ through character or ⋏ where required	ʼ
Start new paragraph	⌐	⌐
Run on (no new paragraph)	⟩	⟩
Centre	[enclosing matter to be centred]	[ ]
Indent	⊏	⊏
Cancel indent	←⊏	⊏
Move matter specified distance to the right	enclosing matter to be moved to the right →|	⊏

Instruction	Textual Mark	Marginal Mark
Take over character(s), word(s) or line to next line, column or page	⌐‾‾‾	⌐‾‾‾
Take back character(s), word(s) or line to previous line, column or page	‾‾‾⌐	‾‾‾⌐
Raise matter	↑ over matter to be raised ⌐_⌐ under matter to be raised	⌐_⌐
Lower matter	⌐‾⌐ over matter to be lowered ↓ under matter to be lowered	⌐‾⌐
Correct horizontal alignment	Single line above and below misaligned matter e.g. $mi_{sa}{}^{li}gn_{e}d$	‾‾‾‾‾ ‾‾‾‾‾
Close up. Delete space between characters or words	linking ⌢ characters	⌣
Insert space between characters	| between characters affected	Y
Insert space between words	between words affected ⌣	Y
Reduce space between characters	| between characters affected	⌠
Reduce space between words	between words affected ⌠	⌠
Make space appear equal between characters or words	between characters or words affected |	⋎⌢

12   The Published Author

The writing income of published authors is not necessarily restricted to the moneys paid to them by their publishers, and it is pleasing to find that other sources bring additional financial benefits.

Public Lending Right

Since 1979 you have been entitled by law to receive a Government-funded payment for borrowings of your books from public libraries in Britain. Once your book has been published, it is your responsibility to register it for PLR, and you can do so by applying to The Registrar, Public Lending Right Office, Bayheath House, Prince Regent Street, Stockton-on-Tees, Cleveland TS18 1DF. Any sums due to you are paid annually in February. You do not have to share PLR income with your publisher, and that applies equally to moneys which you may receive from ALCS (see below).

The principle of a Public Lending Right was first put forward in 1951 by John Brophy, who suggested a payment of 'A Penny a Book'. His efforts to secure this payment failed, but the campaign was revived in the 1970s by the Writers Action Group, with the additional support of the Society of Authors and the Writers' Guild. All authors should be grateful to Maureen Duffy and John Brophy's daughter Brigid, who were the leaders of the Writers Action Group, and whose tireless determination finally won the day.

When PLR became law in 1979, the Government allocated an annual sum of £2 million for its funding, and that sum has since been twice increased, so that it now stands at £3½ million. It may seem curmudgeonly to complain at this addition to the income of British authors, but the moneys available are quite inadequate. To begin with, the sum should now be over £4 million simply in order to have kept pace with inflation, and even that amount would allow for a payment of only very slightly more than 1p per borrowing, which does not begin to compare with the value of John Brophy's 1d in the 1950s. All authors have a duty to campaign for an increase in the funding by writing in the early autumn, when budgets for the ensuing year are under consideration, to the Minister for the Arts and to their own MP.

The Authors' Licensing and Collection Society

In Britain PLR is paid only to authors of British residence, but the PLR scheme in West Germany allows for payment to non-resident authors, provided that the sums due should be paid in bulk to an agency, which will then distribute the sums due to the various authors. Similarly, Belgian and Dutch television companies pay royalties on British television programmes which they broadcast under the system known as 'simultaneous cabling'. In Britain the collecting agency for these moneys is the Authors' Licensing and Collection Society (ALCS). If you are a member of either the Society of Authors or the Writers' Guild, you are automatically a member of ALCS. If you do not belong to either of those organizations, it may pay you to join as an individual member for the current annual fee of £5. You can do this by writing for details to Mrs Janet Hurrell, The General Secretary, ALCS, 7 Ridgmount Street, London WC1E 7AE. German libraries contain quite a large number of books in English, so even if your works are not translated into German, it could be worth joining ALCS. Moreover, PLR is a concept which is gradually being adopted in other countries, and ALCS will certainly be dealing in due course with the resulting payments for British authors.

The ALCS is also closely involved with the Copyright Licensing Agency. This agency exists to license photocopying of published work, which is illegal when unauthorized, except when the photocopied material is minimal in quantity and is for personal use only. It is against the law, unless you have specific written permission, to photocopy complete books or plays or other material, or even large parts thereof. The CLA was set up in 1982 and its main activities to date have been the licensing of various educational authorities, schools and colleges under a scheme whereby a record is kept of the material which has been photocopied, and a royalty paid per page. Half of the money goes to the publisher of the work in question, and the remainder is paid to ALCS, which in turn passes it on to the author concerned.

The CLA is working to extend the range of users of

photocopying machines covered by its scheme, and hopes, for instance, eventually to include the ubiquitous printshops.

The ALCS takes a small percentage from the sums it distributes as a handling charge, but the authors who constitute its council ensure that the whole operation is run with economical efficiency, so that the authors shall see as much of the money as possible.

Public Speaking

Authors of published books are sometimes asked to speak to various organizations. Many authors, despite wizardry with the written word, are inarticulate or inaudible, or both, but for others it may prove a useful addition to income. The Society of Authors and the Writers' Guild recommend that authors should charge a minimum fee of £50 for a public address, but this is unrealistic unless you are famous or unless you speak only to wealthy gatherings. If you speak to a Women's Institute or a Townswomen's Guild you cannot expect a payment of more than about £15, plus travelling expenses, and some organizations will offer less, or indeed nothing at all. Some authors also feel that they should not charge when speaking to a writers' circle, but if it is a professional engagement the labourer is surely worthy of his hire, however tiny the fee may be.

A speaking engagement does, of course, provide an author with useful publicity, and may stimulate sales of his or her books (or, more likely, additional borrowings from the public library), and this is undoubtedly in the minds of those who do not offer fees. In the same way, if you are given an interview on local radio in connection with the publication of a book you will probably not receive any fee, on the grounds that you have been given free publicity. Shame!

Selling Copies of Your Own Books

Most publishers' contracts include a clause allowing the author to buy copies of his work at trade terms, but forbidding their resale. However, you may wish to sell copies of your book at the full retail price at various functions you attend, and publishers will generally allow you to do so, provided that you seek their permission first. If you do sell books in this way, you may be depriving a bookseller of a sale, and you should take that into consideration, for authors need booksellers, many of whom make a precarious enough living. On the other hand, the total quantity of books that you sell privately is unlikely to be really significant.

Grants

The Regional Arts Associations will occasionally provide authors with financial assistance in the form of bursaries to underwrite research or simply to buy time for a proposed work (usually one which has already been contracted for by a publisher), especially if the project is of particular interest in the region concerned. The various RAAs are listed in *The Writers' and Artists' Yearbook*, and you should apply to your local Association for information on whether such grants are available, and how to apply.

Grants are also available in certain circumstances from a number of other sources, such as the Royal Literary Fund. Details can be found in *The Writer's Handbook*.

Prizes

In recent years literary prizes have proliferated, the most prestigious, such as the Booker and Whitbread Prizes, bringing their winners not only very substantial sums of money but vastly increased sales. In most cases, it is the responsibility of the publisher to enter books from his list for such awards, but some are open for entries direct from the author. A list of prizes is included in *The Writer's Handbook*.

Income Tax

All your earnings from your writings are subject to Income Tax, including any profit you make by selling at full price copies of your books which you have bought at trade terms. It is unwise, when you receive a nice cheque for your work, to go out and spend the lot – keep some in reserve for the dear old bloodsuckers of the Inland Revenue service.

The bloodsuckers are not, however, entirely unreasonable, and all your expenses in connection with your writing are chargeable against the income you receive from it. You should therefore retain all receipts for paper, typewriter ribbons, etc., and for any other expenses you incur, such as travel, purchase of reference books, postage, telephone, office furniture, secretarial services, and so on. It is also possible to claim for the use of a room in your house, if it is used only for your writing, and for a proportion of your lighting and heating bills. It is worth noting that if these expenses total more than the earnings you have received from writing, you will be allowed to offset the difference against your other income.

You can of course deal with your tax inspector directly – it will help you if you have kept meticulous records of everything that you have earned from your writing and everything that you have spent in achieving that income – but unless your earnings are minimal, it will probably pay you to employ a good accountant. Search around until you find one who has some knowledge of the way an author works and of those claims which a writer can make and which the Inland Revenue inspectors will consider to be legitimate. An author's income is irregular and unpredictable (except that you can always be sure that the money will come in rather later than you hoped), and a competent accountant will be able to arrange that your tax payments are, at least to some extent, evened out and paid over a period of time.

A good accountant is worth having, incidentally, especially if you a full-time professional writer, not only for tax purposes, but because he or she will be able to advise you on such matters as Social Security contributions, pension schemes for the self-employed, investments, etc.

Organizations for Authors

Writers regularly complain that theirs is a lonely occupation. We are, it sometimes seems to me, a somewhat discontented profession, always wittering on about the agony of writing, our insecurity, the inadequacy of our rewards, the lack of understanding even from our nearest and dearest, and, of course, the wickedness of publishers. It is largely nonsense, because most of us enjoy the work and would not want to do anything else. Perhaps we indulge in such self-pity simply as an expression of the artistic temperament. Nevertheless, we do like to meet fellow authors to discuss our common problems and to agree how hard done by we are, and because we discover that so many of them are charming and interesting people.

There are hundreds of societies and groups for anyone interested in writing, ranging from small local writers' circles to the Book Trust (formerly the National Book League) and such international organizations as PEN, and many authors find it very worthwhile to belong to several of them. A large number of them are listed in *The Writers' and Artists' Yearbook*.

There is no doubt, however, that the two outstanding associations, to which frequent reference has already been made in this chapter, are the Society of Authors and the Writers' Guild of Great Britain.

The Society of Authors was founded in 1884. It is the senior and larger of the two organizations, and its members represent every genre of writing. It contains specialist groups for translators, broadcasters, and educational, children's, technical and medical writers. For more than a hundred years it has worked with considerable success to improve the status of authors and to defend their rights.

The Writers' Guild was founded in 1959 as the Screenwriters' Guild, and although it too covers all forms of writing, it is still perhaps the prime association for those who work in television or films. It has separate committees dealing with writing for television and film, radio, theatre, and books.

The Society of Authors and the Writers' Guild are officially recognized as trade unions, but the Society is not affiliated to the TUC, whereas the Guild is.

Both organizations offer advice to their members on all matters connected with authorship, and there is a considerable degree of co-operation between them, so that they frequently negotiate jointly with government departments on such matters as VAT, PLR and copyright, and in discussing terms with the Publishers Association or with individual publishers, as, for example, in relation to the Minimum Terms Agreement. Representatives of the Society and the Guild serve on the council of ALCS. If the lot of authors has been greatly advanced in the last thirty years or so it is largely due to these combined efforts.

The Society and the Guild both produce regular publications for their members, arrange various social events, seminars and the like, and also offer a number of other benefits, ranging from facilities for buying stationery at favourable terms to pension schemes.

All authors should join one or other of these organizations. The qualifications for membership differ slightly, but publication or at least acceptance of material for publication is essential. The subscription to the Society of Authors is currently £50 per year, while the Guild charges a percentage of a member's income from writing, amounting at the time of writing to a minimum of £30 and a maximum of £480. Details can be obtained from The Society of Authors, 84 Drayton Gardens, London SW10 9SB, or from the Writers' Guild of Great Britain, 430 Edgware Road, London W2 1EH.

The Society and the Guild both have among their members writers whose prime interest lies in articles for magazines and newspapers. However, if you are such an author you may be interested in applying for membership of the Institute of Journalists, Bedford Chambers, Covent Garden, London WC2E 8HA, or the National Union of Journalists, Acorn House, 314 Gray's Inn Road, London WC1X 8DP.

Index

REVISION

An Author's Guide

REVISION
An Author's Guide

MICHAEL LEGAT

Contents

1

The Why, When and How of Revision

The Importance of Revision

The popular view of the author is of someone who lives a much-to-be-envied life, not engaging in honest work, but sitting around waiting for a flash of inspiration; when the Muse has supplied the required idea, the author then writes the book, straight off – a process which demands no effort – sends it to a publisher when it is finished, and makes a lot of money when it is published.

As anyone who has any sort of pretension to being a writer knows, this is a more than somewhat distorted picture. Authors don't wait for inspiration, but create it for themselves, by an attitude of mind – no true writer is ever at a loss for something to write about. Having got their idea, authors then spend a great deal of time in developing it, and working out all its ramifications. This is one of the hardest parts of the writing business – Sir James Barrie, the novelist and playwright, and creator of Peter Pan, was once asked how his new play was coming along, and replied that it was nearly finished since he had only the dialogue to write. The story does not tell how long he had spent or how much mental energy it had taken to get to that point, but we can be sure that it had demanded a great deal of thought

7

and time. The actual writing of a book may be a little less demanding than the preparation for it, but it is still no easy matter to get all the necessary words down on paper, and in an effective way. As for the work being immediately accepted for publication, that happens to very few authors, and mostly only when they have already proved their abilities and have a string of successfully published books behind them. And the thought of making a lot of money is likely to produce pained laughter or some other expression of incredulity from the majority of those whose books get into print.

So the popular idea of authorship is a travesty. As I have set it down above, it also leaves out one vital stage in the writing of a book (or indeed of any written material, whether book-length or not), and that is revision. It is not only the public at large which does not envisage the need to revise – many, many writers feel that once they have written the last words of their book or article it can be sent to a publisher without any further attention, or if they do condescend to recognize a need for revision, they mean by that merely reading through the typescript with the object of correcting any typing errors, rather than a process of looking critically at every aspect of the work to see whether it could be improved.

Few of us have such astounding talent that we can just sit down and write something which is impossible to better – indeed, we're lucky if we can turn out a first draft which is actually readable – and even a genius can usually produce a much improved second version. Most of the world's greatest authors have taken enormous pains over their work. Those who didn't revise in some depth would probably have done so if they had had the time – I am sure that Charles Dickens would be regarded even more highly if his demanding literary schedule had ever allowed him the luxury of careful rewriting. You might think that what I am saying applies only to prose – that the great classic poets were in fact able to wait for inspiration and then set down their thoughts in words which they never needed to change. That may have been so in a few cases – if Coleridge really did dream the whole of 'Kubla Khan', maybe he could leave what he remembered unaltered – but if you look at the original manuscript versions of work by some of our greatest poets, you will find them full of crossings-out and rewritings, and second thoughts.

I think of writing as being a three-stage process: the first stage is the preparation, which includes the initial concept, the elaboration and development of the idea, the solving of the plotting problems, the research, and the putting together of a detailed synopsis; the second is the actual writing; the third is revision. Of these three, the first is the most important. Some writers and some tutors of creative writing would disagree, saying that as soon as you know your subject, you should simply get on with the writing; this method is used by some successful novelists, but I suspect that in most cases the subconscious is in fact doing a great deal of work of which its owner is unaware before the writing begins, and the rest of the planning simply gets integrated into the writing stage. It is not, I believe, the best way to go about things if you are inexperienced, and I would always recommend planning in detail. Of the remaining two parts, revision seems to me to be of greater importance than the writing, even though it can't take place until the writing has been done. It is revision which can transform your work, give it sparkle, and make your type-script stand out from the rest of the submissions in the slushpile; it is revision which, more than anything else, signals the professionalism of your attitude, for professionals revise, amateurs don't.

Revision is hard work. So is writing. If you find it easy to write, you may be naturally talented and indeed brilliant, but it is rather more likely that your work will reveal the lack of effort which has gone into it. The craft has to be worked at – hard – and revision is part of it. On the other hand, it shouldn't be regarded as an unpleasant chore – on the contrary, there can be great excitement and pleasure and fulfilment in altering your work to improve it.

At What Stage in the Writing Should You Revise?

Every author does a certain amount of revising in the course of writing – words are altered, sentences rephrased, chunks crossed out – and while it is quite possible for those who use pen or pencil or a typewriter to work in this way, it becomes even simpler, and indeed habitual, if you graduate to a word processor, because it is so easy to make changes, to insert or delete words, and to move material from one place to another. However, this kind of tinkering as we go along, when we have second thoughts almost in the process of putting the first thoughts down, is not really what we mean by revision, for which we need a certain amount of completed text which we then re-read and amend if necessary. When should one start this process?

For some writers it is very tempting to stop at the end of each paragraph or page and rewrite it as necessary. The problem with this approach is that, as we shall see later, one of the objects of an effective revision is to make sure that the structure of the book, the way that information is conveyed, and the variety and pace of the text are satisfactory, and it is very difficult to see matters of that kind when looking at one paragraph or page only. If you like to work that way, there is no real harm in it, especially if what you are really concentrating on is comparatively minor matters of style, word choice, grammar, punctuation and spelling. Even so, it seems to me a somewhat wasteful approach, since much of the work that you do may have to be amended later when you come to look at what comes before and after the material in question, and indeed at the chapter and the book as a whole.

A common method is to revise when you have finished a longer section of your book. You have reached a natural break, perhaps, or the end of a chapter, and it seems sensible to stop and reread what you have done, and to amend it where necessary before you continue. This works very well, especially if you are in the habit of reading over what you wrote yesterday (or whenever you last worked on the book) before starting today, since you may use the reading as a device to get you back into the spirit of whatever it is that you are writing. It is certainly a better idea than the revision of much smaller pieces, and you will probably have sufficient material to allow you to see the structure of the chapter, its pace and variety and to judge the progress you are making in marshalling your information and getting it across to the reader. But you still can't see the book as whole.

There is also a great danger which entraps many writers who decide on this approach to revision. They write the first chapter, and then revise it; the revisions are, perhaps, fairly substantial, and often so interesting that it seems to the author that it would be a good idea to rewrite the chapter there and then; when it is finished, it is just asking to be revised again, and rewritten again, and the author goes on and on, producing ever more different versions of Chapter 1 and never getting as far as the first words of Chapter 2. This problem occurs most frequently with those inexperienced fiction writers who do not believe in advance planning. New ideas occur to them, demanding rewrites, and since they are not sure exactly where they are going, the siren voices of the latest twists and turns in the story lead them off in uncharted directions, and often into impasse after impasse.

As may already be plain, one of the biggest bees in my bonnet about writing is my fervent belief in the need to plan in advance, to know where you are going, to work out what you are trying to achieve in each chapter that you write. This is when you can make sure that your plot works, testing its development (constantly asking yourself 'how can I make this happen?' and 'what if . . .?' – 'what if this happened?', 'what if he did that?', 'what if she were to say such and such?'); this is when you can build up and really get to know your characters; this is when you can see the shape of your book and plan the chapters. It's a slow, careful process, often taking much longer than the writing of the first draft. In my book, *Plotting the Novel*, I tried to refute the arguments against planning – it really isn't true, for instance, that a plan is a straitjacket and will prevent your book from seeming spontaneous and lively – and I set out seven reasons in favour of producing for yourself a detailed synopsis before you start to write the story. Had I thought of it at the time, I could have added an eighth – that you are far less likely to fall into the trap of endlessly rewriting Chapter 1 – and a ninth, which I shall come to shortly. And in case you are in any doubt, I believe in planning for nonfiction books too, and even for articles.

If you ask me, I think the only really satisfactory time to undertake that essential full-scale revision is when you have come to the end of your first draft of the complete book. Then you have some chance of seeing it as whole and of judging the extent to which it meets the criteria which a successful book demands. Moreover, you will not only be able to consider the overall structure and impact and pattern of the work, and what amendments, large and small, are going to be needed, but when it comes to specific smaller details, including quite minor matters, you will be able to place them in the context of the whole.

The Detached View

One of the most difficult things for all authors to do is to judge their own work. Even if you have a considerable amount of expertise, it isn't easy. After long experience as an editor, and having written twenty books, I still find it hard to be objective about my own material, simply because it is mine and I love it as it is and am too close to it to see its flaws. If you have an editor, or one of those partners to whom books get dedicated 'with thanks for being my severest critic', you may be able to rely on receiving good, disinterested advice, but many writers have not yet succeeded in getting an editor and if they have partners at all have chosen them for their forbearance rather than for their critical faculties. In any case, most of us want to get the book into the best shape we can manage before it is read by anyone else.

So we are the ones who have to try to be detached and disinterested. The only solution that I have ever found to this problem is the effect of time, and I therefore try to put the work on one side when it is finished, and to leave it there for as long as possible – at least a couple of weeks, and preferably more. If you follow my example, the longer you can stay away from the book, the more easily you can eventually come back to it with the eyes of a stranger, and if you can fool yourself into believing that you really *are* a stranger, that will be all to the good. Of course, you won't be able to forget the main elements of the book, whether it is fiction or non-fiction, but you should be able to look at the *way it is written* with a little detachment. Some bits may impress you with the excellence of your writing, while in other parts you will cringe at your ineptitude, but the more you can manage to read it as though it were the work of someone else, the more likely your judgements are to be right and the more easily you will see what needs to be altered. If you do not leave a gap between completion of the first draft and the commencement of revision, you are likely to be so close to the writing that it will not only be totally familiar, but you will probably remember the actual setting down of the words and the difficulty or the ease with which the words were flowing, and your feelings at the time, and none of this will allow you to see any imperfections which may be there.

Similarly, if you work in accordance with the procedures suggested in this book, going through various stages of revision, it is well worth leaving a time-gap of at least several days between each read-through. A break will not only give you a rest, but will help you to achieve a greater detachment.

Many authors, even if they manage to look at their own work fairly objectively, will still end up knowing that something is wrong with their work, but not being able to put their finger on what it is. This book has been written for them, and in the pages to follow this chapter I shall be suggesting all manner of questions which you should ask yourself which will perhaps help to pin down the faults.

How Many Revisions?

It might be better to ask how many times you should go through your typescript in the process of revision. A single shot is better than none at all, but is certainly not enough. On the other hand, once you have accepted the idea that revision is essential, you may get a taste for it, and you must then be careful not to fall into the trap of Permanent Revision Syndrome, which I have already hinted at in regard to constant rewriting of the first chapter. It is even more tempting to do this when you start revising the complete novel, so that as soon as you have finished a revision you have another go at it, and then just one more, and then another, and another, and so on. You must call a halt somewhere. After you have checked the text a number of times and made all the obviously necessary alterations, you may still feel less than one hundred per cent satisfied. Wouldn't a little more tinkering be worthwhile? Well, give it one more run-through if you must, but stop there, and try your luck with getting it published, knowing that you are not alone – that all good authors have just the same inner reservations about their work when they send their creations out into the world. Besides, if you fall victim to Permanent Revision Syndrome, you may not only put off indefinitely the possible publication of the book, but you may even be damaging the text – as with almost everything else, an excess can be bad for you.

The answer to the question of how many times you should go through the book can best be answered by deciding what you are going to do each time. I like to revise my work four, or possibly five, times.

During the first reading, I am looking at the structure of the book, making sure that it says what I want it to say and nothing else, and that it works as a story, or is effective as an instructional book. I am trying to be analytical in depth, looking not only at what I have written, but at what lies beneath it, whether it achieves the effects I intended, whether it is satisfying overall. The criticisms that I make of the material may entail considerable re-writing. I am also looking out for material which can be cut. Like most writers I tend to over-write, and if the book is fiction, I may take out even as much as twenty per cent of it at this stage (although ten to fifteen per cent is more likely). This first stage of revision is a slow process, and cannot be hurried, because there is so much which has to be looked at with painstaking care. It may not be a case of starting at the beginning and going straight on to the end, but of moving back and forth to make sure that if I have altered anything I have picked up every other change which it will necessitate, whether earlier in the book or later. And even if major restructuring does not seem necessary, some passages will get moved, which will almost certainly mean that a number of adjustments have to be made, and other sections will need to be completely rewritten, and new material may have to be added, and all of the changes which are made will have to be looked at to see if they themselves need revising. More details of how to tackle this stage and what to look for are to be found in Chapters 3, 4 and 5.

Because I plan my books in considerable detail before I start writing, and iron out most of the likely problems at that stage, I rarely find it necessary to write another complete draft – that saving of time and effort is the ninth advantage of planning. However, if you have not planned, or if you find that your book really needs rewriting from start to finish, then you may have to work your way through a number of new versions. Each time, you will then need to go through the processes of the first stage of revision before moving on.

If the first reading looks at the wood, the second concentrates on the trees. Page by page, paragraph by paragraph, sentence by sentence, word by word, I look to see whether I have said exactly what I want to say in the best way that I can contrive. Is every word doing a worthwhile job? Again this is a time-consuming business, but it can't be rushed, even if I don't spend as long as Flaubert in the search for *le mot juste*. Much of the material may have to be rewritten, even when the alteration that I am making may seem very minor – swapping one word for another, perhaps in order to avoid an ugly repetition, can sometimes mean that the whole paragraph has to be rejigged. Chapter 6 is concerned with the many aspects of your writing which you should be examining during this second revision.

In the third revision it is the ear which is at work rather than the eye, because this is when I read the book aloud to myself, letting the ear do the editorial work. Revision number four, in contrast with the earlier work, is quickly done, because the idea is to read the whole book without stopping. Nevertheless, although the time required may be shorter, the need for intense concentration is no less. These two forms of revision are discussed in Chapter 7.

Once any amendments resulting from notes taken during the fourth reading have been done, I can usually leave the typescript at that. Sometimes, however, I still have a slight feeling that the book is a bit stodgy, and if so, then a final reading will allow me the opportunity of sharpening the whole thing, and this revision too is covered in Chapter 7.

It may not be that the processes described will suit you. You might want, perhaps, to combine stages one and two, at least to some extent, or you may have left gaps in the

16

book which are to be filled in with suitable material when you have completed your research, and this may call for a further step in the revision. Inevitably too the processes become blurred at the edges, so that you may find yourself doing some of the fine tuning during the first more general revision, and vice versa.

Your format for revision could also depend on your basic approach to the writing of the material. If you write slowly and with great care, thinking everything out in detail before you set it down, working strictly to a full synopsis, and aware all the time of how the words you are putting down will affect the chapters to come, then you will probably be able to dispense entirely with my first stage of revision, and even if you use the other suggested processes, you may not need to spend a great deal of time on them. However, meticulous writers of that kind tend to be rarities, especially among beginners, who, even if they believe in detailed advance planning, often like to get words down on paper or on the computer disc, when they actually start writing, as quickly as possible, not bothering too much about whether they are the best words, because to take time to consider nice points of style and the effect that the words will have would stop the flow. If that's the way you write, you're in good company, because it's exactly what many professional authors do too. But you will need to spend quite a lot of time on revision. That is not to say that you will have to change absolutely everything – undoubtedly you will have managed some excellent bits – but the better the good passages are, the more need there will be to bring the rest of the work up to their standard.

For Those Using Word Processors

Revision is particularly easy if you write on a computer – so easy that it may cause you problems. I am sure you know that you should always have a back-up copy of your text, and it is a good idea to make a habit of taking a copy of what you have written at the end of each day's work. When I have completed my first draft, I like to keep that back-up copy somewhere reasonably safe away from the word processor and any other discs, so that if some kind burglar should decide to remove the computer and all that goes with it, I would still have a basic text. But it is also worth making a second copy of the text before you start any revision, so that if you make an alteration that you later regret, you have not lost the first version. Although a line must be drawn somewhere, it is a good idea to make back-ups of your alterations too, so that if you make yet more changes you can go back to your second draft. Alternatively, you can print out your various drafts, of course, and some writers prefer to revise on paper rather than on the screen.

2
The Length of the Book

Is the Length Right?

Before you start your revision you may want to ask yourself this question, because the answer could affect all the work that you will want to do before you feel that the book is ready to send off to a publisher.

A lot of beginners do not seem to be aware that you should know how long your work is. It is not difficult to work out. You can rely on the word-count facility on your word processor, if you have one, although this does not allow you to count short lines and short pages as if they were full lines or full pages, which most publishers prefer you to do. However, it does give you a rough guide. The best way of calculating the wordage is to count the number of words in ten consecutive full lines on five (or ten if you prefer) different typed pages, then divide the total by fifty (or by one hundred if you have counted a hundred lines) to get the average number of words in one of your lines, assuming that you work throughout to the same width of full lines, as you should. Multiply that average figure by the number of lines you get on a full page (again assuming that you are correctly consistent in this respect), and you know the number of words on an average page. Keep a note of the figure and simply multiply it by the number of pages in your book, and there's your answer. It works whether you write longhand or use a typewriter or word processor. Let me stress that you do not reduce the figure to allow for short lines or short pages.

I have always found it very helpful not to wait to calculate the length of what I have written until I have completed my first draft, but to keep a tally as I go along. It does not need to be exact, but whether you write in longhand or on a typewriter or word processor, if you know roughly how many words go on one of your pages, you can monitor your progress. If you find that you are either over-running or are very much below your proposed length, you may be able to make some effort to solve the problem at that early stage of writing, although before you take any drastic action it is as well to try to work out fairly carefully how many words will go into the rest of the book.

Non-Fiction

If you are writing a non-fiction book, the subject and the market at which you are aiming will virtually dictate the length of the book, although of course it depends on the complexity of the material and the scope of the book too. The range of retail prices for novels is, by convention within the trade, comparatively small, and rarely rises above the norm even if the book is extremely long. Publishers have much more freedom in pricing non-fiction, so the possible shortness of the book is not quite so crucial as it is for fiction. Even so, publishers do not generally like short books (except in certain categories – humour, for instance) and are not likely to look favourably on a book of less than 35,000 words, unless it has some special appeal. The reason for this is that short books are only a little less costly to produce than longer books, and so often have to have a retail price which seems expensive and which therefore diminishes sales. The key is to study the market – see how long other books on similar subjects are, and try too to place yourself in the position of your readers and ask yourself what length of book they would want.

Since it is more and more usual for the writers of non-fiction books to seek a commission from a publisher before embarking on a book, most of them will have discussed the matter of length with the publisher. If you are trying to get a commission it will be important for you to be able to tell the publisher fairly exactly the length that you expect to produce. The publisher may be happy with your proposal or may want to change the extent (that is, the number of words in the book), especially if the book that you are writing is to go into an existing series.

The market at which your book is aimed has a major part to play in decisions about length, as well as content. The economics of the publication are dependent on the size of the potential sale, the question of whether the book will be published in hardcover or as a trade paperback or even as a mass market paperback (or a combination of these formats), the number of competitive works on the subject which are available and how they are priced and in what format, and how your book differs from them – all these and other similar factors must be borne in mind. Your publisher may have some knowledge of the competition for your book, but may not have your own expertise in the field, so you need to be up-to-date and well-informed.

But, having agreed a length with a publisher, what do you do if you discover in the course of writing or when you have completed your first draft that your book is much shorter or much longer than the contract specifies? Two or three thousand words will probably not matter, but a greater discrepancy is going to be a problem. The initial solution, naturally, is to ask yourself in the former case whether there is extra material that you could add without padding the book or repeating yourself, and you might also consider bumping it out, if this has not been previously planned, with the addition of illustrations, diagrams, tables and the like, and an introduction, a bibliography, an index, and so on, provided that these are all relevant and useful and will enhance the book. If it is too long, the solution is usually easier, and is simply a matter of deleting all your over-writing; ask yourself especially whether you have a tendency to explain things that don't need explaining, or to explain more than once things that do; if the book is very substantially over the desired length, you will have to consider how drastic a cut you could make without damaging the book's content and value to potential readers. In either case, it is a good idea to consult the publisher before you do anything at all, giving your reasons for wanting to change the originally agreed length; the publisher may be prepared to accept a revised plan, or may make suggestions which would solve the problem.

Fiction

For fiction it is equally important to study the market. While you are doing your market research so as to decide to which publisher(s) you will submit your novel, check to see what length books those publishers bring out. Of course, the extent of a novel usually depends on the complexity of the plot and sub-plots and the number of major characters whose stories are told – the more involved the story the more likely you are to end up with a thousand-page novel like the splendid *A Suitable Boy* by Vikram Seth. Although a glance at the paperback shelves will tell you that long, fat books are popular, it has to be said that very few first novels by unknown authors with a length of over a quarter of a million words will find a publisher. Of course, if an enormously long book is really of exceptional quality, its length will not be a barrier even for a first-time author, but unless you are convinced of your own genius, it may be a good idea, if your novel runs to a thousand pages to see whether it might be possible to divide it up to make a trilogy or tetralogy.

But what if your book is, in contrast, on the short side? Few, if any, publishers will be interested in anything less than 45,000 words, or thereabouts, and if you have failed to reach that target, you will need to think again. It may be that you are under-writing, and you need to expand everything quite considerably. This is a fault which afflicts some inexperienced writers who are so eager to get their novels down on paper that they rush through them. Have you perhaps simply told your story too baldly, and left the reader not really knowing what is going on? Have you given us enough information about the people in your story, and their backgrounds? Have you used too much narration and not enough action (see pp.68–71), missing the opportunity to show us the more dramatic parts of the story as they happen, rather than after the event? Could you invent any sub-plots which would have relevance and which would in fact enhance the main story? Work on points of that sort might enable you to add sufficient wordage to your book to bring it up to a publishable length.

But you need to beware of padding. Padding, in essence, is simply using more words to say exactly the same thing. For instance, you could take a sentence such as 'She eventually decided to go' and pad it out to read 'She eventually decided, *having weighed up all the pros and cons*, that, *all things considered, it would be much more sensible* to go, *even though at first she had been doubtful about doing so*'. Everything in italics is padding. Padding can also take the form of new material on a previously unmentioned subject which has no relevance to the story and does not help the reader's understanding or interest. It is always visible and irritating, whatever its form, and it makes the reader yawn and say, 'Oh, for heaven's sake, get on with the story!' Everything which you add must be essential to the book, and of real value. A lot of work will be needed.

Another possibility, when your completed story is very

much on the short side, is that the idea is just not suitable for a novel, and should have been a short story; in that case, rather than having under-written, you may in fact have over-written to a considerable degree. You will probably have to abandon hope of turning it into a full-length book. The next time you have an idea for a novel, ask yourself before you start whether the plot is simple, the characters few in number, the time-span brief, the settings limited to one or two. If you have to give affirmative answers to those questions, then you are almost certainly dealing with the basis of a short story, not a novel.

It is impossible to lay down an ideal length for a novel, but for practical purposes of getting published, you are probably in the right area if the book is somewhere between 60,000 and 100,000 words, or possibly even double that if you have written a story with a complex plot covering a long period of time, as in a family saga.

Of course you should always let your novel find its own length rather than targeting a particular wordage (unless you are aiming at a publisher such as Mills & Boon or at others who bring out light fiction intended primarily for the library market and who mostly work to set lengths – you can get information from such publishers about their requirements).

Have You Over-Written?

The fact that your book, whether it is fiction or non-fiction, has come out at what seems to be a reasonable length does not mean that you should not examine it to see whether you have over-written – which you quite probably have, because it's a fault to which very many writers are prone. Over-writing has exactly the same effect as padding – it makes your narrative sag, and is boring to read. You will need to cut – possibly quite drastically. Later in this book we shall be considering the need to cut unnecessary words, like many adverbs and adjectives, and repetitions and a number of other examples of material the disappearance of which will improve your style no end, but at this stage we should be looking for more substantial excisions.

The problem is usually much more likely to be acute if you are writing a novel rather than a non-fiction book. If you were to cut this scene or that, would it really make any difference? Would this or that long stretch of comparatively undramatic dialogue be better rendered in a couple of lines of narration? In your novel, every scene, every character, every piece of descriptive writing, every line of dialogue – every word, in fact – must be there for a purpose, and everything which does not serve a purpose must be cut ruthlessly, however much it pains you and even though some of what has to go will inevitably contain some pieces of what you think of as your very best writing.

It is worth trying an experiment: take one chapter of your book and go through it word by word (literally – looking at every single word), sentence by sentence, paragraph by paragraph, cutting everything that is not essential. I am not suggesting that you should take this to extremes, in which case you might end up with a one-sentence synopsis, but if you do the exercise carefully, weighing every word, you may be surprised to find how much more sparely you could write, and as a result how much more effective the writing would be. Look up the parable of the Good Samaritan in St Luke Chapter 10, in the King James version, and see how strong and telling such simple writing can be.

One of the reasons why it is essential to pare your book down is that modern fiction reflects modern life. Modern life moves fast, and so must modern fiction. There is no time now for the leisurely wordiness of some of the Victorian writers, nor for the much shorter but still slow-moving novels which were current for the first half of the twentieth century. Nowadays, pace is essential, so cut and cut and cut to achieve it – at least from an overall point of view, because clearly not every scene can move with the same rapidity, and you certainly need a variety in the pace (which is another subject to which we shall return later).

As I mentioned in Chapter 1, in my own work I expect to cut between ten and fifteen per cent (very occasionally, more) of my first draft during this initial revision. That may suggest to you that my over-writing has been unusually excessive. Well, yes and no. I doubt if I am alone in producing too many words to that extent – certainly as an editor I have seen many typescripts which could have benefited from even more than that amount being taken out. But, despite my advance planning, one of the things which I have often found is that a scene which seems essential as I plan it and as I write it, turns out to be unnecessary because it holds up the main action or because its content can be more effectively summarized indirectly rather than placed in full before the reader's eyes. 'Make a scene of it' is a good maxim to have in your mind all the time you are writing a novel, but in your anxiety to ensure that you dramatize the story as much as possible, you can be led into excess.

Summing Up

If you feel that the length of your book is about right, not merely from the commercial point of view, but in relation to its content, and if you are confident that you have neither under- nor over-written, you can get on with the rest of your revision without worrying about that aspect. If you feel it is either too short or too long, you must clearly bear that in mind every time you go through the book, looking to see how you can solve the problem.

3
Fiction – The Plot

The First Revision Read-Through

Following the plan set out in Chapter 1, the first read-through of your book in the process of revision is one in which you look at it overall. It is not for fine-tuning, which will come later, but is concerned with structure and content generally, and with the broader aspects of characterization, and conflict and dialogue and backgrounds – all the most important elements in fiction. Taking the overall view seems sometimes to be a difficult concept for inexperienced writers to grasp, since they feel that revision should be primarily concerned with getting the minutiae right. In fact, more books get rejected because of major structural faults than for any other reason (apart from sheer bad writing). An overall assessment is essential, and there is a long series of questions which you need to ask yourself.

At this point, I should make it clear that almost all the points covered in this chapter should not arise if you accept the idea of detailed planning in advance, because it is much easier to see such faults in a synopsis, and then to correct them. (Perhaps if you do prepare a detailed synopsis for yourself before you begin to set the story down on paper, you may find this and the next two chapters of use at that stage rather than when the book is written.) And if you get the plan right and then stick to it, the writing and the revision should both be plain sailing. However, a synopsis is not set in stone – after all, you invented it in the first place, so you are entitled to alter it if you want to – and you might ask what you should do if, having planned carefully, you find yourself drifting away from your synopsis to a serious extent when you are actually writing the story. The answer is once again revision – but this time revision of the synopsis. Go back to it as soon as you realize that you have departed from it, work out what effect the new developments are going to have on the story, and then decide whether you really want to stick to your original plan, or whether to alter it to accommodate the changes you have begun to make.

Whether or not you planned in advance, as we go through the various points in this and the following chapters, you should be aware that in practice one does not consider only one point at a time, so you may be looking at some of the characterizations at the same time as you are considering the general structure of the book, or indeed working on a whole string of different aspects simultaneously. However, when you have done all that you feel is necessary, or if your meticulously planned synopsis means that no structural alterations were needed, it may still be worth checking through the questions to see whether you have missed anything.

One thing which I hope goes without saying is that all the revision processes may involve a considerable amount of re-writing, and that is especially true of this first stage. For many writers the first draft is little more than a first trial shot, and it is only when they revise that the real book begins to emerge. When you decide that a certain passage needs to be rewritten, take your time with it, even though you may be tempted to press on to see what needs to be done in the rest of the story, and write it carefully. That material will itself need to be given the full revision treatment afterwards, and of course you must bear in mind the effect that any rewriting will have on the remainder of the book.

Have You Written the Book You Intended?

If you prepared a detailed synopsis before you began to write, then you probably do not need to ask this question. But if you are one of those writers who like to start off without knowing exactly how you will reach the end of your story, waiting to see where the characters take it, you may find that something has gone a little, or more than a little, astray. Has the book which started out as a romantic novel turned, halfway along, into a detective story? Has your central character faded into the background while some other character has taken over the limelight? Have you allowed your novel to turn into a vehicle for you to promulgate your views on some controversial subject so that characters and plot have been totally overwhelmed by the preaching? To be successful a novel needs a shape and a form – it's not a sort of ragbag into which you can throw anything you like – and it should, first and foremost, tell an interesting story with a strong narrative line. It can have more than one theme, and more than one principal character, and can concern itself with social issues, but it must always entertain and interest its reader, and it will never do that if it confuses him or her by switching horses in midstream.

You may think that only a total fool of an author would fail to recognize major structural weaknesses such as the examples given, but any publisher's reader would tell you that dozens of books of this kind are regularly to be found in the slushpile. And it is exactly this kind of problem, more than any other, which leads the authors of such books to say, 'I know there's something wrong with it, but I just don't know what it is.' They can't see the fault partly because they are too close to the book, but principally because they have not looked at it overall, confining their revision to points of style.

If your novel has structural faults of this nature, you will clearly have a great deal of work to do to sort out the problem. In most cases the first and most effective answer will be a substantial amount of cutting to eliminate the matter which has led you astray. For instance, in the first example, perhaps you need to cut out the romance altogether and start with the detective story; in the second case, you might cut one of the two characters completely, or at least make it clear which one is to be the focus of the reader's attention, and start with that one and give the other a less important role in the story; and in the third case, you must try to integrate the arguments you want to put across into the story, making sure that they are expressed by one or more of your characters, rather than by you as narrator, and probably allowing other characters to present the opposing view as fairly as you can. How do you choose between the various plots? For once, don't listen to your head, but to your heart, which will tell you, if you listen, which version you really want to write.

A rather more subtle way in which you may not have written the book that you originally intended may be apparent to you on the first revision read-through when you realize that there is an important sub-text to the book. This is not a question of a switch in interest or of one of the themes being of major significance and the other of much less weight, but of two ideas struggling for supremacy. One of them has won, but is it the right one? You may have thought, for example, that you were writing a simple love story, but underneath that is an attack on some social issue of the day, which was in fact what drove you to write (even if you did not realize it at the time), or alternatively the novel of big business which you have written is basically more concerned with the love story which appears only as a minor element in the plot. These may seem rather crude examples, and in practice the sub-text is often less easily distinguished than it might be in those cases. It is strange how easy it is not to see the confusion while writing the book – which can only perhaps be explained by the power of the subconscious to dictate what we write without our being aware that anything of the sort is going on. If you do detect this kind of problem in your book, then you first need to think about it and decide which of your themes is really the one you want to exploit, or whether perhaps you want to retain both ideas on a more or less equal footing, and then you will have to go through the text rewriting, possibly from beginning to end, so as to get the balance right, building one up and the other down.

Has the Story Got a Shape?

The shape of a novel is another aspect of structure. Presumably your novel has a beginning, a middle and an end, but it is quite possible that you have never thought beyond that in considering whether it has a shape. I find it very helpful to think in terms of a shape which you could actually draw, rather like a line on a graph, the line indicating the rise and fall of tension within the story. Your novel needs to increase in tension as it progresses, so that in fact it rises to the climax of its ending. At the same time, although the interest should build up, it should not do so at the same pace all the time – variety is needed, so there will be plateaux among the mountains of the graph, and valleys too, as it were. Check to make sure that the plateaux don't extend too far, that the valleys aren't too deep, and that the mountains go on getting higher.

If you find that the shape of the novel, as reflected in a graph of the tension, is too flat, you may be able to solve part of the problem by a fairly drastic shortening of the plateaux and valley sections, and a sharpening of the mountains where the text moves at a quicker pace. But you may also need to go back to your plot and see whether you can inject more tension by the introduction of new twists and turns in the story, and perhaps additional sub-plots. This is a very tricky business, because anything of that sort cannot simply be tacked on – it has to become an integral part of the story, arising naturally from it, and its effect on the rest of the novel has to be worked out with care. It all means a very considerable amount of rewriting, but there really is a vital need to get the shape right at whatever cost.

In particular, in this context, pay attention to the middle of your novel. This is the time during the writing when a great many authors, including practised professionals, tend to feel that their book is dull and boring, that no one will ever want to read it and that the best thing would be to abandon it and start something else. The feeling should be ignored – it is a symptom of fatigue when you have run out of your first wind and haven't yet got your second. Unless there are other reasons for believing that what you are doing is a waste of time, you should press on, and when you come to read the whole book you will probably find that the section which bothered you is not in fact in the least dull and boring. (We authors are mostly rotten judges of our own work – we love the worst bits and underrate the qualities of the better parts.) Sometimes, however, the author's lack of enthusiasm at the midpoint of the novel is justified, because the story is indeed sagging, and the slow pace, the lack of excitement, the sense that the novel has run out of steam, all become evident when the first draft is read through. This time the solution is usually simply some enthusiastic cutting. You may even find that the slow section could disappear altogether without leaving much of a gap, replaced by no more than a couple of sentences.

Yet another problem occurs when, if I may continue the metaphor without straining it too much, the road over your mountains and plateaux towards the highest peak has too many side turnings which lead nowhere except into dead-end valleys. These side turnings are, of course, sub-plots, and sub-plots are very much needed – most novels would seem very thin without a sprinkling of side interests to go along with the main story, but they must all be fully integrated into the principal theme, and have some effect on it, and they should be used, in fact, to drive the central narrative onwards. If there are too many sub-plots and they are not totally relevant, the reader is going to be confused and will lose interest. If that is your problem, cut and cut and cut again. Ask yourself what difference it would make if you were to eliminate this little bunch of characters and their actions, and if the answer is that it would really not affect your central characters and their story, then chop the interlopers out.

Another way of expressing this idea of shape is to think of the novel's narrative as a profile of that mountain road, with sharp bends and steep ascents and other parts where the going is easier. Will the reader feel, right from the beginning, a desire which grows in intensity to carry on to the mountain top to find out exactly what happens? Or perhaps, to be more precise, I should say 'exactly *how* whatever it is happens', because when we read novels we are rarely surprised by the final outcome, but only by how it is reached. Starting a murder story, we expect to know by the end whodunit; if we read romantic novels, we can be pretty sure that the heroine is going to end up in the arms of Mr Right; if we discover at the beginning of the book that its hero is an attractive, ambitious, talented young man without a bean in the world, it's odds on that he's going to end up as a success. What intrigues us in fiction is finding out that the murderer was not the person we suspected, that the course of our heroine's true love ran anything but smoothly, or that the young man reached his goal by an altogether unexpected route. There is an inevitability about the outcome, but as far as possible it must be disguised from the reader, so that there is always the possibility, however faint, that the murderer will get away with it, that the heroine will marry Mr Wrong, that the young man will end up a failure. But the point is that having once planted in the reader's mind a desire to find out how everything happens, the author must not allow that interest to fall away, either by the introduction of irrelevant and confusing subplots and characters, or by writing long boring chapters in which nothing much happens.

And do make sure that the climax of the story really is a climax, that it is a satisfying outcome to all that has gone before, and that, preferably, there is some feeling of excitement as well as fulfilment about it, which can often be achieved if it includes an element of surprise – not, as I have already said, in the final resolution, but in the way it is brought about and revealed to the reader. Although this climax will come towards the end of the book, it may not be the actual ending, but may be followed by pages in which the story is brought to what in music is called a full close, and its loose ends are tied up – the revision of those last pages is a matter of technique, rather than to do with plotting, and will be dealt with in Chapter 5.

Before leaving the subject of the structural shape of a novel, I should make it clear that the author has a great deal of flexibility – there are no rules about the number of peaks and plateaux and valleys in your story or how regularly they should occur, although it has to be admitted that there are a few genres which the publishers require to be written to a structural formula – notably the currently fashionable erotic novels for women, in which torrid sex scenes have to be included every so many pages.

Is the Story Too Closely Based on Real Life?

Many a novel is directly inspired by its author's own experience, not of life in general on which all writing must be based, but of events in which the writer played a part, and of which she or he has written a faithful account, turning it into fiction by changing the names and perhaps inventing some of the scenes and dialogue. If this is the kind of book that you have written, you must be very much aware, as you read it through, of the danger that you have been too faithful to what actually happened. Real life, as well as being fairly chaotic, is often anticlimactic, and your own experiences nearly always need to be expanded, dramatized, manipulated in order to make them into a strong story. To say 'but that's really what happened' is no excuse for a long period of inaction in your novel, or an excitement which completely fizzles out. It is always very difficult, I think, if you have based your story too closely on truth to see where it does not really work, but I would like to suggest that you should make frequent stops as you read through, think of your favourite author, and then ask yourself each time what would happen at that point if it had been a novel by Catherine Cookson, or Anita Brookner, or Wilbur Smith or Graham Swift, or whoever you admire.

Re-Arranging the Material

Sometimes, as you read through the book, you may realize that it would work better if the various events of the story were told in a different sequence. Perhaps an early scene in the novel would have more effect if told in flashback at a later point, or maybe you could bring about a splendid piece of dramatic irony by letting the reader know in advance of something in store for your main character. This kind of adjustment is often needed if, despite having planned the book in detail before starting to write, you altered it as you went along, perhaps because a character 'came to life' in an interesting way, or simply because you had a brilliant new idea. And if you are not a planner, then you are very likely to need to do some juggling of the happenings in the story, and you will need to remember that the movement of material from one place to another may leave gaps or rough edges which you will need to tidy up.

Is Your Novel Event-Driven?

A problem with many novels is that their authors have concentrated almost entirely on the events of the story, neglecting the characterizations. It is a fault to which writers of thrillers are particularly prone.

As tutors of Creative Writing never tire of telling their students, plots are derived from characters. It is because of the people that they are that everything happens; it is because of their actions and reactions and the effect that they have on each other that the story is advanced. This is one of the reasons why the tough guy at the centre of a thriller has a relationship with a beautiful woman – it is not simply to enable the author to include a steamy, blow-by-blow sex scene, or even to provide contrast with the hero's struggles against the machinations of the villain, important though that may be, but to allow this central character to be more than just a fighting machine, to give him some humanity, to make him a character rather than a cipher.

If you have written a thriller, a western, a science fiction or fantasy novel, or a horror story there may be some justification for concentrating on events rather than characters, but the more you have done so, the greater the need, when revising, to try to put more depth into your characters.

Do the Events of the Novel Grow Out of Each Other?

Everything which happens in your novel should have an effect on what follows. Real life is shapeless, at least in detail, but the novel requires a much more tidy approach. If, in real life, you lose an earring, or miss a train, or have a disagreement with your partner, or it rains, or England lose a Test Match, although such occurrences could be momentous for you, depending on circumstances, in most cases they will make little difference – you may be upset about the earring, you may be late for an appointment, and so on, but none of these things will have a major effect on your life. In a novel, anything like that must be there for a purpose, and out of it the story must grow.

The growth must not stop, however, with one incident and its consequence. One way of looking at the plot of a novel is to consider it as a chain of causes and effects – because this happened, the result was that something else occurred, and that led to yet another development, and so on – a rolling sequence of events giving rise to other events – cause and effect, cause and effect, cause and effect. To put it another way, in this sequence of rolling cause and effect, each effect becomes a new cause, driving us on to the next incident or crisis in the story. This is why, although we may not put it in so many words, especially not in the novel itself, there should always be the sense of the storyteller saying not simply, '. . . and then . . . and then . . . and then . . .', but, with a more logical progression, '. . . and then, as a result . . . and that led to . . . and because of that . . . and the consequence was. . .' and so on.

Of course, some of the causes may combine to lead to a joint effect. To give a simple example (which also demonstrates the way in which cause and effect can solve a plotting problem), let us suppose that you want your heroine to meet the man who is to become the love of her life, but that there is no reason, other than an unconvincing whim or coincidence, why she should be in the right place at the right time for the meeting; let her lose one of an expensive pair of earrings given to her by her present fiancé (Mr Wrong, whom she will ditch later), and be eager to replace it before he finds out that it is lost; then let her try in vain to get a replacement in the shop where the earrings were originally bought; coming out of the shop, worried and not looking where she is going, she nearly knocks a young woman over; because it is pouring with rain they stay chatting, she tells the young woman about the missing earring, and the young woman suggests that she should try her cousin's shop in a nearby town; in that shop she is served by Mr Right, whom she takes to be the cousin, but who is in fact standing in for him (this will give rise to various confusions later). You have then used two simple causes – the missing earring and the chance meeting with the young woman – to achieve one important effect, and have done it in a more interesting way, perhaps, than simply letting the heroine and Mr Right meet at a party. To make this work properly the earrings should continue in some way to play more than a casual part in the novel (perhaps Mr Right decides that he will also give the lady a pair of earrings, and there are decisions to be made about which pair she wears and unexpected changes in relationship result from her choice) and the casual rainstorm acquaintance and her cousin should also be woven into the story so that they do not disappear, but are significantly involved in the rest of the plot.

Make sure during this first revision read-through that the events of your novel grow out of each other in this way, and cut out anything which does not have an effect on the story, leading on to another development.

Are the Sub-Plots Sufficiently Interwoven with the Main Theme?

Sub-plots are necessary to most novels, but it is very important that those which you introduce should be integrated into the principal storyline, and indeed should affect it. Sub-plots usually develop from two principal sources – they are concerned either with the secondary interest or interests of the main character or characters (for instance, the story may be principally about the heroine's search for

true love, but she may also be a career girl and some attention will be focused on that side of her life), or they come
from the interests and actions of the friends and relations of
the main characters. If those subsidiary characters do not
play a part in the main story, affecting the lives of the prin-
cipals, then, however interesting they may be in themselves, they should be cut, or amended so that they do, in
fact, have a strict relevance to the central theme. There is a
great temptation, especially in historical novels set in
Victorian times, or the early twentieth century, to give the
central characters a whole tribe of brothers and sisters,
which seems true to life because so many families at that
period were large ones. But once you have conjured up all
those siblings, you have to try to invent something for them
to do, some part for them to play which will affect the main
story; it isn't always easy and what often happens is that
you end up with a string of sub-plots which really have no
connection with your principal theme. If you are writing a
story set in this period, remember that small families
existed too, and there is no point in having a whole slew of
extra characters who have no part to play simply because
the popular conception of Victorian families is of at least
half a dozen children. The principle applies not only to
Victorian families, but to the circumstances which surround
any story – use only the essential elements.

It might be said that sub-plots and sub-themes can be
either constructive or destructive. The former contribute to
the achievement of the central character's aims and ambitions, while the latter place obstacles along the way. The
inclusion of both varieties is essential to the novel.

However many sub-plots you may have – and there can
be no rules about such matters, because it depends entirely
on the design and scope of your novel – they must have a
close relationship with the principal narrative. If you have
any doubt about the validity of a sub-plot, simply ask yourself what the effect would be if you removed it altogether.
The excision should be a painful business, leaving you with

gaps in your story which would have to be filled in some other way if the sub-plot were to go. On the other hand, if it all comes out with the greatest of ease, and you can hardly see where it's been, as it were, then it shouldn't have been included in the first place, and if you insist on including it, you will have to amend it so that it is really knitted into the main narrative, and could not then be removed without difficulty.

Is There Sufficient Conflict in the Story?

Unless you are trying to produce that kind of literary novel in which storytelling often takes second place to fine writing, brilliant but unorthodox construction, deep psychological characterization, social comment, and other such elements, you will probably be using, in some form or other, the basic formula for fiction of giving your central character an aim or ambition and then placing a series of obstacles in the way of achieving the goal. The barriers which the central character has to surmount provide conflict in the story, and conflict is not only the essence of drama, but the essence of good storytelling.

Conflict does not necessarily mean argument or fighting, but simply anything which causes difficulties for your hero or heroine. Most often it occurs because of the actions of other people, pursuing their own aims and ambitions, but it can also be a matter of the protagonist being torn between two opposing self-interests, or of misunderstandings.

A good sprinkling of conflict throughout the book is needed. It would be absurd to suggest that a major problem should arrive every twenty pages – formulae of that kind just don't work, and although some books have been written in that way, the result is invariably a mechanical, lifeless story. But you do need to see that the tension is maintained in the novel by frequent doses of conflict. It will, of course, have to be woven into the story, which will probably involve some preparation for it, and certainly a follow-up to it. If the scene for it is not set, and it has no consequences, then it will be obvious that it has been inserted as an after-thought, and is not an integral part of the story.

Is There Sufficient Variety in the Story?

It is all very well to talk of a series of metaphorical barriers over which the principal character has to climb in order to achieve the desired ending, but it is important that there should be variety in them, that the various crises should have differing causes and effects. The plot should twist and turn, so that just as everything seems straightforward, something happens which diverts the central character from the proposed course, and leads to further complica-tions, and so on. Sub-plots should have their own variety. And although successful novels have been written with the same setting throughout, and all within the timespan of a few hours, it takes considerable skill to keep the reader's interest alive, and a preferable variety can be provided by changes of scene, time and characters.

A change of pace is important too, so a quick-moving scene, physically or emotionally violent, gains in intensity if it is preceded and followed by something rather quieter. And, as we shall be discussing later when we come to the subject of cliffhangers, a switch of background and mood just as a moment of crisis is reached can be extremely effec-tive in keeping the tension going. But the curious thing about tension is that it works best when it tightens almost to breaking point, and is then slackened off before becom-ing taut again. This is of course the well-known reason for the clowns and other absurd figures who appear somewhat strangely in the middle of Shakespeare's most serious tragedies – non-stop tension is unbearable, and so we need comic relief. He uses the same device in the comedies, too think of Lancelot Gobbo in *The Merchant of Venice* or

Dogberry in *Much Ado About Nothing* – even though the tension is not at such a high level, it still needs breaking periodically.

Variety really is the spice of novels, as well as of life, but it has to be appropriate and it has to belong in the story.

Is the Plot Clear?

Check to make sure that you have given your readers all the information they will need to understand your story. It is remarkably easy to leave out essential information simply because you are so familiar with it. Readers always like to use their imaginations and work some things out for themselves, and they find it irritating if the author keeps telling them things which are fairly obvious, (which is partly why tutors of Creative Writing often offer the maxim, 'Never explain'). But if you have left out some major part of the plot, it is asking too much of your readers to expect them to guess at it.

In fact, it isn't only major omissions which can pose this kind of problem for readers – sometimes something which is of very little significance can cause bafflement, so it is advisable to check that at all points in the development of the story the reader has all the necessary information, or can reasonably be expected to guess at it.

Is the Story Credible?

We all know that life is full of coincidences, and that people behave irrationally and totally out of character from time to time, and that all sorts of things happen unexpectedly for no rhyme or reason that we can see. It is no wonder that people say life is stranger than fiction. It is. And the simple reason why fiction is less strange is that readers somehow feel cheated if a story or its development depends on the kind of action or happening which departs from the norm, even though those actions or happenings are entirely acceptable when they form part of their real lives. Look out, therefore, for any credulity-straining incident in your novel, especially if you have based it on a real-life happening; real-life truth and fictional truth are very different animals.

Preventing your reader from asking awkward questions is of prime importance when considering the ins and outs of the plot. We have already considered the building up of the plot by the use of cause and effect, but it won't work unless the effect is the logical outcome of the cause. It must all make sense.

Comparatively minor matters must be checked too, such as the time taken for a journey (could the hero actually walk from his house to the pub in under two minutes?), or financial matters (if the heroine has to fly to Australia, has she got enough money to pay the fare?), or, to quote a true example from the work of a bestselling American author, is it likely that an impoverished student would live in an apartment in London's Cheapside? Check your facts. Make sure that your research covers little details as well as major backgrounds.

One of the worst faults that many beginners make in the matter of credibility is in rounding off their story and solving all their principal characters' problems by the sudden, unannounced creation of a long-lost relative (usually an extremely wealthy uncle who suddenly arrives from Australia, bringing with him enormous sums of money which he lavishes on the hero and heroine, enabling them to get married, buy an impressive house and set about the business of living happily ever after). An alternative to the Australian uncle nowadays is a monster win on the National Lottery. The device, which need not be concerned with money, but which always solves the problems in the story, is known as *deus ex machina* (god from the machine), a term which derives from the Greek classical theatre, when actors playing gods were suspended over the stage in a kind of box which was lowered at the end of the play so that the gods could appear and set everything to rights. It may have worked in ancient Greece, but nowadays it is regarded as cheating, and it won't be accepted by a publisher's editor, let alone your readers. Characters have to find their own solutions, and if you must use a wealthy Australian uncle, then he ought to appear earlier in the story, and play a real part in it, and you must contrive very good reasons for his sudden appearance and his willingness to get the central character out of all existing financial difficulties – but, no, that's a waste of time, because it still won't work.

There are novels, of course, which do not set out to be credible at all, or at least not in relation to the world as we know it. Most science fantasy stories depend on the reader's suspension of disbelief. Another world is described, and we accept it, but all that follows must still adhere to the conventions of that world as they have been relayed to us, and the strange creatures which inhabit it must behave logically in accordance with their nature.

In a rather different sphere, it is permissible to invent a character and set him or her in a real historical setting among people who actually existed – a story, for example, about an affair between the Prince Regent (who was real) and your invented heroine (who was not). Provided that everyone behaves in a manner suitable to high society in the early 19th century, and that you do not alter any historical events (wars, Prinny's marriage to Mrs Fitzherbert, etc), readers will accept your invention. But you do have to be careful and logical, and think long and hard about everything that you write, so that it sounds right.

This is a point, perhaps, at which to emphasize that readers are far less passive than many authors realize. In a way, the act of reading is creative, as the reader adds her or his intelligence to that of the author and brings it to bear on the book. The reader is remarkably sensitive to the author's intentions, and to the author's foibles and errors. We shall be looking at this point more than once as we continue, but in fact it should be borne in mind at all times – never underestimate your reader.

Have You Surprised the Reader?

Although everything in your story should be credible, and therefore to some extent predictable, arising out of the characters and the rolling cause and effect of their relationships and actions, at the same time you do need to surprise your reader with unexpected developments in the plot. The surprises must never seem like cheating, which they will if you allow the people in your story to behave out of character or if you use the kind of coincidence or the *deus ex machina* device that I was talking about in the paragraphs immediately above. But if, for instance, your heroine is faced with deciding between two alternatives, one of which is the obvious choice and the other far less likely, then let her pick the second, provided that it is not out of character to do so.

Sometimes it is possible, without anticipating the surprise, to prepare for it, by using the device which I refer to as 'little clouds'. A 'little cloud' (the term is a reference to the story in the First Book of Kings, Chapter 18, verses 41 to 45) is really just like a clue in a detective story, which the author drops in almost surreptitiously early in the story in order to prepare for something which is to follow much later on. To give an example, let us suppose that at a fairly late stage in your novel you want your central character to decide to go on a long and arduous journey, despite the fact that some easier alternative is available; early in the book you allow that character to say something like, 'When I was a kid, we used to go to France for holidays, just driving around. We never knew where we would be for the night, and we didn't care – we could sleep in the car if we had to. It was great – travelling's fun.' You don't make any more of it than that (indeed, that example rather labours its point), but when the decision comes up later in the novel, although choosing to go on the journey is the less obvious option, a hint of its likelihood will have been given, and the reader will probably accept it.

Readers are extremely adept at noticing little clouds. I don't mean that they actually keep a sort of running list of any hints that you have dropped as they go on reading, but that clues do register in the subconscious, which says to itself, 'That's interesting – I wonder why the author told me that.' Then, when the hint bears fruit, as it were, the reader remembers and accepts the surprise more readily, and indeed feels some satisfaction at recalling the little clue. For that reason you must be careful not to put in little clouds which you are not going to make use of. It's back yet again to the old rule that nothing must appear in your novel without a purpose, and one of the reasons why that is so important is that the reader, subconsciously at least, expects you to have stuck to the rule, and notices if you do not.

The purpose of surprising the reader is to keep his or her interest going. This does not necessarily mean that the surprises need have any element of the unusual about them, or put even the tiniest strain on the reader's credulity. Sometimes it is a matter of a development in the story which is reasonably natural, but simply unpredicted. For instance, if you were writing a family story of some kind you might have a young hero who marries well and apparently has a long and happy married life ahead of him, which will allow him to concentrate on his business (which is the main background of your story); but suppose that his young wife unexpectedly dies in childbirth – then the reader will be wondering what he will do, what effect will it have on him, how he will look after the child, and so on. Making the reader want to know what happens next is one of the most important parts of successful novel-writing, and you can often achieve it by plot developments of this kind. When you read through your typescript, check that you have put in sufficient material to keep the reader's interest, whether in the form of fairly startling surprises or of happenings which take the story off in a new direction.

4
Fiction – Characterization

Whose Story Is It?

In this chapter we are still dealing with the first read-through of the typescript, when we look to see what major revisions are needed. Chapter 3 began by asking whether you had written the book you intended, and in similar vein you should now make sure whose story you have written and whether he or she is the person you wanted to write about. You can, of course, have more than one main character, and they can be of more or less equal importance. But in most cases, you will have set out to tell the story of one central person, and you do need to check whether you have strayed away from him or her so that a different character has taken over the star role.

Alternatively, while the story is still that of your intended protagonist, have you allowed a character of lesser importance to become more interesting, to come vibrantly to life, to play a dominant role in the development of the plot, so that the reader will feel that the story should really have been about that person? This point is valid only if your main character is very much overshadowed by the interloper – it would not apply, for instance to *Macbeth*, for although Lady Macbeth is the driving force behind her husband and a fascinating character, Shakespeare never allowed her to become of more importance than Macbeth himself. But if your protagonist has constantly been pushed into the background you will need to think again, and perhaps rewrite the whole novel.

The Focus of Attention

I believe that readers like to know very early on in a novel which characters they should be interested in, and you can indicate this by introducing at an early stage those who have a major part to play. In particular, it seems to be sensible to present your principal character as soon as you possibly can – certainly on the first page, if not in the first paragraph or sentence – and to keep the focus on that person for the rest of the scene, even if it is quite a brief one. Presuming that what you say about the character or what she or he does is interesting, the reader will understand straight away that this person is of considerable importance in your story, and indeed is probably the central character. I would also name the character, unless there is some specific plot-related reason for not doing so, because this is another signal to the reader that the character has some standing, and is not just a supernumerary. (For the same reason, never name people who appear in very minor parts in the story and have no real effect on it – who are just background, as it were – such as a taxi-driver, or the receptionist in an office building. As soon as you give a name to a character, you give them importance, and the reader subconsciously feels a need to remember them.) If you begin the story with someone of lesser importance, your reader will possibly be confused and feel betrayed when the spotlight changes later to focus on the main character.

Do also beware of introducing too many characters in the first pages of your novel – if you bring in a dozen or more named characters, the reader won't be able to remember them, or distinguish them one from another, and will have no idea which is to be the most important. If your plot demands that a great many people appear in your first scene, all of them having a significant part to play in the story and therefore needing to be named, then at least follow the advice of starting with the principal character and spending enough time on him or her to engage the reader's attention, and make sure that he or she does not disappear for the rest of the scene, but continues to stand out in it.

Are There Too Many Characters?

Presuming that you have already eliminated any unnecessary sub-plots, as advised in Chapter 3, and therefore any characters who appeared only in those parts of the story, you may still find, if you put yourself in the reader's place, that there are too many people. In a long family saga, especially one in which the stories of a large number of members of the family are told in some detail, it may be necessary to include a family tree, or what might be called a cast list, so that the reader can keep track of them. If it is a really long book or is perhaps a trilogy or tetralogy, the device is justifiable, but even so it always seems a pity if the reader has to break off and turn to the list in order to jog the memory about a certain character and how she or he fits into the overall picture. One way of solving the problem is to give the reader an occasional clue – you might, for instance, say, 'The next time she saw Cousin Mary' rather than 'The next time she saw Mary' – but be careful to make it sound natural and to use the device only when the character re-enters the narrative after a long gap, when the reader will not resent the reminder.

If you still feel that you have too many characters, you might ask yourself when you come to look at a particular character whether his or her function in the story really is essential, even if she or he has a part to play in some incident which has a major effect on your main characters. Is this person involved in a sub-plot of importance, or merely in this incident? It is sometimes possible to circumvent such a situation, and therefore to do without the character altogether. What would the book lose if this 'vital part' were simply blue-pencilled? What would it do to the balance between the various characters in the story? You might find that it actually strengthened the protagonist. And would taking out this section weaken the variety and interest of the novel as a whole, or is the story already so complex that to make it just a little simpler would be a good idea?

You might also be able to alleviate the difficulty of too many characters, at least to some extent, by diminishing the importance of some of the minor characters, cutting down on their characterizations, giving comparatively little information about them, and making it plain that they are not closely involved with your central characters. You must, of course, still try to retain their individuality, because you certainly don't want them to turn into cardboard figures. You must leave some life in them, if you can, but treat them, as it were, casually. This approach does make things easier for the reader, who, struggling to keep track of who is who, notices such treatments, and uses them to decide which characters need not be so firmly slotted into the memory.

Another possibility, which is often worth considering, is to combine two minor characters into one, even if both of them have a vital function in the book. For instance, if X is the person who brings your principal characters, A and B, together, but then fades out of the story, and Y is the person who discovers and tells A that B is unfaithful, is it possible, with a little rejigging, that X could be both bringer-together and informant? Can you do the same sort of thing with some of the other minor characters in the novel? It might even be possible to condense more than two characters into one, but whatever you do in this direction will not only have the benefit of cutting the number of people that the reader has to remember, but of strengthening those to whom the extra functions are given, and of probably improving the whole novel as a result.

There is, incidentally, a converse to this suggestion. Sometimes if you look through the functions of the various characters in the story, you may find that it would be effective to make two characters out of an existing one, provided, of course, that they will both have a job to do in the story, and this may be particularly helpful if you feel that your novel is somewhat lacking in texture and has too simple a storyline.

Are Your Characters Alive?

If you talk to successful novelists they will tell you that their characters are very real to them, that they know them at least as well as their friends and often as intimately as the members of their close family. It is by knowing them through and through that they come alive on the page. It has often been suggested that before starting to write about a character you should make yourself a list of everything you might need to know about her or him – physical appearance, family background, upbringing and education, occupation, beliefs, aims in life, etc, etc, and especially the psychology, the mind and the soul. If you carry out the exercise in depth, the character will be very real to you, and you will be sure of how he or she will react in any given situation, which can be of great value. Of course, you are not going to put everything you know about this person on the page – if you do, you will inevitably include information which the reader does not need, and which would be without purpose in your story, although it is important for you in your behind-the-scenes efforts to clothe the character in flesh and blood. But do make sure that enough has been put in to make your characters real people, which means, among other things, giving them weaknesses as well as strengths. Remember that characters are revealed in their actions and reactions – little things, such as the way they behave towards a family pet, for instance, can be as important in this respect as the way they act in a highly dramatic situation – and are often extremely effectively shown by the way that other characters react towards them. It is also a useful device to reveal your characters' thoughts at appropriate moments (and you will find that it works very well to do it in the form of dialogue – ' "I really must try not to offend her," he told himself' – rather than using indirect speech), especially when the thoughts are in contrast with what the person actually says or does. It can also help to give your central character a confidant to whom he or she can reveal beliefs, feelings, motives which no one else in the story may be aware of.

If, when you are reading through, your characters do not seem to be alive, you may need to go back and think of them rather more deeply, and then insert material which will give them more individuality, stronger emotions, clearer backgrounds and attitudes to life. Do beware, however, of trying to bring your characters to life by writing a complete character sketch or a full physical description when they first appear – spread the information out, so that the reader can absorb it in small doses, building the picture up gradually. In any case, characterizations are seen more vividly in actions and reactions rather than in a kind of list of virtues and vices. And at no point is it necessary to describe your characters' physical appearance in point by point detail – the more you go on, the less memorable it all becomes, and in any case you have deprived the reader of the happy need to use a little imagination to 'see' the person clearly.

Are Your Characters Believable in Their Actions and Reactions?

We have already discussed, in Chapter 3, the need for your story to be credible. You should also make sure that your characters behave in a believable and consistent way. In real life we all do odd things at times – we may be suddenly generous, or mean, we may decide to divorce after forty years of apparent married bliss, we may, despite seeming to be of an equable disposition, give in to road rage, or even commit murder – but all these things astonish other people only if they don't know us well enough to be aware that the apparently uncharacteristic behaviour is in fact part of our deep, basic nature. In a novel we expect to have so clear an understanding of the characters that we can accept whatever outlandish things they do. If we cannot, then your characterization is faulty. You may be able to solve the problem by preparing the reader for the 'out of character' action at an earlier stage (see the remarks on 'little clouds' on pp.45–6). Alternatively, of course, a character can be completely changed as a result of certain experiences – for instance, it would have been quite unbelievable if Scrooge had suddenly said, for no reason, 'Oh, what an awful old so-and-so I've been. I think I'll turn over a new leaf and start being nice to people', but the lessons taught by his nocturnal visitors justify the change. So perhaps you can give the character some experience which will make his or her subsequent actions credible.

Your characters' dialogue must fit them and be as believable and consistent as their actions. The way characters express themselves results from their background, education, and interests, and from their basic characteristics. Despite all efforts to bring about a classless society, the words and phrases which people use still give an indication of the social stratum from which they come, and this fact can be a useful tool for the novelist, provided that it is used with consistency. Poorer, less well educated characters are not only likely to speak ungrammatically, and to be generally less articulate than those farther up the social scale, but may also (but not necessarily) use swear words and clichés and the meaningless 'you know' rather more freely. There are the subtleties of U and Non-U language to think of too – who says 'lavatory' and who says 'toilet' and who says 'Pleased to meet you' and who says 'How do you do'? Special interests will mean that the characters concerned will use the appropriate technical terms correctly and with familiarity. Age also has an effect – the different generations often have different styles of speech and references, and of course this is especially noticeable if you are writing about teenagers, who tend to have a new slang vocabulary every year. And as well as all these considerations you have to make sure that your gentle characters speak gently, and your hotheads with passion, and so on, and that they are always believable.

There is one fairly simple way of checking this problem of credibility and that is to ask yourself at every possible point, 'Would she really do that?', 'Would he really say that?'. You should, of course, have asked yourself similar questions while actually writing the material – 'How will she react to that?', 'What will he say in reply?', and so on – but sometimes the needs of the plot will have driven you into something which doesn't quite fit.

If you find anything which doesn't seem to be in character, you really must do something about it. Some of the matters which we shall be talking about in this book may not demand alterations quite so crucially, but the truth of your characters and of the way they behave and speak must never be compromised. In some cases a small amendment will solve the problem, but what should you do if any alteration to fit your characterizations will have an unwanted effect on the story, perhaps taking it off in a new direction? The answer is either to change the story, which will probably involve a vast amount of rewriting and which you will not wish to do, or to change the character, which will still demand a great deal of revision, but may be the easier option.

Are Your Main Characters Sympathetic?

Although it is possible to write a successful novel centred on someone who is not very likeable, it is an extremely difficult task. Generally speaking, readers want to identify with the central figure in a novel, and cannot easily do so if the character is unpleasant. Fairy stories for adults, such as *A Christmas Carol*, in which the theme is the reformation of a nasty piece of work, are not much in vogue nowadays, so if you want to write about a miser or a villain of some kind or about boring or pompous people, you will either have to attempt a comic novel (which is not easy), in which you laugh at their failings, or you must include them only as minor characters. Your hero or your heroine should be admirable, with a fair sprinkling of the qualities which we all admire – kindness, honesty, courage, the capacity to love, generosity, honour, and so on – and with ambitions which are in keeping with such characteristics. Moreover, they need to have a certain amount of 'get-up-and-go' about them – they take action, they make things happen and don't just lie back and allow themselves to be carried along passively by other people or by outside events, and indeed they should always solve their own problems, rather than allowing others to make things easy for them. They should also care about something, whether it is another person or a cause or something else, and we should be able to admire them for their concern about whatever it may be. We also need to see them coping with adversity, which does not mean that they succeed in overcoming every difficulty which faces them – that too could affect their credibility – but they should not, at least for any length of time, be overcome by despair. Indeed, when we identify with characters in a novel, we want them to succeed and to achieve their aims – a novel about someone who is one of life's lame ducks and remains a failure to the very end is unlikely to appeal greatly, despite the fact that it mirrors the experience of many readers, because when we read we often want to escape from ourselves and our inadequacies. At the same time, a degree of vulnerability is a quality which arouses sympathy in the reader.

A special case is the genre in which the central character has very few admirable qualities, but makes up for it by an enormous amount of charm. He (it is almost invariably a man) is a rogue, irresistible to women, amusing, living very successfully on his wits, and a constant scourge of people in authority, especially if they are full of their own importance. This is the picaresque novel. It works because the hero really is charming, and because those whom he cheats and makes fools of deserve everything they get. It is, however, an extremely difficult genre, especially for the beginner, and it is likely that a very large majority of the readers of this book will be dealing with a more ordinary protagonist, who will certainly need to have the qualities which will make us approve of him or her.

At the same time, none of your characters should be perfect, because they then become unbelievable. They should have some of the normal human weaknesses, such as a tendency to impatience, or the occasional thoughtlessness, and especially perhaps (because it is such a useful device for the purposes of plotting) a willingness to allow themselves to tell a lie now and then. The main character's failings in any respect can sometimes be used very effectively as an obstacle to the achievement of his or her goal.

The desirability of making your hero and/or heroine humanly less than perfect also applies, in the opposite direction to your villains, who will not be believable if you depict them as unpleasant in every possible way. It may be that there are some people in real life who could be characterized as totally evil and repulsive, but such a character rarely seems to work well in fiction (except in certain cases which I will come to in a moment) and it is almost always better to give your villains some justification for their beliefs and ambitions and to let them show some of the better human characteristics. In other words, they should not really be the dyed-in-the-wool villains of melodrama, and it might be better to forget the word 'villain', use 'antagonist' instead, and think of someone who opposes and causes problems for the hero or heroine, but is still very human.

It is interesting to note, however, that all that I have so far said applies in a slightly different way to the heroes and villains of certain forms of what is sometimes termed 'genre fiction', which is to say thrillers, westerns, and science fiction. The reader still wants to identify with the hero, who is usually tough, ruthless, egocentric and arrogant, and in fact in real life would be few people's idea of a likeable person; but of course, he has right on his side and he's indestructible and is going to win in the end. The villain in such stories, on the other hand, can be as nasty as you like, and doesn't really need any redeeming qualities.

It is often very difficult for authors to tell how likeable the central characters in their novels will be to readers – having been so closely involved with them while writing the book, they probably love them all. You do have to try to be objective, however, and to make sure that your hero or heroine fulfils the conditions described above. One of the surest ways of evoking the reader's sympathy is by making your central character the victim of an injustice of some kind, and this is indeed a mainspring of many plots. But if we are looking primarily at characteristics, there are two which have not so far been mentioned, and which in this context can be of immense value, and they are humour and enjoyment of life. If you suspect that your main characters are less likeable than you would wish, revise their presentation by giving them a sense of humour and it will go a long way towards solving the problem. This does not mean that you have to fill up the pages with a stream of witty one-liners, nor even make them tell jokes. Just allow them to laugh now and then, especially at themselves, and you will remove some at least of their pomposity, and give them a warmth in place of it. And allowing the characters to enjoy life and to be happy when they have good cause, makes the reader happy too. It can also be useful in plotting, since when we are really euphoric we often do foolish things – think of Gene Kelly singin' in the rain, which is not just a song and dance, but an expression of delight at being in love – and foolish actions can lead to interesting developments in the story, and often to what you might think of as 'morning-after' problems.

As for your villains, one of the best devices for giving them some genuine humanity is to allow them to have someone whom they love – or even a pet. Love may or may not make the world go round, but it is an emotion to which we all warm.

Political correctness needs to be considered. Some of your characters may have politically incorrect attitudes, especially if you are writing about a period in which such views were the norm. You need to make sure that it is clear that the incorrectness belongs to the character rather than to you, and preferably that you do not approve of it.

While you are working through this stage of revision, look at all your characters as objectively as you can and if necessary amend them, however much rewriting may be involved. The more trouble you take, the better the results will be.

Do Your Characters Grow and Change?

The importance of this question depends on the kind of novel which you are writing. If you are producing an all-action thriller, for instance, the emphasis will almost certainly be on the events of the story, the physical action, and the thrills, and the characters may be pretty much ciphers, who will exhibit little in the way of development and change between the first page and the last. The same can be true in other forms of genre writing such as the western, some science fiction or fantasy, horror, and the detective story. It all depends on the extent to which the emotions of the characters are involved. I am not saying, of course, that there is never any emotional content in thrillers, westerns, science fiction, fantasy and detective stories, but it is in romances, family sagas, historical fiction, and what is often called, for want of a better term, the 'straight' novel, that the emotions are normally of prime interest. And it is essential that the characters who experience these various emotions should change and grow.

To understand why, we need to look at what readers want from a novel. A novel is primarily a work of entertainment – we may learn something from it along the way, especially if the author has set out to tell us all about some unfamiliar background, or to make an important social point, but the research and the crusading approach will go for nothing if we are not interested. Since the only thing which really interests the whole human race as a whole is other human beings, we look for our entertainment in the characters of the novel. Now the author who knows, or should know, her or his characters through and through, could simply give us all possible information about them and leave it at that, but then we should have nothing more than a collection of character studies – interesting, but only up to a point. What we look for is a story about these characters, because only when the characters are involved in certain situations and faced with certain problems do we become involved. So we want a plot, and, as we have already seen in an earlier chapter, the story or plot is a matter of cause and effect, cause and effect, rolling on and on until the end. But the effect is only interesting if it affects a character. If it rains (cause), the roof may leak (effect), but that, by itself, is dull; what the owner of the house does about it, what effect it has on his or her future and particularly his or her relationships with other people – that is what is interesting. We are looking for something as mundane as a leaking roof to make a difference to the owner emotionally, in his or her character. We learn by experience, but we are also changed by experience. By the end of the story our main character should have grown and changed, and the process should in fact have been a gradual one as the story progressed.

You probably do not need to worry a great deal about this point if you are writing a family saga, or indeed any novel which takes place over a long period of time, because the mere fact that the characters grow older will undoubtedly result in their growth and change. And, as I have already suggested, there is little problem with much genre fiction – at the end of the thriller, the intrepid hero may have saved the world from being taken over by the Russians or the Chinese or drug barons, but otherwise will still be the same fairly wooden figure. But make sure, in the novel in which your characters are emotionally involved with each other, that your plot allows their essential development to take place. And, by the way, that includes antagonists – they should grow too.

Have You Libelled Anyone?

If in your novel you have included an uncomplimentary but recognizable portrait of a real-life person, you will be running the risk of an action for libel. It will be libellous only if the material is damaging to the person's reputation, but will be considered to be more damning if it affects his or her ability to earn a living. Disguising a real-life person by giving the character a different name, appearance and situation in life is rarely sufficient, because his or her friends will still say, 'Oh, that's meant to be old So-and-so', and as soon as they do that the victim has a case for libel. You also need to be careful that you don't libel someone unintentionally, which is most likely to happen if you give your wholly imaginary but entirely villainous character the name of a real-life person in a fairly prominent social position, such as a doctor, or lawyer, or clergyman. Such professions have lists of those who belong to them, and it is worth checking to see that the name you select is not on the list. Since unpleasant people are all around us and that fact must be reflected in fiction, it is just about impossible to avoid including baddies in your story, perpetrating various degrees of villainy – indeed, they are essential because they are usually the cause of the conflict and drama which make the story interesting. Just make sure that they are not even remotely based on anyone you know. One consolation, mainly for the historical novelist, is that you can't libel people who are dead – although even in that case there is a caveat, because you can by inference libel the dead person's descendants. It's a minefield – check with care, and revise as necessary.

5

Fiction – Story-Telling Technique

If the content of the novel seems satisfactory, or if you have decided on and carried out various structural changes, you now need to look at the way you have actually written your story – its technique – but again, since we are still concerned with the first revision read-through, in general terms.

Does the Novel Begin Effectively?

As any Creative Writing tutor will tell you the first page of a novel is vitally important. It must grab the reader's attention, and if it can do so in the very first line, that is all to the good. Consider the following opening lines:

'Hale knew, before he had been in Brighton three hours, that they meant to murder him.' Graham Greene, *Brighton Rock*.

'It was at a love-spinning that I saw Kester first.' Mary Webb, *Precious Bane*.

'Suppose you are contemplating an island. It is not any island known to you.' Jill Paton Waloh, *Knowledge of Angels*.

'High, high above the North Pole, on the first day of

1969, two professors of English Literature approached each other at a combined velocity of 1200 miles per hour.' David Lodge, *Changing Places*.

'It is cold at six-forty in the morning of a March day in Paris, and seems even colder when a man is about to be executed by firing squad.' Frederick Forsyth, *The Day of the Jackal*.

' "Take my camel, dear," said my aunt Dot as she climbed down from this animal on her return from High Mass.' Rose Macaulay, *The Towers of Trebizond*.

All six have the essential quality of arousing the reader's curiosity. (Why did they mean to murder Hale, and who are 'they'? Who is Kester, who is the 'I' of the story (and what is a love-spinning)? What and where is the island, and why should we be interested in it? Who are the two professors and is there some reason why they should apparently be travelling in opposite directions? Who is being executed? And are we in Egypt, and who is aunt Dot and to whom is she speaking, and where will that person take the camel?) Moreover, all these openings plunge straight into the story, without going into long descriptions of the background or the circumstances, which can come later, and they also, at least in most cases, give some indication, which a perceptive reader will have no difficulty in picking up, of what sort of story is to follow.

They do all that in a matter of a couple of lines. Does your novel start as effectively? If you can achieve the same sort of effect as those six extracts do, you will straightway engage the attention of an editor. Mind you, it is as well to avoid an opening line which is so shocking ('He plunged the dagger into his mother's breast!') that you will never be able to achieve the same kind of tension again. On the other hand, you may feel that a direct and immediate appeal to the reader's emotions is not for you, because it does not suit the style of the book you have written, and this may be particularly true of the novel which seeks to amuse, to entertain, and even perhaps to instruct, but does not set out to shock or excite. Well, you don't necessarily have to start with something startling enough to be what article-writers call 'an eye-opener', but you certainly need to make sure that on that very first page you put questions into the reader's mind (who is this speaking? what is going on? why is he doing that? where is this taking place?). Arousing curiosity is one of the most important parts of the story-teller's craft; once you get some way into the novel, the reader's principal query will be 'what happens next?', and he or she should go on asking that until the very end, but at the start we are probably thinking rather more in terms of Kipling's honest serving-men, What and Why and When and How and Where and Who.

The most important of the serving-men, in any context, is Who, but that is particularly true for fiction, since it is characters who form the story and about whom we want to read. As I have already mentioned, I think it is important to introduce your principal character on the first page of your book, focusing attention on him or her and launching him or her straight into action of some kind. Keep the introduction of other characters to a minimum in the first pages of the story, so that the spotlight remains on your hero or heroine, and if at a very early point you can expose the protagonist's emotions, even if only to a small degree, you stand a good chance of getting the reader to begin identifying with that person.

Action – something happening – is the next essential ingredient. Donna Baker, in her book *How to Write Stories for Magazines*, suggests that a short story should begin at or immediately before a moment of crisis. It is true of novels too, and the sooner you involve the reader in the events of the story the better. It may be very important to put across all sorts of relevant information, but it can wait. Once you have your hooks well and truly into the reader, you will be able to go on to other details without fear of losing his or her attention, provided, of course, that you don't allow yourself to become boring, but for the moment something of interest must be taking place. In other words, using a metaphor drawn from the detective story, put the body on page one.

It is almost always advisable to give some indication right at the beginning of the kind of story which is to follow, particularly if it is genre writing, such as a thriller, or a historical novel, science fiction, or a humorous tale. It may not always suit the construction of the book to do so, if, for example, you are planning to surprise the reader by moving from a gentle beginning into full-blown horror, but in most cases it is helpful. Similarly, hints as to the period and scene, especially if subtly done, may add to the reader's interest.

One last piece of advice is not to overwhelm the reader with attention-grabbing devices. Keep her or him guessing, but not confused, and although you may give promise of complexities to come, let your opening pages have a certain simplicity about them.

Because the first page is of such great importance, it is possible to become obsessional about it, and to go on revising and revising until you probably need to rewrite the rest of the book to match it, or until, feeling that you will never get it right, you abandon the whole novel. Avoid a fixation, but be aware that poorly-written, over-complicated, diffuse, and plain dull first pages are the reason why so many books do not get read by the publishers to whom they are submitted. The opening page is your shop window for the editor and eventually the reader – make sure that it is well stocked and dressed, and if it isn't, then have another go at it, remembering the criteria discussed above.

Have you Shown instead of Telling?

Tutors of Creative Writing frequently advise their students, 'Show, don't tell', or they use the terms 'action' and 'narration' when making the same point. Action does not necessarily involve physical movement, but is used to mean a scene in a novel which takes place, as it were, before the reader's eyes, unfolding as we read. It almost invariably uses a great deal of dialogue. Narration, on the other hand, is the term used when the author tells us what happens (or, very often, what has happened) without us seeing it take place – it is all off-stage. Narration is usually very much more succinct than action, but has far less impact. To give an example, the three words 'They quarrelled bitterly' is narration, short and to the point, but if instead we were to be given something like this:

'You stupid idiot!' Angela said, her eyes flashing. 'How could you have forgotten?'

'Now, wait a minute . . .'

'It's just typical! You're selfish, Tom, utterly selfish. You never think of—'

'Darling, please! I wish I could make you understand.'

'Oh, I understand only too well. The only thing you care about is your precious business. Nothing else matters, does it? I don't matter. Emma doesn't matter. Nothing matters, except your stupid computers.

Tom struggled for a moment to maintain a conciliatory tone, but when he spoke the words came out with an icy contempt. 'Have you finished? I might remind you that my stupid computers pay for us to live – they pay for you and they pay for Emma, and if you weren't so bloody extravagant . . . You call me stupid, you call me selfish, but you're the stupid one, Angie, you're the selfish one. It's time we called it a day.'

The scene could go on for several pages, provided that interesting facts about Tom and Angela and their relationship and background keep on emerging – many have already – items which would have an effect on the rest of the plot. The scene could have been summed up in the three words of narration, 'They quarrelled bitterly', or it could have been expanded to cover some of the topics in the conversation, but action is so much more revealing and interesting because it tells us about character and motives, and it leads on to developments in the plot.

Although some novels have been successfully written without any narration at all, that approach demands great skill, and because the effect is somewhat wearing, published novels in this style have usually been quite short. On the other hand, unalloyed narration is likely to be life-less, which is why when readers flick through a novel before buying it, they are usually looking to see whether or not there is plenty of dialogue – dialogue means action. The answer therefore is to use both techniques, interspersing the action with passages of narration, which gives contrast and variety, and in fact results in a strengthening of the action scenes.

One slight danger when writing action is that, if the scene is a very long one, the action will become too relent-less. Just as a long section which is very emotional may need a touch of comic relief to break the tension, so a para-graph or two of narration inserted into a long stretch of action will enhance it.

Make sure, then, when you are engaged in your first revi-sion read-through, that you not only have that kind of contrast and variety, but much more importantly that you have used action for all the moments of crisis in your story, employing narration mainly for the essential linking mate-rial between the main scenes. It is quite easy, as I know from my own experience, to miss an opportunity for a dramatic action scene; in one of my novels one of the major charac-ters dies, to the great distress of the hero, but in the draft which I submitted to my publisher the death occurred off-stage, and my editor pointed out that if my hero could be at the deathbed it would make an effective, touching scene, and would add another dimension to the portrait of the hero. It was easily put right, but I should have seen the mistake for myself during my revision. It is such a common error that you should constantly ask yourself, as you revise, whether you have missed a chance to make a scene of some quite important part of your story.

Have You Chosen the Right Viewpoint – and Kept to It?

By 'viewpoint' teachers of Creative Writing usually mean whether the story is told in the first person, or in the third person but with the focus of attention very firmly on a central character, or in the third person taking what is sometimes called the 'God's eye view'.

In the first person narrative, which has the benefit of immediacy and ease of reader-identification, the problem is that nothing in the story should be there if the central character, who is the narrator, does not know about it or is not present when it happens. Various devices are available to overcome the difficulties – the protagonist can be told by a friend about things of which otherwise he or she would be ignorant, or can read essential information in a letter or a newspaper, and the reader can even learn about the narrator's appearance if he or she looks in a mirror and describes the reflection.

As a variation on the first person narrative, the story may be told by an observer who is engaged only on the fringes of the action, and, being perceptive but not emotionally involved in whatever is happening, can give a comprehensive account of events. However, this rarely works well, precisely because of this narrator's lack of participation in the central events of the novel.

The God's eye view enables the author to disclose to the reader the actions and thoughts of each character in turn, and to move the story from one set of characters to another without any problems of communication. The approach has the disadvantage of making the author more noticeably the

71

narrator, and it sometimes gives a very detached atmosphere to the story, when reader identification becomes less easy.

The story told in the third person, but through the eyes of the main character gives more freedom than the first person narrative, without the lack of focus associated with the God's eye view. It is the most popular approach, especially when combined with occasional brief use of the God's eye view. You will still have some problems, because when the focus of attention is on the central character – and you should not move away from it until you shift to another scene – she or he cannot always tell what the others in the story are thinking, so that the picture is not a complete one, but you can often overcome that difficulty by allowing her or him to guess, or by giving the reader information about what the others have in mind – including perhaps their reactions to the main character – in a later God's eye scene.

There are two questions on the matter of viewpoint to ask yourself when you are engaged in your initial revision read-through. The first is whether you have chosen the right approach. The first person narrative and the God's eye view are likely to be the viewpoints which may turn out to be less than satisfactory. If you have written in the first person, have you challenged the reader's credulity at any point by making your central character aware of happenings or of other characters' motives of which he or she could actually know nothing? If so, is there any way you can get around the problem, or will you in fact, because you really can't cheat in such matters, have to rewrite from the beginning? If you chose the God's eye view in the first place because you intended to spread your attention and the reader's among several characters, does it really work, or has one character grown so much that you should re-write, making sure that the focus of attention is firmly on that one character?

The second important question is whether at any point in the story you have switched the viewpoint in the middle of a scene. As I have already suggested, you should not do so. Even if you are using the God's eye view, it is preferable that each scene in your story should be centred on a single character – if you switch viewpoint in mid-stream to put the focus of attention on someone else, the reader is liable to feel confused. Choose a viewpoint at the beginning of each scene, and stick to it.

Does the Dialogue Take the Story Forward?

We have already looked in Chapter 4 at the need to ensure that the dialogue is in character, and now we must consider what the dialogue achieves. Because of the requirement, even in fantasy, to convince the reader of the reality of whatever is happening, inexperienced writers often feel that it is vital to reflect real life as closely as possible. Nothing could be farther from the truth – fiction is not a reflection of life as it is. It may make very important comments on real life, it may have entirely recognizable characters and situations, it may be concerned with every-day issues – in short, it may have a ring of truth about it, but it is selective, shaped, presented from a particular angle, so that if it is a reflection of real life it is one which is seen in a slightly distorting mirror. Real life is untidy, disorganized, trivial, and often extremely dull – and the novel should be none of those things. Think of a novel as a painting in which the artist composes the picture, chooses the way in which the theme is presented, altering reality at will, and uses colour and light and shade to make a comment on the subject rather than a wholly accurate representation; a novel is not a photograph.

One aspect in particular where the writer must never try to reflect reality with total exactitude is dialogue. Listen to two people talking and you will find that the conversation contains an enormous amount of what might be called social chit-chat – the kind of thing that we say automatically because it is polite and conventional to do so – 'good morning' and 'nice day' and 'how are you?' and 'did you sleep well?', etc, etc. Additionally there are the interjections we make to show that we are still listening – 'really?' and 'did he?' and 'I know' and 'm'm'. What is more, we are all guilty of the faults in that popular panel game, 'Just a Minute' – repetition, hesitation, deviation. And sometimes we don't say what we mean, although it is not our intention to deceive, and we don't always listen properly, so that we have to ask for information to be repeated. Real life dialogue is a mess, and if you put it in your story exactly as it is, the result is boring and virtually unreadable. What you have to do is to make the dialogue sound natural, but get rid of all the irrelevancies and general sloppiness, remembering that your reader will happily take them for granted. When your characters meet, readers will accept without being told that they will go through our habitual conversational rituals.

So, no chit-chat, but make sure that the dialogue is actually doing a job by helping to tell the story or revealing aspects of the speaker's character. Of course, you will occasionally be forced into using a line of dialogue here and there which is unproductive, but keep such instances to the minimum. Remember the value of misunderstandings, lies and other deceptions, Freudian slips, humour, teasing, and use such dialogue devices not only to leaven the straightforward sincerity of the rest of what is said, but because they can often effectively advance the story. Every chunk of dialogue needs to have a purpose, to be part of the plot, to be productive in terms of moving the story forward. Be ruthless in your editing of pointless dialogue.

Does Your Research Show?

Because, even in fantasy, readers demand verisimilitude, most writers have realized that research is essential if only to provide an authentic background to the main story. Even if you know the subject backwards, there are always little points which need checking, just to make sure. Once you have discovered how much you can find out simply by keeping your eyes open, and how willingly most experts will share their knowledge and just how much information is readily available in libraries, museums and from the archives of most large organizations, research becomes easy and fascinating. And the more you find out, the more intriguing it is to quarry even more, and the more you learn about a given subject, the more tempting it is to share your knowledge with your readers.

There are two dangers. The first is that, because you find it so interesting, you will include chunks of your research which really have nothing to do with the story. The novelist and publisher Diane Pearson once said, 'Research is like manure – a little here and there makes everything blossom and grow, but in large lumps it is horrid.' Large lumps of research are indeed unacceptable, but it is really extraordinary how even the briefest of casual references based on a piece of research stands out if it is not strictly relevant to the story. Research has not only to be spread thinly but must bring essential information to the novel. Cut any details, however fascinating they may be, which add nothing other than their own content, and if you find that you have included long, solid chunks of research which are in fact vital to the story, rewrite so that the information is spaced out, and you don't give too much to the reader at any one time.

An extremely useful device for getting your research across as painlessly as possible is to let your main character be ignorant of certain facts which, for the sake of the plot, it is essential that he or she should learn about; then put into the story an expert on the subject who will explain those facts to the protagonist and so, indirectly, to the reader. But it must be natural for the expert to do so. For instance, if your hero is required, for the purposes of the story, to learn how the big supermarkets work, then let him join a branch of Sainsbury or Tesco or Asda as a trainee, and whoever is looking after him can pass on all the vital information (slowly, in small bites, rather than in large indigestible lumps), or if your heroine needs to know how to paddle a canoe through white water, then let her be told by an instructor. And in either case, refuse the temptation to include anything which is not strictly relevant, even though you feel that it would add interest – what it will add instead is a feeling in the reader that she or he is being got at, that the author is showing off, that the research is obtrusive.

Have You Kept Yourself Out Of The Book?

If your novel has a theme which interests you deeply, it may be difficult sometimes to keep yourself and your beliefs and prejudices out of the story. If when reading through you become aware that you, as the author, are speaking directly to the reader, then rewrite so that your views are expressed by the characters – and of course it must be natural for them to do so. There are some similarities in this matter with those dollops of research mentioned above – once the characters become transparent, so that it is your emotions, not theirs, which can be seen, it will be apparent that you are lecturing the reader, just as you are showing off your knowledge if you include a large section of research which is not directly related to your story and your characters. Never, ever lecture the reader. Moreover, if you have an antagonist in your story who is entirely opposed to the views which, through your main character, you wish to propagate, then you must try to present that baddie with understanding, and be careful not to make your own disagreement with her or his views clearly visible to the reader by an obviously prejudiced approach. The goodies, on your side, are bound to win, so there is no need to show the opposition as either villainous or idiotic.

Have You Ended Your Chapters Effectively?

Beginners often worry a great deal about chapters. The query which arises most frequently is 'How will I know when to end a chapter?' The answer is that you can usually see quite easily where chapter breaks should occur if you look at the structure of your novel. The story will be made up of different elements and sub-elements – the beginning, in which characters are introduced and the theme is set, the various events and incidents and sub-plots which form the long middle part of the book, and the denouement, when everything is brought to a satisfying end. Each of these elements and sub-elements may form a chapter, especially when there is a change of time or scene or of viewpoint or characters. To take a simple example, let us suppose that 'Cinderella' is a novel rather than a story: Chapter 1 will introduce us to Cinderella, her father and her step-sisters, and show us the way in which they live, and might end with the arrival of the invitation to Prince Charming's Ball; Chapter 2 will show Cinderella meeting and helping the old woman who later turns out to be her Fairy Godmother; Chapter 3 shows the step-sisters getting ready for the Ball; in Chapter 4 the Fairy Godmother arrives and turns Cinderella into a princess for the evening; Chapter 5 takes place at the Ball, with Prince Charming falling in love with the beautiful and mysterious stranger, and ends with the dramatic striking of midnight; Chapter 6 tells of the Prince's search for the owner of the glass slipper, his visit to Hardup Hall, and his discovery of Cinderella; and Chapter 7 describes the wedding (and possibly, nowadays, the bedding). If we add sub-plots and other characters – giving the Ugly Sisters other concerns besides catching husbands, and perhaps explaining and justifying their treatment of Cinderella, and if we also bring Dandini and Buttons into the story and give them real parts to play in it – we shall probably need more than those seven chapters. Looking at the simpler plan, however, we can say that most stories fall just as naturally as that into chapters or sections. You might also think of any ITV programme, but perhaps particularly of dramas and sit-coms – the advertisement breaks are often called 'natural breaks' because they are precisely that – they come when an episode, an event, a section of the story has been completed. Look a little more deeply into the question, and you will see that the breaks come after a climax. Just as the novel as a whole works towards a climax, so should each chapter.

Perhaps you have had little difficulty in dividing your novel into chapters. You may also have sub-divided chapters into sections separated by blank lines, each section being related to the main theme of the chapter, but possibly involving a different place or time or focusing on different characters. However, the use of the 'natural breaks' in your story may not be the best way of telling it, and one of the points which you should look for during your initial revision read-through is whether you have ended the chapters in such a way that your reader will want to know what happens next, and the best way of doing this is to end in the middle of a moment of crisis, not resolving it at that point. Thus in our novel about Cinderella, Chapter 1 would end not just with the Ugly Sisters telling Cinders that she is not to go to the Ball, but with Cinderella saying that she will appeal to her father about it. The reader (who, for the purposes of this illustration, does not already know the story) is left until at least the next chapter wondering what Baron Hardup will say.

What we are talking about here is the cliffhanger, which is one of the most useful devices available to an author, and you should check to make sure that you have not neglected it, and that if you have used it you have done so in the best way. 'Cliffhanger' is a term derived from the days of serial movies, which often concerned themselves with a young woman in danger; she might find herself hanging on a cliff, with a vertiginous drop below and no hope of rescue – and at that point the week's episode would end, and it would not be until their next visit to the cinema that the audience would know how she got out of danger. That was a 'cliffhanger'. The same term came to be used for any similar situation, even if it did not involve a cliff – when the heroine was left tied to the railway lines, with an express rapidly approaching, for instance. Some of the best examples of cliffhangers today are to be found in the radio serial, *The Archers* – if one of the characters says, 'I've had a letter ... and I'm worried about it ... very worried,' you can be pretty sure that the familiar signature tune is about to break in, leaving the listener wanting to know what the letter says until the next episode is broadcast the next day. Cliffhangers are in fact hooks which the author sinks into the reader, making her or him want to know what happens next.

One danger with the cliffhanger is that of a feeling of let-down when you go back to the crisis point if it turns out hardly to be a crisis after all. The writers of *The Archers*, who have to come up with a daily cliffhanger, don't always follow up satisfactorily – the letter which worried the character at the end of yesterday's episode may turn out to be a complete fizzle. Try to make sure that when you return to it the crisis is still in full swing, and that the way out of it is dramatic – if the approaching express train suddenly swings all by itself on to a different line, avoiding the heroine tied to the rails, that might be quite exciting, but it would be much better if the hero arrives in the nick of time and switches the points.

Having checked that cliffhangers are there in your story, you need to ask yourself whether you have given them their maximum power. They work best if you can move at the beginning of the next chapter to a different scene, or time, or set of characters, and especially a different mood (probably a lot less tense), leaving your crisis metaphorically hanging on that cliff, and not resolving it until the following chapter. However, it has to be said that this is often easier to contrive in a God's eye view story than if you are using a less detached viewpoint.

Cliffhangers can come in varying strengths, as it were – the interrupted crisis need not necessarily be a life and death matter – and you can use them at the end of sections within a chapter as well as to round off the chapters themselves. Beware of using too many powerful cliffhangers – like anything else, repetition can cloy – but do try to create suspense throughout the story. Suspense exists whenever you make the reader want to know what happens next. That well-worn piece of advice from Charles Reade – 'Make 'em laugh, make 'em cry, but make 'em wait' – is really relevant.

Do Your Changes of Scene and Time Work Smoothly?

In the course of a novel there are likely to be many changes of scene and time, and when checking through you should make sure that the reader is never confused as to where and when events are taking place. This does not mean that you have to account for every hour that passes or every slight change of scenery – readers are quite good at assuming for instance that several hours will pass between the time that a character leaves for work and gets home again, or that a train will pass through a number of stations on its way to a desired destination – there is no need to tell us anything about those lapsed hours or the details of the train journey unless they are relevant to the story. Sometimes, however, it is essential to specify the time and place of a new scene fairly exactly. There is nothing wrong with that, but it is preferable, if you can, to avoid the clumsiness of constantly beginning sections with 'The next day' or 'Two months later' or information about where the action is taking place. You can, of course, preface each chapter or section with a date and location as a heading, and that can be quite effective, because it not only gets the information across but does so in the most economical and least boring way. However, a more subtle approach can often be used. For instance, if a chapter ends at night and the next chapter begins with the information that the sun is shining, the reader will take it for granted, unless you indicate otherwise, that it is the next morning; if your characters notice the daffodils in flower, we know that it is spring, and if they can see the Eiffel Tower we don't need to be told that we are in Paris.

One of the problems with the handling of time in a novel is concerned with flashbacks, which are a very useful device, enabling the author either to withhold certain information until a more effective point in the story (Charles Reade's 'make 'em wait' again), or to put across some essential facts which, if inserted earlier, in chronological order, would have held up the narrative at a time when it was more important to get on with the action, or again to vary the way in which important details are conveyed to the reader. Like most of the more obvious devices which are available to authors, such as cliffhangers and dramatic irony, flashbacks need to be used sparingly. The main problem which inexperienced writers find with flashbacks is the pluperfect tense: your story is being narrated in the simple past, and then when you come to a flashback you need to say something like, 'She had been to visit Alexandra and had had an interesting discussion with her. After that they had had lunch and had then gone to the museum, where they had seen . . .' and so on; the 'hads' get more and more obtrusive. The same is true when 'would' is used instead of 'had' – 'She remembered how she would get up each morning and would go to work in a daze, and would come home tired and would go to bed early' – the 'woulds' go on and on. If this problem occurs in your novel, the answer is simply to leave the first one or two 'hads' or 'woulds' in place – probably those in the first sentence – and then revert to the ordinary past tense: 'She had been to visit Alexandra and had had an interesting conversation with her. After that they had lunch and then went to the museum, where they saw . . .' The reader will assume that the story is continuing in flashback, until, when you come to the end of it, you give some indication that we are back in the time of the main story. The switch back can easily be achieved if you do not open a chapter or section with the flashback, but interrupt your story for it, as it were – for example, your heroine is talking to your hero, she stops to remember in flashback something which happened in the past, and then returns to her conversation with the hero – that technique will present the reader with no difficulty in understanding what is happening and when.

If you use flashbacks, I think you should make sure that you have not done so in the first few pages of the book, because it seems to me a mistake to take the reader away from the scene and the characters with which you begin before you have established them firmly. And although it is possible to write a whole novel in flashback, framing it perhaps with the first and last chapters taking place in the present, and you can certainly put a whole chapter into flashback, on the whole it is wise not to let flashbacks go on too long, since they tend to hold up the flow of the narrative, even when they impart essential information.

Are Your Descriptions of Backgrounds Effective?

Most of the Victorian novelists were prone to indulge in the detailed description of scenery, and their scene-setting sometimes seems interminable to modern eyes. Scenery and other background details are, of course, important, and can have a great effect on the mood of your novel or of events in it, but, as with the portrayal of characters, long chunks of description tend to bore the reader, and it is preferable to bring the information out gradually, rather than in a solid lump. And do look to see whether you have a tendency to start off each new section of your book by describing the background at some length before getting on with the story; if you do, then make changes – get the reader interested first in the action, and once the hook is in you can afford to set the scene. Note too how much can be achieved with a considerable economy – tell the reader, for instance, that a sitting room is furnished with the utmost luxury, or that a room in a small cottage has a dirt floor and is almost bare of furniture, and the reader will be able, with a little imagination, to supply the rest of the description.

A great many novelists 'see' their characters and their backgrounds as they write, almost as though they were watching a play, putting down on paper what they see, and, perhaps because it is so obviously effective, using colour as one of the most important elements in bringing the scene to life. Many also 'hear' the scene, and record what they hear. Television makes us accustomed to colour and sound. But the other senses can be equally potent. Smells of all kinds, whether pleasant or disgusting, are very evocative, and so are touch and taste, and descriptions which use all the senses stay in the reader's mind more clearly. While looking generally to cut down on scene-setting, check your work to see whether at any point you can enhance the effect by adding in (economically, of course) the sometimes neglected senses.

Background material is not always concerned with scenery, of course – the information may be about what happened before the novel proper began or some fact essential to understanding the story. Whatever it may be, cut it to the minimum and don't try to put it across in indigestible dollops.

Have You Included Any Humour?

In the chapter concerned with characterization I mentioned the value of giving your central character a sense of humour. Humour is an extremely useful ingredient in the novel as a whole, serving a number of purposes: it acts in exactly the same way as the comic relief in a Shakespearean play, providing a contrast to highly dramatic scenes and releasing the tension; it stops your work from seeming over-solemn and portentous; and, if it is witty or truly funny it has a value of its own to which the reader will respond. Of course, it does not mean sprinkling jokes and funny comments about indiscriminately – any comedy in the story must arise naturally from the characters and the plot – but if you can amuse your readers they will enjoy it.

Is the Ending Right?

Referring to her own three-volume novel, Miss Prism, the comic governess in Oscar Wilde's *The Importance of Being Earnest*, said, 'The good ended happily, and the bad unhappily. That is what fiction means.' It is a joke, of course, but in fact to some extent it is true of almost all novels. The happiness or unhappiness may not be total, but generally speaking we like stories to end in an upbeat way, and the central character's achievement of his or her goals and ambitions is what we always hope for. If the protagonist is not about to attain fulfilment in marriage or wealth or power or a combination of some or all of those and of any other desirable objectives, then at least the character should find some kind of contentment, even if only in the way of being sadder but wiser. We also want to see the antagonists receive their come-uppances, especially if they are the perpetrators of some injustice against the central character. On the other hand, it is possible that they should not end unhappily at all, but that the obstacles which they placed in the way of the heroine or hero's ambitions will have been largely overcome, and (unless you are planning a series of stories which will involve the same main characters and their adversaries) they will disappear at the end of the novel with their propensity to harm neutralized.

Of course the novel can be ended in an almost totally inconclusive way, leaving the reader to try to work out what happens subsequently. It can work, but needs to be done with great skill, without which it is likely to disappoint. Ending in this way is rather like those television plays which we have all seen in which, just as it seems to get really interesting, the credits come up and it is all over. A brilliant playwright can get away with it, because in fact it is only superficially that it seems incomplete – if you dig into it, it will reveal itself as a finished work of art. But in most cases that kind of skill hasn't been used, and the result is a dissatisfied viewer.

All this is fairly obvious, but there are four major mistakes about the ending of a novel which inexperienced authors make, and when you are revising it is worth checking to see that you have not been guilty of any of them.

The first of these faults is the hurried ending, in which the author seems to feel, having reached the climax of the story, that the developments arising from that climax should be got over as quickly as possible. The result is that the final chapter moves so much more speedily than the rest of the story that the pace itself becomes obtrusive and the reader really does feel rushed. Moreover, it seems almost as though the author had lost interest, wanting to finish as soon as possible, and if that ever happens, the reader's interest also disappears. You may argue that there is nothing much to say after the climax has been reached and that there is no justification for dragging the story on when it has already finished, and this is a valid point to which I shall come in a moment. But I am referring here to the kind of story in which some tying up of ends is required after the climax, especially if there have been important sub-plots which have not finally been resolved. The fault often results from an abandonment of action in favour of narration – a tendency, to take an imaginary situation as an example, to say, 'X and Y were quickly reconciled', rather than presenting us with a scene in which, using dialogue,

the reconciliation is effected – and it can be cured by drama-
tizing the material.

The second and third faults are both concerned with the
tying up of ends, but using opposite approaches. Readers
do generally like to know what happens not only to the
main characters, but to the secondary people in the novel,
and, if there have been fairly important sub-plots, to know
the outcome of the problems with which they were
concerned. Some of these questions may be resolved in the
course of the story, but others will still remain after the
main climax as loose ends. The inexperienced writer sometimes falls into the trap of either leaving too many ends
untied or of relentlessly knotting every single one. The
former fault leaves the reader mentally unsatisfied, protest-
ing, 'Yes, but what happened to So-and-so, and about such-
and such?'. The latter frequently turns into a kind of boring
list, detailing what happens to even the most minor of characters. The ideal normally lies somewhere in between these
two approaches. You may be able to see what is needed in
the way of resolution by looking at the people and the
issues in the story and making a somewhat arbitrary
distinction between those which really engaged your interest while you were writing, and those which were periph-
eral. Tie up the loose ends of the former, and leave the rest.

The fourth fault which is frequently found in the work of
amateur writers in the final chapter is that of going on too
long, either by supplying unnecessary explanations or by
telling the reader things about additional developments
which he or she is perfectly capable of working out. The
problem nearly always concerns the principal characters.
Apart from the unravelling of the mystery at the end of a
whodunit, or in some similar kind of story, explanation
should never be necessary at any stage in the book – your
readers should always be able to work out why the characters behave as they do, and if they can't, then it is too late to
explain matters at the end of the book, and you need to go
back farther in the story and make sure that the ground-

work is laid then for what is to come. As for prolonging the story with unnecessary detail, any editor will tell you how often the final paragraph or page of a novel by an inexperienced author could be cut without its loss being noticed. Look at the story of 'Cinderella': conventionally, because it is a fairy story and all fairy stories end like this, it ends with the words 'and they got married and lived happily ever after', but the adult reader does not need to be told that – for him or her the story is over once the glass slipper fits. Indeed, in my imaginary novel based on the Cinderella story (see p.77) we wouldn't need Chapter 7 at all (unless the wedding is to be the occasion for finding husbands for the Ugly Sisters and letting Baron Hardup win the lottery – or unless the bedding is so delightfully erotic that it would be a shame to do without it). Never tell us things that we can work out for ourselves.

6
Fiction – Style

The Second Stage of Revision

Having used the first revision read-through to check and alter where necessary the structure, the characterizations and the technique of telling your story and keeping the reader interested, you may need to write a complete new draft, revising again and repeating the process until you feel that you have no more alterations to make in accordance with the suggestions put forward up until now in this manual. Each time that you revise it is advisable to leave a time gap before tackling the script again – to go through several revision processes continuously diminishes both your powers of concentration and your objectivity.

We now come to the much more detailed work of the second revision read-through, when we shall be looking to polish the prose to make it as effective as possible, and to eliminate some of the faults in writing to which most of us are prone.

What to Look For

If you read what you have written with really careful atten-tion, taking it paragraph by paragraph, sentence by sentence, word by word, you may be surprised, firstly, to find how much unnecessary waffle you have written, and you should ask yourself, as you read through, why you have put in this phrase, why you have used that word, and whether it would make any difference, other than improvement, if you cut them. Secondly, you may discover that you have failed to avoid irrelevance, repetition, clumsiness, and other similar faults, and that the narrative does not flow easily and effectively as it should.

For the purposes of illustration, I am printing in the next few pages the opening of an imaginary novel as it might have appeared in the first draft. It is a pretty disastrous piece of writing – far worse than anyone with even a little experience would produce – and as such is barely credible, but I have deliberately tried to include in it many of the faults which regularly appear in beginners' efforts. The fact that so many errors are crammed into a fairly short extract makes them obvious as well as ludicrous, but although such mistakes might not be nearly so noticeable if spread out through the typescript of a novel, they still need attention. You will almost certainly not be guilty of all of these faults, but when you are engaged in this detailed stage of revision, it is worth looking out for the odd lapse which may have slipped through, and although the errors in the extract have been exaggerated in order to make my point, subtler versions are still in need of correction. So here it is – the start of a novel – with every fifth line numbered for ease of reference:

The Eventide Retirement Home was situated in the northern suburbs of Leeds. It was a large, three-storied, yellow-brick, building in Victorian style, standing in extensive grounds. The board outside swung creaking in the breeze.

I had had a difficult job trying to track down my Great Uncle Fred and had

5.   been to the Social Services, and had been given the information that he was resident in the Eventide Retirement Home. I had had a long journey across the city that afternoon to find it, but had eventually reached it, had walked up it's wide, gravell path, and had rung the bell. Little did I know what I would find.

A young and pretty nurse answered the door. A badge on her dress

10.   proclaimed the fact that she was Deirdre Watkins. 'Yes?' she enquired.

'Could I please see Mr Jones?' I responded, tentatively.

She looked the young man up and down. 'Of course', she smiled. 'I will show

you into the waiting-room, and go and fetch him.'

The waiting room was small, and crammed with heavy, Victorian furniture, I

15.   sat down and waited, and after some five minutes, the door opened, and an

elderly man came slowly into the room, gazing about him short-sightedly. He was

quite tall, but seemed shorter, because of a pronounced stoop. His shoulders

were broad, and obviously he had been quite a fine figure of a man in his day! He

leant heavily on a knobbly, chestnut-wood, stick, with a large, rubber, ferrule

20.   on the end. He was dressed in an old, grey, check, sports coat, a white shirt with

a badly-tied blue tie, and dark grey trousers. He wore old but comfortable, down-

at-heel, carpet slippers on his feet. His wispy white hair floated untidily above his

ears. His eyes were watery, narrow-lidded, and blue, and seemed unable to focus

clearly. As he frowned the many lines on his weather-beaten face creased quickly

25.   .into deep, time-worn wrinkles. His large hands were covered in the liver spots of

old age. His fingers were thick and knarled and ended in horny yellow fingernails.

Slowly he shuffled towards a chair, covered in dark brown dralon, and

lowered himself into it gingerly, obviously finding it painful to do so. As he did so

the handsome, mahogany long-case clock struck three, the loud, melodious,

30.   chimes echoed round the tiny room.

'There's old grandfather', the old man chuckled wheezily.

'Mr Jones', I ventured. He seemed not to hear. 'Mr Jones', I repeated,

enunciating more loudly and clearly.

'What is he after?' the old man thought. He gazed at me through watery eyes.

35.   'Did you say something?' he queried warily.

'Yes', I smiled, carefully. 'Good afternoon, Mr Jones.'

He gazed at me suspiciously. 'What do you want?' he questioned.

'Er - ' I began hesitantly. 'I am not quite sure how to put this.'

He gazed at me unwaveringly. 'Come on!' he grumbled, obviously irritated.

40.   'Spit it out!!!' He paused. 'I have not got all day', he went on, testily.

       'Its like this', I pronounced tentatively. 'In 1937 my grandfather John Jones

       emigrated to live in Melbourne, Australia. He met a girl there called Mary

       and married her. They had five children, Mabel, Alfred, Edith, Wayne, and Violet.

       Mabel got married to a man called Smith, and went to live in Sydney, Alfred was

45.   killed in a road accident in 1949, Edith didn't marry and when John and Mary

       died she inherited the house in Melbourne where they lived and she is still there,

       gaining a meagre and uncertain remuneration by knitting, Violet married a

       chartered surveyor and is domiciled in Perth with her husband and three

       children, and Wayne courted a Polish girl called Milly Rzewuski, and they were

50.   joined in matrimony, and I am their son - indeed, I confess to being their only

       child. I was born in 1972, and I was educated at the local high school and at

       university in Melbourne, reading history, and after my graduation I made a

       resolution on the spur of the moment to take the bull by the horns and make an

       expedition to England, and the last thing I promised my Mother before I departed

55.   from Melbourne was that when I arrived in England I would try to find some of

       my relatives, because I know that my Grandfather had a couple of brothers, and

       he was the only one to go to Australia, and although we had lost touch with them

       my Mother said she thought they were still resident, somewhere in the Leeds

       area, and it would be pleasant if the family could be reunited again, because after

60.   all is said and done, blood is thicker than water, is it not, so I agreed and I

       promised her faithfully that I would. She said I should look up my cousins, Jean

       and Joan, too. Well, with one thing and another, I did not get round to it for quite

       a while - you know how it is, do you not? But eventually I came to Leeds, and I

       did not know how to find out about them, and then on the spur of the moment, I

65.   went to the social services to pursue my investigations, because I thought they

       must be advanced in years by now, and the social services might know about

       them, and they did and they told me that you were living here, and so I came

       here, and I think you are my Great-Uncle Fred', I finished happily, feeling that I

       had achieved my object, and how gratified Mother would be. I gazed at the old

70.   man with anxious, pleading eyes, hoping that he would be gratified to meet his

Great Nephew.

The old man gazed at me with incomprehension. 'Eh?' he boomed, inquiringly.

I realized that he had obviously not heard what I had to say! I began again,
75. shouting loudly, telling him about my grandfather and his family and how I had come to England and had tried to trace him.

At that moment a young, dark-haired, male, nurse, called Jonathan Richards, came in with tray bearing a cup of tea and a plate of bread and butter for my Great-Uncle. 'Will he eat his tea?' the nurse wondered silently. He put his tea in
80. his hand, but he did not take his bread and butter and he stood there hesitantly, obviously uncertain as to whether he would take his bread and butter or whether he should take it back, and he shook his head, and went out.

Outside the room's window stood a silver birch, through which the sun had been shining brightly, like a lover's smile, into the room, tracing a filigree of
85. coloratura on the bare, white-washed, walls. The gently flickering movement of the leaves had formed a delicate, golden, ballet, a dancing, motley pattern of choreography, gilding the room's heavy furniture, glittering like the dappled surface of a mountain stream in the early morning light.

When I had finished, the old man nodded, obviously moved. 'Happen I am', he
90. confirmed. Then his eyes narrowed suspiciously, and he gazed at me penetratingly. 'Eh, bah gum!' he exploded. 'I knaws what thee are abaht. Thart arter me brass, lad', he gritted. 'Of course not, great-uncle', I countered.

'Art speakin' t'truth, lad?' came the swift rejoinder.

'Of course, Greatuncle', I swore.

95. He gazed at me quizzically, obviously trying to make up his mind as to whether to believe in the veracity of my protestation.

'Thart a reet bonny lad', he judged, finally. 'Coom, gie thy old uncle a hug.' He rose to his feet, swaying unsteadily.

As the young man moved towards him, he was horrified to see his Great-
100. uncle clutch at his chest, and fall back into his chair.

An Overall Comment

There is so much wrong with this piece that I hardly know where to begin (when I have finished my list of criticisms, you may find it amusing to see how many other faults you can pick out yourself), but the first thing to point out is that it takes some 1,250 words to say what could have been better put in less than half that number. The whole thing is woolly, repetitive, lacking in suspense, and without any narrative flow. We are given vast amounts of unnecessary and uninteresting information – lines 1 to 13 could be cut without their absence being noted and so could the sentence about the clock, and the little sequence involving the male nurse (unless, of course, these references are going to be used as 'little clouds' and followed up later). The only information given in these passages which might be of importance is that the scene is taking place in a nursing home for old people, but any reader with a glimmer of intelligence would soon realize that, and in any case, until the location of the conversation becomes clear, not being certain of it functions as a minor piece of suspense. One wonders too just how much of the information about the narrator's family will serve any useful purpose in the rest of the story. Apart from such chunks, which are obvious candidates for cutting, words and phrases and sentences could be chopped out throughout, and we shall be looking at some of these in later paragraphs.

Adjectives and Adverbs

This piece is excessively besprinkled with adjectives and adverbs, almost every verb being qualified by an adverb, and many of the nouns by one, two or three adjectives. Inexperienced writers tend to scatter adjectives and adverbs around liberally in the belief that they add colour and definition. In fact, the curious thing about these words is that the more you use, the less effective they become. As many of them as possible should be removed, and the piece would gain in strength as a result. In particular, anyone writing in this style should watch out for tautological adjectives and adverbs – can wrinkles be anything but time-worn? can you shout in any way other than loudly? when a character starts by saying, 'Er –,' do we really need to be told that he is speaking hesitantly? Such usages are even more superfluous than the others.

This does not mean, of course, that you have to eliminate all adjectives and adverbs, which would be extremely difficult. It is an instructive exercise to try to write a brief story or a description of some activity without using any adjectives or adverbs at all – and it is even more interesting if you then allow yourself to put in just one – either an adjective or an adverb; it may be quite difficult to choose just the right word and exactly where to place it, and it is fascinating to realize the power that it assumes simply because it has no competition. Adverbs and adjectives can be very useful, and sometimes essential; they not only define verbs and nouns, sometimes giving the reader vital information, but do indeed add colour, and very often help to lend the prose an underlying rhythm; but their use should be strictly controlled, and they must never be used to excess.

Repetitions

No doubt you noticed in lines 69 and 70 the repetition of the word 'gratified' and the 'bread and butter' twice in lines 80 and 81 – in both cases the two uses are so close together that they can hardly be missed. But you almost certainly also picked up the two appearances, in lines 53 and 64, of the phrase 'on the spur of the moment', even though they were a bit farther apart. It is really quite astonishing how jarring a repetition of that kind can be. In some instances it may be impossible to avoid using certain words or phrases over and over again in close juxtaposition, and this is especially true in non-fiction – if you are writing a section of a book dealing with characterization, it will be very difficult not to repeat the word 'character', even if you try to ring the changes now and then with 'person', 'personage', 'protagonist', 'antagonist' and the like. It is always a difficult problem, and it is worth taking plenty of time to try to arrive at as good a solution as you can. In fiction, however, there is rarely much need to repeat yourself – English is versatile and usually has a number of possible alternatives for any given word – and you should certainly do your best not to duplicate a phrase like 'on the spur of the moment', which the reader will notice. However, as with most things in life, you have to bring a certain amount of common sense and moderation to the problem, because if it becomes too obvious that you are searching through the thesaurus for more and more alternatives, that can be even more obtrusive than the occasional repetition would be, quite apart from the fact that the substitutions you find, although synonyms, may not always carry the exact flavour that you want. The one word which you need rarely worry about repeating is 'said' when it is used as an attribution (attributions are phrases such as 'he said', 'she replied', used in dialogue), but we shall come to that when we move on to discuss the dialogue in this piece.

Of course, deliberate repetition for effect is quite legitimate, and can be a useful device – 'He laughed when I said I would fight him, he laughed as I stripped off my shirt, he laughed as I approached him, my fists balled, and he laughed as he floored me with one blow.' The trick should be used very sparingly – probably no more than once in a novel – because the device itself will be a repetition on its second appearance.

Repetition does not only refer to words and phrases. In this piece we are told, twice, for instance, about the narrator visiting the Social Services in order to find his great-uncle, and about the heavy furniture of the waiting room. A problem of this kind is easily dealt with by the use of your blue pencil. We also have a different form of repetition when Fred does not hear all that the narrator has said, and the latter then tells him (which means telling the reader for the second time) what he said, when all he need have told us is 'I repeated my story'. Repetition of information can occasionally be valid, if the author wishes to underline its importance to the reader, but generally its use should be restricted to essential occasions.

Finally, the piece we are considering is guilty of yet another form of repetition – the use of repetitive rhythms. This fault is most easily detected during the third revision read-through when you read the work aloud, because it is something which the ear can pick up far more readily than the eye. The eye is not entirely incapable of detecting it, however, and sometimes finds such writing unsatisfactory without perhaps knowing exactly why. If something that you read seems boring, try reading it aloud, and you may find that the problem is largely a matter of repetitive rhythms. If you read aloud lines 17 to 26 you will probably see what I mean, because this passage is made up of ten sentences all of which have roughly the same shape and rhythm. The paragraph needs to be reworded with some of the sentences being rephrased altogether, and others joined by conjunctions. Repetitive rhythm can be an effective device as in the 'he laughed' example above, but it needs to be handled with great care and rarely, if ever, repeated in a single work.

Habit Words

We all have habit words, which we tend to put in without thinking, rather in the way that it has become fashionable in recent years to lard a conversation with regular injections of 'you know'. Habit words are of course repetitions, but they are in a somewhat different category, because they have been put in without conscious thought, almost as punctuation, rather than as part of the narrative. In this case, the imaginary author's favourite habit word is 'obviously', and, if you will pardon me for saying so, this obviously has to be cut out as often as possible. You might also note that the author never allows his characters to 'look' at anything – they always 'gaze', and this comes very close to being a habit word, rather than simply a repetition.

Other habit words (which I have myself to beware of using too often) are 'indeed', 'in fact' and 'of course'. I also have a tendency to start a great many sentences with 'There are . . .' or 'There is . . .' Precisely because of their habitual quality, it is easy when reading through to be unaware of them, so it is a good idea to discover, if you are not already sure, what your habit words are so that you can be on the look-out for them.

Characterization

Although some small attempt has been made to indicate what sort of person Fred Jones is, his characterization is in fact as skimpy as it could be, but at least it is better than that of the narrator, about whom we learn nothing except that he is apparently obedient to his mother, is in his twenties, and speaks in a remarkably boring way. He reveals nothing of himself in anything that he says, we do not know what he thinks or feels, and we are given no indication of what he is doing in England other than visiting his great-uncle. Since he is presumably to be the central character in the book, this is a major fault. I have written earlier of how vital it is to grab the reader on the very first page, and have also suggested that the principal character should make a very early appearance. This protagonist certainly pops up straight away, but far from hooking the reader, he is a big turn-off, despite the fact that it is a first-person narrative, which usually makes reader identification and interest easier. We should have quickly learnt enough about him to make us interested, and we should have some inkling of what problems he has or what his aims are, by which I mean a hint of something rather more riveting than simply identifying an old man in a nursing home as a relative. Perhaps Great-uncle Fred is wealthy and the narrator is hoping to squeeze a sizeable cheque out of him for some worthy or nefarious purpose, or perhaps the old man is the only one who can unravel a family mystery set in the distant past. Whatever it may be, give us a clue.

The author has not given any indication either of the narrator's physical appearance (not that it is necessary at this stage), but has done his best to tell us exactly what Uncle Fred looks like, presumably feeling that this is the best way of fixing him in the reader's mind. I don't think it is. It would have been much better to allow the old man to speak more freely and to describe his actions and facial expressions, which will give a stronger impression of his character. In any case, the physical description goes on far too long and includes far too many details, and a passage like that will just wash over the reader, who will remember hardly any of it. Keep the physical description down to essentials, and spread the information out, so that we get it in little dribs and drabs, preferably at an appropriate moment – for example, if the old man is puzzled, he might scratch his head, and it is then that we could learn that his hair is wispy and white.

Don't Explain

The behaviour of your characters and the meaning of what they say should never need explanation. Quite apart from the fact that you are probably being tautological, you are forgetting that reading is not a passive business. Readers contribute actively to what they read by understanding, by anticipation, by involvement with the characters and simultaneously by distancing themselves from them so that they can observe them. And one of the things which readers enjoy most of all is working things out for themselves. In lines 69 to 71 of this piece the narrator gazes at the old man 'with anxious, pleading eyes, hoping that he would be gratified to meet his Great Nephew'. The whole sentence is unnecessary, but the worst part of it is 'hoping that he would be gratified to meet his Great Nephew', because the reader can work out from the context what the narrator is hoping. This is in fact a fairly innocuous example of what I am talking about; some inexperienced writers go to great lengths to explain exactly what their characters are thinking, what their motives are, what effect it will have on the other characters, and so on, and it is all unnecessary – unless, of course, the character is thinking or doing something which is in complete contradiction to what is being said, and even then, if it is possible for the reader to work out the truth – maybe you will need to drop in a subtle clue – it is much better to leave out the explanation, and let him or her have the pleasure of puzzling out exactly what is going on.

Suspense

I said earlier that we were not given information about the narrator's reasons for coming to find his great-uncle, but the author might say that he is deliberately withholding the details in order to create suspense. That is fair enough, but a slight hint is still needed to the effect that the meeting is crucial to the narrator, without necessarily saying what his problem or object is – 'As I sat in the waiting-room, I prayed that I had found the right man, and that he would have the answer I needed.' A sentence of that sort will go a long way towards hooking the reader. Even if the author still wanted to hold up various pieces of information, the material that we are left with could have been presented in a far more

intriguing way. I have already suggested that the first thir-
teen lines of the piece could be cut because they add nothing essential or interesting to the story, but another even
stronger reason for dispensing with them is that the author
has destroyed what little suspense could exist in these few
pages by telling us in the first paragraph exactly what is
going to happen; as any fiction-reader will know, the
sentence here which begins the second paragraph is as
strong an indication as you can get that the 'I' of the story is
about to meet Great-uncle Fred. If we had not known what
the narrator was doing there and who Mr Jones was, we
might have allowed ourselves a little flicker of interest. The
author could also have intrigued us rather more at the end
of the piece if, instead of greeting the narrator so warmly,
the old man, while making it clear to the reader by his reactions that he was in fact Great-uncle Fred, for some
unknown reason denied the relationship. That would make
the last couple of lines into a really strong ending, and
would sink a good hook into us to make us want to read
more.

The last two lines, in which the old man collapses, are
possibly the best thing in the whole piece. They are a good
example of a cliff-hanger, and the author should now
change the scene, leaving us wondering whether Great-
uncle Fred has died or will recover. If the denial of his relationship to the narrator has been included, the reader will
also want to know why he was lying. Undoubtedly,
however, a writer as incompetent as this one would call in
the nursing staff, allow Great-uncle Fred to recover and
explain that he wasn't really trying to mislead the narrator
at all.

Did you notice the sentence in line 8 – 'Little did I
know . . .'? That phrase is calculated to make any editor
shudder, partly because it is such a dreadful cliché, but also
because it attempts to create suspense, but does so in a way
which patronizes the reader. It is as though the author were
saying, 'Oh, I've got some marvellous surprises in store for

you!' It is irritating and old-fashioned, and if you have used it yourself, I'd ask you to cut it out.

Viewpoint

The author has chosen to write this piece in the first person, which is not the easiest of methods, but one which, well handled, has the advantage of a close involvement of the reader in the story, and usually a tight, driving narrative. But if you choose a particular viewpoint, you must, as I have already said, stick to it. In this example, the author has switched viewpoint four times – in line 12, when the nurse looks at the young man, in lines 34 and 79, when we are told the thoughts of the old man in the first case and of the male nurse in the second, each of these being a move to the viewpoint of the person concerned, and then in line 99, when the narrator suddenly turns into 'the young man' and the viewpoint has changed to that of the author, using the third person. These are major errors, which are quite easy to correct, but before simply altering the offending lines, the author should perhaps ask himself whether he is really happy with the restrictions of the first person mode of narrative. If you ever find yourself writing in the first person but lapsing from it occasionally, those accidental switches of viewpoint are a clear sign that you might be much happier using a less restrictive approach.

Flashback

Although the whole beginning of the piece is to be cut, have a look at lines 4 to 8, which are a flashback. As I said in Chapter 5, flashbacks are a useful device for conveying essential information, but in this case, one would have to question the value of the information given, which the reader really doesn't need to know. And how clumsy and irritating all those repetitions of 'had' are; after the first sentence, the paragraph works perfectly well if it moves directly into the simple past, rather than continuing in the pluperfect.

Names of Characters

As I indicated in an earlier chapter, I think it is a mistake to name very minor characters, and unless the nurses Deirdre Watkins and Jonathan Richards are to play a part in the story later, it would be much better to leave them unnamed.

When we come to the narrator's long speech (lines 41 to 68) we meet two different problems. First of all, we are introduced to too many people in a very short space, which means that it will be almost impossible for us to remember later who they all are. They don't all need to be mentioned at this stage, and in fact some mileage might be made later out of a scene in which Great-uncle Fred asks the narrator about his Australian relations, and if they are to play a part in the story, the narrator can respond with much more detail. And if they have no relevance to the story – poor old Alfred, killed in a car accident, for instance – they can not merely not be mentioned, but actually eliminated altogether. Secondly, although parents can be eccentric in the naming of their children and go against all the current trends, readers often treat first names as signals referring to the period when the holders of the names were born. Although the narrator's mother, uncles and aunts were born in the late 1930's or in the 1940's, the names Mabel, Edith, Violet and Alfred belong primarily to an earlier time – more like the first two decades of the twentieth century – while the second uncle, Wayne, has a name which was not in vogue until the 1960's and 70's. If you have any doubts about choosing the right names for the period you are writing about, *The Guinness Book of Names* by Leslie Dunkling is an invaluable and highly entertaining guide.

A further point arises because three members of the family have names which all begin with M. This can be confusing for the reader, especially if the appearances of these characters in the novel are fairly fleeting and scattered. The problem worsens when the narrator mentions his cousins, Jean and Joan. The author can help the reader to keep track of the characters (and this is particularly important if there are a great many of them) by ensuring that they all have fairly distinct names which are not likely to be confused with each other. Mabel, Edith, Violet, George and Wayne meet this requirement, but Jean and Joan are far too close in spelling and even in pronunciation. I think it is a good idea to avoid using names with the same initial, and to choose a good mixture of differing syllable lengths – John, David, Christopher, Alexander, or Jean, Mary, Amanda, Elizabeth, for example. I apply the same principle to the characters' surnames.

Even though we read silently (or most of us do), we do have some sense of hearing what we read, and it is irritating if we cannot pronounce to ourselves any words in the book, and this is most likely to occur with names, and especially foreign names, such as the maiden name of the narrator's mother. If you have any foreign characters, try to choose names which the average linguistically-handicapped English reader would not stumble over.

Dialogue

The dialogue in this piece is quite appalling – surely no one could write quite as badly as that unless, as was the case here, the intention was to illustrate a number of faults. If I did not know that, I would have said that the first point to be made is that the author had cloth ears – he had never *listened* to anyone talking. To write good, or even reasonable dialogue it is true that you have to know the character who is speaking, and when you know that person through and through all you have to do is to let him or her speak in your mind, and write down what is said. But you also need to know how people in real life talk, and you learn that by listening. You have to be an artist, of course, rather than a photographer – fiction is false not only because the story it tells is imaginary, but because it does not provide an accurate reproduction of life as it is. Even if you want your novel to be 'true to life' you have to select and adapt. That applies to the whole book, but especially to dialogue, as has already been pointed out. If real-life conversation is a confused mess and needs to be completely remodelled, why is it essential to listen to it if we want to write good dialogue? Because when we have edited out all the nonsense, we can at least learn what sort of words people use and how they string them together, and it is only when we have that kind of knowledge that we can hope to give our dialogue the appearance of truth. We should certainly recognize that no one talks at all like the narrator in our piece – his dialogue is very stilted.

One of the reasons why the narrator's speeches sound anything but natural is the author's penchant for long words with Latin roots and for formal phraseology. Many beginners write in this way, feeling that it gives their work dignity, whereas the result is pomposity and awkwardness. They also have the idea that you need this kind of heavy-handed solemnity in order to achieve 'style', not realizing that style is simply the way you write and that good style is almost always simple and easily understood. So in this piece we need to get rid of words and phrases like 'remuneration', 'is domiciled', 'made a resolution', 'make an expedition', etc, substituting 'living', 'lives', 'decided', 'go'. And instead of a phrase like 'whether to believe the veracity of my protestation' we could simply have 'whether to believe me'. There is nothing wrong with long words of Latin or Romance-language derivation, of course, when they are used in the right place, and if you try to exclude them altogether, your wording will lack the variety that they can bring, but the simplicity which is a part of good style comes largely from the use of words of Anglo-Saxon origin. In any case, unless they are deliberately trying to be pompous, people just don't talk in strings of long words and the kind of phrasing which is found in official documents.

Next, the author should look at the fact that he never uses contractions – insert 'I'm' and 'haven't', 'didn't' and 'don't you', instead of 'I am', 'have not', 'did not' and 'do you not' and the dialogue immediately begins to sound a little more natural. The informality of contractions often worries beginners, particularly those who are old enough to have been brought up in an age when teachers imposed all sorts of formal rules on their written English. The answer is that there are only two rules: one is that what you write must convey your intended meaning to the reader, and the second is that it must sound right, and no contemporary dialogue will sound natural if you don't use contractions. Sometimes in period novels the more formal approach can work, but even then you need to be careful to avoid sounding stilted.

In the last lines of the piece the author has decided to make the old man speak in dialect. This is another disaster, especially because it doesn't ring true and certainly doesn't sound like the Yorkshire dialect that is intended (it seems to stray all over the North Country). Dialect is rarely easy, and even if you can convey an accent satisfactorily, this will usually mean a plethora of apostrophes and odd spellings and a sprinkling of unintelligible words. Such usages become very irritating to the reader. The same thing is true of 'Godwottery' – the use of supposedly period words in historical novels set in the 16th century or earlier. As far as dialect is concerned, it often works simply to tell the reader when the character in question first speaks that she or he has a strong Yorkshire (Scottish, Irish, West Country, Birmingham, etc) accent, and leave the rest to the reader's imagination.

In the long speech by the narrator the author has made an attempt at realism in the sentence which runs from line 51 to line 61. We do indeed often talk like this, in long sentences covering a number of different topics, without any pauses. The problem is that it is not at all easy to read an involved sentence of this kind, especially in the middle of a long speech, without losing track. The sentence could easily be split more than once – after 'England' (line 54), after 'Australia' (line 57), and after 'is it not' (line 60). For that matter, the whole speech would be better if it were more radically broken up. A new paragraph could begin after 'child' (line 51) and it might be a good idea at an appropriate point to change from speech to a short piece of narration – something like: 'I looked at the old man, hoping to see some reaction, but he was staring at me impassively. I decided that, having started, I would have to go on.' Generally speaking, it is always advisable to break up very long speeches – a little breather part way through helps the reader to grasp all that is being said, and stops him or her from thinking, 'Would the character really have gone on at such length without being interrupted?' Apart from the inordinate length in this piece, too much information is given in too short a space. If these details are necessary to the plot, some of them could be left until later in the chapter, while others could perhaps be expanded into a more vivid form.

The imaginary author of this piece was very worried about attributions. Trying to avoid repetitions and feeling that 'said' is a dull word anyway, he came up with a wide variety of alternatives – 'responded', 'questioned', 'grumbled', 'boomed', 'confirmed', 'exploded', 'gritted', 'countered', and so on; none is repeated, and no doubt if the work were completed he would pride himself on maintaining that record throughout. Quite apart from the fact that not all of the attributions are appropriate to what is said, in most cases 'said' or 'asked' or 'replied' – the attributions which authors use most often – would be preferable. 'Boomed' and 'exploded' should be avoided unless the person speaking really is booming or exploding, 'gritted' is quite dreadful, and worst of all (at least, in my opinion) is 'came the swift rejoinder' or any other similar phrases, which always make me shudder, and which, if I came across them in a typescript in the days when I was an editor, were almost enough to make me stop reading and send the book straight back. As I have already mentioned earlier, you can repeat 'she said', 'he said' as often as you like and your reader will not find it repetitious, and 'asked' and 'replied' can be used almost as freely. 'Shouted' or 'whispered' and other verbs which indicate tone or volume are acceptable, but must not be used too often or too closely together. For many speeches you can do without attributions, especially if you are dealing with a duologue, although you must avoid the kind of conversation in a novel which has no attributions at all and no indications of which of the two people is speaking (such as using the other person's name) so that the reader has to count back to see who says what – that situation should rarely arise in any case, because the speeches themselves should reveal which character is speaking by their content and individuality.

I mentioned earlier that the piece has far too many adverbs, and many of these are linked to the attributions. When we speak we have at our command tones, and rising and falling inflexions, and various degrees of emphasis, and differing speeds of speaking, and pauses, and other vocal devices, and we also use facial expressions and gestures to help convey our meaning. In written dialogue we have nothing but printed words on the page, plus a few punctuation marks, and the ability occasionally to indicate emphasis by the use of italics. We can also describe pauses, or allow a character to break off in the middle of a speech, or to be interrupted. But if we want to give an idea of tone and expression, we are often forced into using adverbs. It is preferable always to word the dialogue, if you can, so that your intention is immediately clear, and so that the speech

could be said only in the way you mean. Sometimes this is
fairly easy to achieve because of the context, but often you
will have to struggle to get it right. It is worth spending a
lot of time on it at this stage of the revision, and also when
you come to read the work aloud, and if you are successful,
you will be able to dispense with a great many of those
adverbs.

Finally, you might have noted that in line 92 the author
has joined a speech by the narrator on to the same paragraph as speeches by the old man. And the opposite effect
is to be seen in line 97, which has been made a new paragraph, whereas it could have followed on after 'protestation'. It always seems to me preferable to start a new paragraph for each speaker. The paragraph can also contain
narration relating to the person who is speaking, as in the
passage from line 89 to 'gritted' in line 92. It is as though the
paragraph belongs to the character.

Inconsistencies and Forgetfulness

You may be able to rely on a long-suffering copy-editor to
correct your inconsistencies, but it is much better to get it
right yourself, before you submit your book to a publisher.
Like so many other apparently trivial matters, while minor
variations in spellings or capitalizations can easily be
corrected, their appearance in a typescript gives an impression of amateurishness. In the piece under consideration
the author cannot apparently make up his mind between
'Social Services' with capitals and 'social services' without
(the capitals seem preferable) and he uses 'Great Uncle',
'Great-Uncle', great-uncle' and 'Greatuncle' – and no doubt
'Great-uncle' and 'greatuncle' would appear later in the
book ('great-uncle' seems to be the most acceptable form,
except when it is a title or when the gentleman in question
is being addressed in dialogue, when 'Great uncle' should
be used – and 'great-nephew' is better than 'Great Nephew,

or any other variant). When such alternatives exist, it isn't always easy to remember which of them you really want to use – are you going to say 'Village Hall' or 'village hall' and are you going to write 'bestseller' all in one word, or hyphenate it into 'best-seller' or split it into 'best seller'? I find it useful, both when writing and while revising, to have by me a list of any words of this sort with the spelling I have decided to use, so that as I go through I can check that I am being consistent.

It is sometimes more difficult to find places where the inconsistency comes about less through carelessness than because you have been forgetful. When you are revising (and although I raise the matter now, this is probably much better done in your fourth revision, when you read the whole book in one day) look out for this kind of slip. Check to see whether you have, for instance, put your heroine in a trouser suit and later talked of her skirt, or whether you have mentioned a vase of chrysanthemums on the table, forgetting that it is Spring, and daffodils are more likely, or whether you have described, as I once did in a book written in collaboration, how your main character gets up in the morning, rides on his bicycle to a friend's house, leaves the bicycle there while he goes off in the friend's car, is delivered back to his cottage that evening by the car, and then gets up the next morning and gets on his bicycle again (incidentally, this mistake was not noticed by my collaborator, nor by the publisher who accepted the book – it was my wife who spotted it, fortunately in time for correction before publication).

Fine Writing

Every now and then writers of quite mundane stories feel a sudden urge to be poetic, to indulge in striking similes and metaphors, to choose an exciting vocabulary, to paint a picture in words with an artist's eye. The author of this piece has done so in lines 83 to 88. They should be cut. The fact that in this particular case they aren't very good has little to do with it – fine writing, when it is deliberately inserted is almost invariably self-conscious, out of place, and, what is worse, self-indulgent. Dr Johnson reported that an old college tutor said to his pupils, 'Read over your composition, and wherever you meet with a passage which you think is particularly fine, strike it out.' That advice is so well known that you may be bored to read it again, but I repeat it because it is so sensible.

Is there then no place for striking, evocative writing, for words which have been chosen with the utmost care for their beauty as well as the depth of meaning which they convey, for prose which has been honed and polished? Yes, of course, but not simply in a little burst in the middle of a novel which is far more prosaic – the whole book needs to be in that style (and will probably be 'Literary'). The problem in any case with 'fine writing' like the example in the piece we have been considering is that it usually tends to be over-lush and complex, whereas the best prose, and indeed the best poetry, is spare and simple.

Confused and Ambiguous Writing

If you look at lines 79 to 82 you will see a good example of what I mean by 'confused writing'. Read it carefully and there is no doubt about which person the various uses of 'he' and 'his' refer to, but you will probably have to go over it twice before it becomes clear. It is very easy, because you know exactly what you mean, to find yourself making this kind of error, and you should be on the look-out for it when you revise. Another example is to be found in line 65 in which, on a first reading, you might think that 'they' refers to the Social Services.

Ambiguity often comes from the misplacing of words. My favourite example of this is a notice which appears at every entrance to some public gardens in a South Coast resort: 'Only dogs on leads admitted'; well, we all know what they mean, but what they have actually said is that no one but dogs on leads is allowed in – humans must presumably wait outside until the dogs come out and collect them. The problem results from the fact that we are rarely conscious of all the rules of syntax when we talk, but despite this other people know what we mean, or if they don't we can soon put them right. When the words are down in cold print (or on a metal notice stuck in the ground) we need to take more care, because the reader may read them more literally than we intended. You need to strike a balance, of course, because too much pedantry will make your work irritating and dull. But at least, when you are revising, look out for ambiguities which can be misinterpreted (to give another example, you have probably seen the notice which often appears on doors nowadays – 'These doors are alarmed,' it says, and although I know perfectly well what is meant, I always want to ask what has frightened them).

Malapropisms

I am sure that all my readers 'reprehend the true meaning of what they are saying', but if you have used an unusual word which is perhaps not normally in your vocabulary, it is worth checking at this stage to see that you have not made some stupid blunder. In line 84 of this piece the author has been led into error by his wish to write a beautiful, 'poetic' paragraph, and has put 'coloratura' when he meant 'chiaroscuro' (at least, I think that's what he intended).

Clichés

Few things do more to make your writing seem tired than a whole string of clichés. I always think it is a shame

112

about clichés, because they are mostly very vivid and interesting – think about 'as busy as a bee', for instance, or 'as cool as a cucumber', which are brilliant similes, or were, until overuse turned them into tired clichés. It is interesting, incidentally, that clichés used in a metaphorical way usually seem slightly less boring than those which are direct similes – 'that's right up his street' or 'a storm in a teacup'. Then there are phrases like 'blissful ignorance' or 'piping hot', which are equally to be avoided.

In the piece above, clichés are to be found in the dialogue (lines 53, 60 and 64), which is perhaps acceptable, because we all use them in speech, but even in dialogue it would be preferable not to overwork them.

If you have read this book carefully you will probably have noticed that I don't always take my own advice (which is foolish of me, because my suggestions are always sensible), and this is certainly true as far as clichés are concerned – I have talked of 'bees in my bonnet', of 'plain sailing', of 'switching horses in midstream', and so on. These, and others that I have used, are all clichés in the form of metaphors, but such phrases are undeniably useful, because they are immediately understood and they act as a sort of shorthand, conveying a great deal in a very few words. Maybe I should have eliminated them, but I decided against (which raises the important point that you can break any 'rule' in writing, but it is best if you know that you are doing so).

Clichés exist in other forms than written phrases: in characters, for instance, where they may be called stereotypes, or in plots, where they may be called entirely predictable. Wherever this sort of cliché is found in your book, whatever form it takes, now is the time to get rid of it, making certain that your people are live individuals rather than stock cardboard characters, and that your story twists and turns so that the reader is never certain of what will happen next.

Punctuation, Grammar and Spelling

Our imaginary author has a pepperpot full of commas which he sprinkles everywhere, especially after each adjective. This really isn't necessary, and you might fill in an idle ten minutes by going through the piece and seeing how many commas you can get rid of. I make it well over thirty, and I am not counting the cases in lines 14 and 29 (and also in the long section about the narrator's Australian family) where full stops, or possibly semi-colons would be preferable to commas. When you come to read your work aloud, you should listen to the pauses that you make and the different tones that you use – if the break is more than very brief and if the tone changes, you almost certainly need a full stop rather than a comma.

It is interesting to note, by the way, that in lines 23 and 43 the author has used the 'serial comma', which is to say that a comma has been added in a list in front of the 'and' which brings the list to an end. This is an American habit, I believe. In most cases that extra comma is unnecessary.

A great many authors have difficulty in deciding where punctuation should go in dialogue. Should the comma or full stop or question mark or exclamation mark come inside the quotation marks or outside? This author seems to put most of the commas outside, but the other marks inside. The usually accepted convention is to have all the punctuation marks which belong to the speech inside the inverted comma(s).

Do be careful about exclamation marks. Generally speaking, they should never be used in narration, because they are an intrusion by the author – the author who puts in exclamation marks is saying to the reader, 'Isn't that strange?' or 'Isn't that funny?' Authors should keep such comments out of their stories. Exclamation marks should certainly not have been used in lines 18 and 74. They are permissible in dialogue, and indeed may help to indicate the way in which something is said, but do make sure that the speech actually

114

needs the mark – neither of the examples in lines 39 and 40 is really needed, and even if it were legitimate, one would be sufficient in line 40, rather than three.

A different problem occurs in line 60 where a question ('is it not') comes in the middle of a sentence. Do you put in a question mark, or not? I would suggest that the best answer is to put one in, and then start the next word with a capital letter as the beginning of a new sentence. A problem which I have encountered in this book is of how to punctuate a series of questions which share the same introduction. My solution, as you may have noticed, is to give each question a question mark, but to start the next word with a small letter rather than a capital.

I have suggested that 'is it not' should be changed to 'isn't'. Do note, if you have any doubts, where the apostrophe goes – it represents a letter which has been dropped, which in this case is the 'o' in 'not', so 'isn't' is correct, and 'is'nt' isn't. Talking of apostrophes, there should really be one in the contraction 'th'art' in lines 91 and 97.

You will surely have noticed that the apostrophes are wrong in lines 7 and 41. 'It's' is short for 'it is', while 'its' is the possessive form of 'it', so the wording in line 7 should have 'its' and in line 41 'it's'.

If you are addicted, as I confess I am, to the use of brackets or pairs of dashes to separate some comment from the rest of the sentence it appears in, you will probably have to keep an eye open for the occasions when you have not put the closing bracket in, or have used a comma instead of a closing dash. This can easily happen, especially if the material in the brackets or pair of dashes is fairly lengthy.

On a similar theme, make sure that you have always closed the inverted commas at the ends of speeches (it doesn't much matter, incidentally, whether you use double or single quotes, as long as you are consistent). If you break a very long speech into paragraphs, of course you put the closing quotation mark only at the end of the last paragraph of the speech; by not putting it at the end of the earlier paragraphs you are telling the reader that the same person is still speaking.

Do check your spelling. You probably picked up 'gravell' in line 8, and 'knarled' in line 26. Use a dictionary whenever you are doubtful. Many word processors nowadays have spell-checks, which are useful, although they will not call your attention to anything which is a normal word, even though it may not be the spelling you require (if you had written 'bill of fair', for example, the spell-check would not suggest that it should be 'fare', because 'fair' is an acceptable word to it).

The piece above is pretty free of grammatical errors, although you may have noticed in line 19 that the author has written 'leant', the past participle of the verb, when he should have put 'leaned', which is the simple past. That comment is perhaps pedantic, and I dare say that only one in a hundred readers would notice the mistake. Nevertheless, I would prefer to get it right, and at this stage of revision I would be looking for anything of that kind, or, for instance, especially when the sentence is a complex one, including perhaps more than one sub-clause, any use of a singular verb with a plural subject, or vice versa.

Other Amendments

Readers will no doubt be relieved to know that at this point I am abandoning that dreadful opening to what was undoubtedly a totally unpublishable novel, and moving on to a number of suggestions for possible revisions to which that piece is not very relevant.

Breaking Up Overlong Passages

I have already mentioned the need to break up excessively long speeches in your dialogue, but you should also look at any lengthy passages in the narrative and consider whether you could make them easier to read by splitting them into paragraphs. Readers of books are usually less demanding than those of the popular press, who want their paragraphs restricted to a couple of sentences and three lines at the most, but even those who take the *Times* can be put off if your book contains too many page-long chunks of text without a break. Split any such passages into paragraphs, and check whether a certain amount of rewriting can bring a greater feeling of variety to the prose, allowing one paragraph to contrast with its immediate predecessor, for instance.

Strength in Words and Constructions

Be aware of the relative strengths of different words. There is usually little problem in recognizing those which are doing a big, effective job, and those which are vaguer and willowy. I like to cite a sentence from *A Distant Trumpet* by Paul Horgan, which occurs in a scene when a small American town is waiting for Abraham Lincoln's train – 'The firehouse band was standing loosely about the station much too early'. What a brilliant use of 'loosely', and how strong it is! It works, of course, because of its context – it is clever and effective writing. On a much simpler basis, without the need to place the word in a particular sentence, the contrast in the relative strengths of words is seen most clearly perhaps in specific as opposed to general words – 'Labrador' is stronger than 'dog', and 'spaghetti' is stronger than 'pasta', and 'scarlet' is stronger than 'red'.

The position of a given word in a sentence may make a great difference to its strength. If the sentence quoted above were changed to 'The firehouse band was standing about the station loosely and much too early' then 'loosely' has lost most of its impact. Similarly, if you write ' "I hate him!" she screamed. "And I wish he were dead." ' that is much stronger than ' "I hate him, and I wish he were dead," she screamed.' On the whole, the strongest parts of a complex sentence are the beginning and the ending, and in just the same way the strongest sentences in a paragraph are the first, which introduces the subject, and the last, which wraps it up. Sometimes rearrangement of a sentence or paragraph will help tremendously in the creation of a stronger effect, and this, incidentally, is something which you should look out for not only at this stage, but later when you come to read the book aloud, because the effect will then be more obvious.

As an exercise, look at the possibilities for a brief narrative consisting of the following elements: 'a man was lying on the floor', 'the man was heavily built', 'a knife protruded from his chest', 'the room was spattered in blood', 'the blood seemed to be everywhere except on the rumpled sheets of the bed', 'there were long scratches on the man's face'. Put the elements in various orders, rewriting them as necessary to make short or complex sentences which will form a paragraph. (Remember to avoid repetitive rhythms.) Note how the elements are strengthened or weakened by their position in the narrative. It is also interesting to see the effect that is achieved by combining some of the elements – for instance, you could say 'a heavily built man was lying on the floor' instead of giving his build a separate clause.

You should be aware too of the different effects of using active or passive verbs. The active voice is usually to be preferred, because by its very nature it is more immediate and alive, although sometimes a different emphasis may result from the alternative forms; if you compare the passive in 'She was met by jeers when she made her entrance' with the active version, 'Jeers met her when she made her entrance', you will see that the passive voice in this case puts the emphasis on the person, while the active focuses on the jeers. It also happens that the passive version is more euphonic. On occasion a change from one voice to the other may have the benefit of adding variety.

Informality, Slang and Swear Words

I have already said that it is almost mandatory in dialogue to use contractions such as 'don't', 'isn't' and 'shan't' (the last of which, if you want to be really pedantic, should be written as 'sha'n't' – but nobody bothers with that). What worries some writers, however, is the question of whether you are allowed to use contractions in narration. Of course you may – you can do anything you like, provided that it sounds right in its context and conveys its meaning clearly to the reader. Whether you write, 'She wasn't at all pleased to learn...' or 'She was not at all pleased to learn...' depends on you and the style of your book and the slightly different emphasis that one or the other usage may give. If you feel the informal tone is right, then use it.

In the same way, although grammar and syntax are important, and you really ought to understand their principles before you start playing around with the basic rules, you should not feel constrained by old-fashioned ideas. Everyone who is at all interested in writing has probably heard of Winston Churchill's famous 'up with which I will not put', mocking the rule that you should not end a sentence with a preposition. And there's no reason at all why you should feel guilty if you begin a sentence with 'And' or 'But', provided that you understand that it will probably give the sentence a stronger emphasis than it would have if it were tied to the previous sentence with a comma separating the two ideas. You can even use 'nice' if you want to, despite all the teachers who tried in days gone by to stop their pupils from putting the word in their essays; they disliked 'nice' because it is a weak word – and even that isn't always true. Don't therefore feel, when you are revising, that you must eliminate any informality.

Slang (make sure that it is in period) can often be used in dialogue, and, if it seems right in the context, in narration too.

As for swear words, use them as often as you like,

including the 'worst' ones, but it is worth remembering two things: first, although nowadays it would seem that anything goes, there are some readers who find swear words offensive, and secondly, although they can still have a shock effect, this is lost if you repeat them too often. The answer is to use them fearlessly when the context demands them, but not otherwise.

The same applies to sex scenes. Don't try to write a detailed sex scene unless you feel at ease doing so and in fact enjoy it – if you write that kind of material almost or completely against your better judgment, because you think it is commercial, the result is likely to sound false and will reveal your own unease. If, when reading through your work you have any feeling that a sex scene is embarrassing or simply clumsy, for heaven's sake cut it altogether.

Anachronisms

This is a problem which applies mainly to historical novels, but even if you are writing a story with a contemporary setting there may be flashbacks which take you far enough back in time for it to be necessary to check that you are not being anachronistic. In the historical novel, it is very easy, especially if you are trying very hard to capture the atmosphere of a long-gone period, to slip up every now and then. My favourite example comes from a truly awful American novel in which Mary Queen of Scots was given this line of dialogue: 'Say, Boswell, honey, why don't you fix yourself a sandwich?' That is probably apocryphal, but lesser mistakes can easily be made. In one of my novels, set in Victorian times, I wanted one character to tell another just what he thought of him, and it sounded right for him to say, 'You stupid git!' 'Git', I thought, must be a word of some antiquity – I could imagine a mediaeval knight saying, 'Thou whoreson git!' But when I looked it up in the dictionary, I found that it came into the language no earlier than

1946. So watch out for sandwiches and gits and the like, and always read the history, and especially the social history, of any period about which you are writing, and study it in some detail. That should prevent errors, but check again during your revision.

Suiting the Words to the Action

If you have any scenes of violent physical action in your book, or equally if you have quiet romantic passages, check to see that you are using the right sort of words to describe them. Physical action demands short sharp words with plosive consonants – 'cut', 'kill', 'strike', 'clash', 'bang' and of course, going to extremes, the 'zap' and 'pow' of cartoon comics, and they need to be used in short, pithy sentences (although you must not forget to give them a certain variety of structure). On the other hand, a gentler scene uses softer sounds and sibilant consonants – 'kiss', 'caress', 'shimmering', and so on, and its sentences tend to be longer and more flowing. Similarly, if you are trying to convey excitement, or perhaps speed, you need to give an impression of breathlessness, again with sibilants and aspirates and short hurrying sentences. It is all a kind of variation on the figure of speech known as onomatopoeia, in which words are used to imitate the sound of what they are describing.

Individuality

As has already been mentioned, style is simply the way you write. Whether it is good style or not depends on many of the matters discussed in this chapter, but one simple way of looking at it is to say that you are never really conscious of good style while you are reading it – it does not get in the way of the content. This does not mean to say that it has to be bland and featureless. I think there are three main points to strive for: simplicity, clarity and variety.

Simplicity and clarity are somewhat similar, but the former is a matter of making sure that your prose is never too complex, so that the reader gets lost in long, convoluted sentences, while the latter is concerned with communication, so that what you have written conveys to your readers exactly what you want them to know or to understand.

Variety is vital. A string of long words of Latin origin sounds pompous, but put one in among a lot of Anglo-Saxon words and it gives colour and life to the sentence. Use different styles to describe different kinds of events and actions. Add a figure of speech now and then – a vivid simile or metaphor can enliven a description and make the reader see much more clearly whatever it is that you are depicting. But, of course, don't overdo the search for variety – moderation in all things.

You may be afraid that if you follow too closely all the advice that you are given, your style will no longer be your own – that it will lack individuality. But this is a groundless fear. If you write from your heart, your style will always be recognizable as yours. It is bound to contain various personal quirks, favourite words, habits of phrasing, sentence shapes, and so on. When you are revising, don't try to eliminate all these elements unless at any point they begin to jar – they are the factors which give your style the individuality that you want.

7

Fiction – The Third and Fourth Revisions

Reading the Book Aloud

The third revision is the one when you read the work aloud. This will include any changes you have made during the first two revisions. You must try again, as far as possible, to distance yourself from the work, especially if you are reading it yourself, and listen as though it had been written by a stranger and you were hearing it for the first time on a tape. The reason why this revision works so well, as has already been suggested, is simply that the ear is in many respects a much better editor than the eye. It hears those faulty rhythms and unintentional repetitions, it picks up infelicities of phrasing, and of course it is excellent at detecting stilted or out-of-character dialogue. And the mind is marginally better at remembering what it hears than what it reads, so that it will be more aware of echoes occurring later in the book, which may not always be desirable, of earlier material.

The total detachment you need is quite difficult to achieve. Putting the whole thing on tape, if you have the facility to do so, can be very helpful, but it is even better

to get someone else to read your work to you, and preferably someone who doesn't know anything about the book.
If you read it yourself, you will know where you intend
the stress to be placed in this or that sentence, you will
know the tone in which a certain line of dialogue is to be
read, you will know all sorts of things about your text
which, however detached you manage to be, you cannot
fail to insert in the reading; if someone else is reading, he
or she will see what is on the page and no more, and you
will catch the moments when what you hear is not giving
the impression you intended. For instance, if you have
written a line of dialogue which says, 'She will go to
Edinburgh', without indicating any stress on the 'will', it
may seem obvious to you, especially given the context,
that this is a stern father saying that she will go there
whether she likes it or not, but the reader may interpret it
simply as a statement that she is going there at some time
in the future. So you make a note for yourself to clarify the
text at that point to ensure that your future readers will
get the right message. Of course, this does not apply only
to dialogue, and you should check for any occasions when
what you have written could be misinterpreted by a
reader.

The person reading the book can also provide you with
even more vital information than the fact that a certain
word or phrase needs to be changed, because it is almost
certain that she or he will not be able to conceal any
personal reactions; it may be flattering to see the amount
of interest and indeed excitement that your book arouses
in the reader, but if there are signs of boredom, you will
certainly want to see if you can discover why. However,
don't ask at the time – wait until the whole book has been
read, because the one problem with using someone in this
way is that you need a partner or friend who is willing to
spend a lot of time on it, and it is asking a bit much to
expect whoever it is to wait while you sort out necessary
alterations or to break off reading for a discussion of vari-

ous points. You simply have to make notes for yourself as the reading progresses. The ideal would probably be to bully or cajole someone into recording the whole thing on tape, which you could then listen to as long and as often as you liked, and you may be able to obtain useful information about the reader's reactions in a separate discussion.

The first revision read-through, when you are looking at the structure of what you have written, should not be rushed – take it slowly, examining each component of your plot and your characterization. Alter things as you go along, which may mean going back to amend earlier passages, and then check to see that you have got it right – or at least that it is an improvement on the first version. When you have finished, leave a time gap, if you can bear to do so, of at least a week, and preferably longer, before you start looking at the style. This is another slow revision, because you are examining each word and phrase and paragraph so carefully, and again rewriting as you go. It may be tempting then, when you come to read your book aloud, after yet another time gap, to gallop through it, but again, at least if you are reading it yourself, I would advise a slow, measured approach, because you really must listen closely to the words, and may sometimes have to read passages more than once. Additionally, when you have altered anything, you will have to read it again to make sure that the new version is right. You won't easily be able to do this if you get someone else to read the book to you unless whoever it may be has enormous amounts of time and reserves of patience, and it may be worth your while after you have made any amendments in line with your notes, to have another go at the whole book, this time reading it aloud yourself.

As well as looking for all the possible faults which have already been mentioned, one other use of the reading-aloud revision is that you may notice missing words which have previously escaped you. Whether we write with pencil or pen or on a typewriter or a word processor, our minds work faster than our fingers can, and in the haste of trying to keep abreast of the stream of words going through our brains, our fingers can sometimes skip a word. When we are engaged in the initial revisions, the eye moves rapidly over the written lines, and sometimes, expecting the missing word to be there, doesn't notice its absence. Although the eye is of course again involved in the reading-aloud revision, it is slowed down by the need to speak the words, and you will probably pick up the mistake.

The Non-Stop Read-Through

When you have completed the reading-aloud exercise and all the alterations that it has thrown up, you come at last (again preferably after waiting some time) to the quick read-through – the fourth revision, when you try to read the whole thing as so far revised in one long sitting, without interruptions. Solitude is needed. If you are on your own, you should probably take the telephone off the hook and refuse to answer any callers at the door, if you can bear to do so, and prepare something to eat and drink before you begin, so that you don't have to stop. Another possibility is to go somewhere away from home where you will not be disturbed – the reading room in your public library for instance, or in warm, dry weather a seat in a park, but the trouble with such places is that it is easy to get distracted. If you have a partner, maybe he or she will be willing to stand guard over you for the hours that it takes, protecting you from interruptions, and silently providing inner sustenance.

This is the time when, because you read the whole book from beginning to end without stopping, you can really see it as a whole. By this stage you should have ironed out all the problems of structure and characterization and technique and style, so what are you looking for? Well, it is surprising how easily, when you are checking the details or even making a broader but still close examination, you can miss things that you should have spotted. There are four main questions in my mind as I go through this reading. The first is whether the general balance of the book, after the cutting that I've done and the re-ordering and the major alterations and the fine tuning, seems right. Do I perhaps need to make further fairly major adjustments? Secondly, I ask myself whether I have been a forgetful author. I have already mentioned the misplaced bicycle (see p.110), and to give a slightly different example, I discovered in one of my novels that I had managed to use the same name for two very minor characters (the two men appeared a long way from each other, and very briefly, in a 200,000-word text, with a large cast of characters, and I had just not noticed the repetition in the previous revisions). I also look to see whether I dropped in a little hint at an early stage in the book about something I intended to bring in later, and then forgot the follow-up piece. The third question is whether any of the changes I have made in earlier revisions have left awkward gaps or untidy ends which need to be smoothed out. I might have deleted something early in the novel, but have not removed a later reference to it, or I may have added something and then forgotten to follow it up. And odd deletions and amendments can sometimes produce new ambiguities and repetitions and awkward-nesses and all the things that I have been striving so hard to eliminate. And lastly I watch myself with a part of my brain to see if at any stage in the book I am bored. It is often diffi-cult to avoid a certain smidgen of boredom with what you write – after all, you've been over it time and time again, you know it backwards, and sideways and upside-down – yet at the same time, because it is your creation, your child, you can usually keep your interest sufficiently alive to smother the hint of tediousness. But if you sense boredom during this reading, then take note, and try to analyze the cause.

When you are reading the whole book in one sitting, don't ever stop to make alterations. Jot down a page number and the briefest of notes of what you need to attend to when you have finished the read-through. Try your hardest to make the note intelligible – it is so easy to find that you have scribbled something cryptic which means nothing when you come to read it later.

The Last Polish

When you have carried out all the amendments and alterations that the fourth revision brought up, you have finished, and your novel is ready for a final typing or print out (perhaps with a last spelling check, if your word processor has the facility, not necessarily to correct spelling mistakes so much as to find any typing errors) and you can then send it off to a publisher.

As I have already said, revision must stop somewhere. Your book may not be perfect, but to go on tinkering with it for weeks or months or years will probably bring it very little nearer to a state where no further improvement is possible, so leave it alone. Unless . . .

. . . unless you feel in your heart of hearts that one vital element is missing. I usually do, and the something which I feel is lacking is sparkle. So I go through the book one more time (and it really is the last time, saving the possibility that a publisher will ask for alterations) trying to cut it by a further five per cent. That means on average one-and-a-half lines per A4 page, which is not very much. I take out a word here, a phrase there, a sentence, sometimes even a whole paragraph. I cannot always manage the five per cent target, because I have already been fairly ruthless in cutting, but there is invariably something which can come out without being missed – mostly, as I say, little things – and it really does help to provide the sparkle I want.

Go through that fifth revision and then you've finally finished.

8
Non-Fiction

Is Revision of Non-fiction Different?

There are many similarities in the approaches to the revision of fiction and of non-fiction, but some differences too. It seems to me that the four revising stages which I described in Chapter 1, and have elaborated since, apply whatever kind of book you are writing, but clearly non-fiction writers are not going to have to bother with a plot, or characterization or dialogue, or any other elements which belong only to fiction. There are therefore some differences in the first two revisions, but numbers three and four (and possibly five) are as valid for non-fiction as for fiction.

So now let us look at some of the special points to be considered when revising a non-fiction book.

Have You Pitched the Book at the Right Level?

Books can be written in a very popular, down-market style, and this is often the approach used if they are aimed at beginners in the subject, as an introduction to it.

Alternatively, they can be complex and abstruse, with no concessions to lack of expertise. Some books move chapter by chapter from a simple base to much more difficult concepts, and for certain subjects this may work very well. Generally, however, books should probably maintain the same level of demand on the reader's intellect throughout. The question now, as you read through your draft, is whether you have in fact been successful in writing it for the specific class of reader for which it is intended – expert or novice, the public at large or the specialist, the sophisticated, well-educated person who will recognize literary allusions, or the reader whose usual fare is the crasser television programmes, but who might just be tempted into reading a book if it is not too long, not too demanding (and preferably on some particularly enticing subject, such as sex).

In particular, there are two faults to beware of. The first is of including in a book intended for beginners various terms which are a part of your own everyday language, but which may be all Greek to your readers. You must not take your reader's knowledge for granted. In writing this book I have assumed that the reader is intelligent and will understand what I mean, but it is possible that she or he may not be familiar, for instance, with the technical use of the term 'attribution', and so, when it first appears in Chapter 6, I have explained it. The second fault is the reverse of the first, when in a book aimed at a fairly expert reader, you explain terms or give information which no one but a complete tyro would need to have spelt out. In both cases it is not just a matter of the odd word or technical term – the problem can arise with references, with jokes, with all sorts of things which your reader may find either incomprehensible or condescending.

As you revise, therefore, you must keep your reader permanently in mind, trying to gauge his or her reaction to what you have written, and to strike just the right balance in your text which will suit her or him. If you feel that you are explaining too much, you can sometimes make it seem

132

less condescending by the use of phrases such as 'It goes without saying that . . .' or 'As most of my readers will know . . .' but that can also sound like rather woolly writing, so it may not be the best answer.

The Structure

In a novel there is usually an obvious progression, from the beginning, into the middle, and on to the end, and although there may be flashbacks and other time changes, on the whole it is usually a matter of proceeding in chronological order – unless, of course, the novelist is writing in an experimental mode which dispenses with some if not all of the conventional ideas of story-telling.

Non-fiction books often do not have nearly so firm a structure – a biography or history may do, and if your book is to be part of a series (on various aspects of gardening, perhaps, or on looking after different pets, or something similar), the publisher may have already established a basic plan for all the books in the series so that they all follow the same course, and you will have little problem in working out where various pieces of information should go. But in many cases you will face problems of structure.

To take this book as an example, when I was planning it, initially my idea was that there would be an introductory chapter dealing in broad terms with why, when and how to revise; this would be followed by a chapter on each of the four stages of revision which I intended to recommend, all relating to fiction, then would come a chapter on non-fiction, and a final piece about checking your material before you send it to a publisher and on revisions following submission in the light of comments from the publisher (this chapter having, in fact, been suggested by my publisher). As I thought more about it, I came to the conclusion that the first stage of revision could be split fairly easily and suitably into three chapters, dealing with plot, characters and story-telling techniques. The material relating to the second revision would consist of fairly short pieces on the many aspects of style which I intended to cover, but I could see no way of splitting them up into chapters, and therefore decided that this section would have to be very much longer than the others. This would result in a lack of balance but I could see no way round that problem. Looking at revision stages three and four, I considered that there would not really be enough to say about them to give them a chapter each, and they would be better put together in one. The plan for the last two chapters on the revision of non-fiction and on revision before and after submission seemed to be all right.

Then I came up against other questions. In what order should I place the various points within the chapters? This applied particularly to the long chapter on style. Some kind of progression was needed, so that the reader would not feel simply that I was flitting about from one subject to another without any logical approach. The problem was partially solved when I decided to draw object lessons from a piece of prose riddled with elementary errors, for this seemed to dictate a reasonable sequence of comments. Of course, other writers might have used a different order – questions of this kind can only be answered by the author concerned, and the choice is his or hers.

Another matter which exercised me considerably was where to place a longish piece on the length of a book. Since it is the first matter to be considered when the draft of a book is completed, it seemed logical to put it at the beginning of Chapter 2. But Chapter 2 was about the plot of a novel. My next idea was to tack it on to the end of chapter 1, but it didn't really belong in that introduction either. Finally, I stumbled on the idea that it would make a Chapter on its own, and it became Chapter 2, with the examination of the plot moving on to become Chapter 3. As you read this book, that may seem to you a very obvious solution which should have occurred to me without much thought; with hindsight I agree, but in practice I know that it is not always easy for any author to see straight away how to deal with a problem of that sort. The structure of the book and the structure of chapters are important aspects of planning, but also of revision, because the plan may not always work out exactly as expected, and of course if you haven't planned at all, you will certainly need to take a good hard look at the structure when you revise. Everything should seem logical, everything should flow.

One thought may perhaps help you to decide on how your material should be broken up, and that is to start with sentences and build up from there. A sentence normally contains one thought or idea or statement, although further elements can be added by the use of the conjunctions 'and' and 'but', or by tacking on sub-clauses of various kinds. However complex the sentence may be, it has at its core the one unifying idea with which it is concerned. A paragraph is made up of sentences which are closely related, because they develop the idea of the opening sentence in the group. Paragraphs then are put together to make up a sub-division of a chapter, or perhaps a whole chapter, and they belong together because they are all centred on a specific theme. When that major theme changes, then a new chapter is required. It is a bit like making up parcels to contain differing contents – all the food in one, all the clothes in another, all the toys in a third, and so on.

Consider also the fact that, like a complete novel, sentences, paragraphs and chapters have beginnings, middles and ends, which need to be carefully structured, so that each element of your prose plays its appropriate part in the larger component of which it is part.

Style

Much of the advice contained in Chapter 6 applies just as much to non-fiction as to fiction – you will need to watch out for repetitions, both of words and rhythms, and over-long passages and unnecessary explanations and habit words and inconsistencies, and other similar faults, all of which will have to be cut or amended, and you will want to make sure that the grammar, punctuation and spelling are up to scratch. However, one aspect of your style probably needs particular emphasis, and this is the question of clarity. In fiction your prose can sometimes be imaginative, poetic, fanciful (although you should beware, as I have already said, of 'fine writing' or 'purple passages'). In a novel you may also at times deliberately wish to confuse or mislead your reader in terms of the plot (as in a murder story when you want suspicion to fall on various characters who turn out in the end to be innocent). In non-fiction, clarity is an absolute requirement. So check your material to see that it does not contain ambiguities, or contradictions, or sentences which are so involved that it is difficult to make head or tail of them. And while there is no need to write in words of one syllable, keep the language simple so that your meaning is always completely clear. Stick to the point too – it is very easy to indulge in a certain amount of fairly meaningless waffle (I am prone to it myself), and this needs to be cut. At the same time, a certain amount of variety is needed, and sometimes some of the waffle will help to take the dryness out of what you are writing – especially if you can manage to make it amusing or otherwise interesting, and provided of course that it has some relevance to your subject. There is no reason why you should not enliven your material with a little humour, nor should you be afraid of the occasional informality ('don't', for example, rather than 'do not') despite the fact that you are writing non-fiction.

Political correctness is often a problem, especially when it comes to pronouns. It used to be possible to use 'he', 'him', 'his' to cover both sexes, but that is no longer acceptable, and the writer is forced into using 'he or she', 'him or her', 'his or her' and 'his or hers', which are always clumsy, varying the style by putting the feminine pronoun first, which sounds even clumsier. The problem can occasionally be solved by completely recasting the sentence, but this is laborious and the result can seem stilted. An easier solution is to use plurals – when I refer to 'readers' I can then follow with 'they, 'them', 'their' and 'theirs' – but this is not always possible because of the context. You need to check (especially if you are a man) that you have not left a male pronoun in a place where you should have given the alternatives.

The need for political correctness does not apply only to pronouns, and it goes without saying that if your book contains anything of a racist or otherwise offensive nature you should take it out.

Accuracy

A non-fiction book is likely to be full of facts, or statements purporting to be facts, and it is vital that you should be accurate. Even if you know your subject backwards, you should check your own accuracy, and should make sure that all the information you give is as up-to-date as possible.

If you are writing an instructional book, make sure that everything works, and that the reader will be able to follow the directions you give without difficulty. I have always been impressed by the story behind a book called *Make Your Own Classical Guitar*. The author, Stanley Doubtfire, had made guitars regularly, and knew exactly what had to be done, but when the book was finished he set about making a new guitar following to the letter his own instructions as given in the book. This allowed him to check the accuracy and completeness of what he had written.

If your book has involved you in research, ensure that the details you are using are correct, and check them with alternative sources if you can. During the research you should make careful (and legible) notes of where the material came from, and when you are revising, if you are doubtful of any points, you will know where to go to check them once more. Your notes will also be helpful if you need to clear the copyright of any material you are using.

One other important matter to be checked is that nothing in the book is (or might possibly be) dangerous to the reader. For instance, have you remembered to say that the electricity should be shut off at the mains before carrying out an electrical repair? You have to assume, in matters of safety, however patronizing it may seem, that your reader is both totally inexperienced and lacking in common sense.

Making It Personal

Viewpoint does not apply to non-fiction, but the question of how often the personal pronoun should appear is worth considering. If you are writing an autobiography or a travel book your text will naturally contain a pretty heavy use of 'I', but in other kinds of non-fiction it is probably best avoided. If you keep repeating 'I' it sounds like an ego-trip, and is an intrusion by the author – in a curious way, authors need to keep some distance between their readers and themselves. On the other hand, as you will have noticed, I do not attempt in a book such as this to leave myself out of it altogether. Books about writing are perhaps something of a special case, simply because there are no rules – hardly anything can be laid down in a didactic way, saying that you absolutely must do this that or the other. There is a great deal of freedom, and I like to take the position, when giving advice, that this is what I do or that is what I think, based on my experience, leaving you with the option of accepting or ignoring whatever it is that I say. Besides which, and despite my strictures above, I think the use of the personal pronoun, provided that it is not overdone, makes the approach more friendly. I hope my readers like it – if they don't, I'm sorry, but it is the way of writing which comes naturally to me, and I hope that they in turn will write in whatever way suits them.

Libel, Plagiarism and the Use of Copyright Material

It should not be easy when you are writing your book to forget about libel, but it is possible to do so in the heat of the moment. Enmity or hatred may lead you into excess. If you write damaging material about someone, you may be in serious trouble if the person concerned becomes aware of what you have written (and in non-fiction it is quite likely that you have actually named him or her, so that there is no question of doubt about who is meant). In some cases, the apparent libel may be intentional because you want publicly to destroy the person's reputation, but you must be aware of the consequences. Even though what you have written is the truth – and truth is a perfect defence in a libel action, provided that you can prove it – you and your publisher will suffer an extremely fraught time and will probably have to bear substantial legal costs. The best thing, if you have any doubts about the inclusion of possibly libellous material, is to take legal advice before you finish your revision. If you don't do that, then at least let the publisher know, if you find one, and before you sign the contract, that there is a problem of this nature.

It is to be hoped that you have not plagiarized anyone else's work, copying what she or he has written and passing it off as your own. If you have done so, you are on dangerous ground, and are unlikely to get away with it, because the readers of your book, being interested in your subject, will probably have read the book from which you copied the material and will recognize it – and if they don't, the author of the previous book probably will. You should never plagiarize. If you have done so, rewrite anything that you have copied while you are engaged in revision; rewrite drastically, changing everything – the words, the phrasing, the way the ideas are presented – and change it all so fundamentally that it becomes your own writing rather than the original author's. If you have pinched someone else's basic idea for the book and all their original thoughts, then your best course of action is to abandon it – and probably to abandon writing too – before you are branded as a thief. Infringement of copyright is a crime, but when it takes the form of plagiarism it is worse, because you have added deception to theft.

The use of copyright material which you are *not* pretending is your own work is a different matter. Often quotations from another author's work, especially if he or she is an authority, give weight to your own arguments, and at the same time add a little variety. But if you use any such material, it must be fully acknowledged, which is to say that you must attribute the passage to the author concerned and name the work in which it appeared. You will almost certainly also need permission to quote it. The law states, under a provision known as 'fair dealing', that you may quote a short extract (basically not more than about two hundred words) from someone else's work, but only in the course of criticism or review. In practice, few authors or publishers will object if, while you are presenting your own argument, you quote a few words from work in which they own or control the copyright, but even so you should obtain permission, and you must of course acknowledge the source of the quotation in full. You may feel, with some justice, that this is a matter which can be sorted out once your book has been accepted for publication, but it seems to me sensible to do it at the stage of revision. If you are unwilling to do so, at least take the opportunity of making a list of all copyright material which you have used, and let your publisher know that you have all these details and intend to clear them for publication if your book is accepted.

Illustrations, Maps, Diagrams, etc.

While engaged in your revision, make sure that any references to illustrations, maps and diagrams are correct, and especially that they are consistent. The last comment applies particularly to maps – you might, for instance, refer throughout your book to 'Padua', whereas the map, originating in Italy, shows the city as 'Padova'.

The Third and Fourth Revisions

With reference to Chapter 7, I find that it is just as important to read a non-fiction book aloud for revision purposes as it is for fiction, and the same applies to the fourth step of reading the whole thing at a sitting. The final five per cent cut will do no harm either.

9

Before and After Submission

Preparation of the Typescript

You might not think that preparation of the typescript had much to do with revision, but if you haven't got it right, you had better start revising it. The rules are short and simple (those who have heard Creative Writing tutors banging on and on about this, and who have taken the instructions to heart, should skip to the next headed section): your work must be typed in double spacing (1½ spacing won't do, and single spacing will probably mean that your masterpiece will remain unread) on one side of the paper only. Additional advice includes leaving good margins (a minimum of 1" or 3 cm all round), and sticking to the same number of lines per page except at the beginning and end of chapters – a new chapter should always start on a fresh page. Indent your paragraphs and don't leave blank lines between them unless you want to indicate a change of scene, or characters, or viewpoint or subject. Put the title of the work and your name or pseudonym on the first page, and your real name and address at the foot. Indicate the length of the book, using the method outlined in Chapter 2. Do not put 'FBSR' or 'First British Serial Rights' on the typescript – you will look like a total ignoramus if you do. First British Serial Rights are what you offer when submitting a short story or an article to a magazine, not what book publishers will want to buy. Their requirement is normally Volume Rights, but it is not necessary to include those words on the typescript – the publisher will take it for granted that that is what you are offering.

Nowadays the ease of correction which word processors provide has largely eliminated the messy typescript covered with the author's longhand corrections, but if you are still using a typewriter the process is comparatively laborious and you will not want to retype everything so that it looks perfect. Well, some corrections are acceptable, provided that there are not too many, and that they are all entirely legible and your intention is clear. But as soon as the typescript begins to look untidy, then you just must retype. The same thing applies if you have to keep sending your work to different publishers in the search for an acceptance; after a time, the typescript is bound to look a little tired, and it is certainly worth retyping any tatty-looking pages, including almost certainly the title page, or running off further copies on the word processor. Messy submissions, like poor punctuation, spelling and grammar, speak of authors who have no apparent pride in their work.

Making Sure that Everything is There

This advice is really for writers of non-fiction books. Do make sure when you send off your typescript that any extraneous material which should form part of the submission is there. This includes not only the obvious extras such as illustrations, maps and diagrams, which are an integral part of the book, but also details of permissions either obtained or needed for the use of copyright material, any warnings about potential libel, and so on. In the case of illustrations, maps and diagrams you should make sure, if you can, that they are suitable for reproduction, and relevant, and that their captions are consistent with the main text. Such material should be separate from the text, rather than pasted into it, but if the intention is that it should be integrated into the text, a clear indication of where it is to go should be given.

You should also indicate what material is still to come, and that may include not only an index, but perhaps further pages which should preferably not be written until a later stage in order to make the book, when published, as up-to-date as possible. However, the last provision is certainly not an invitation to send in a work which is incomplete because you haven't yet had time to do the necessary research, or even to write it. If some additional material is to follow, whatever it may be, it will be helpful if you can tell the publisher the extent of what is missing.

Unless the book has been commissioned, in which case all such matters will already have been discussed, it is important to send the publishers details about yourself and your qualifications for writing the book, information, if you have it, of what else on the subject is already on the market, and an indication of why your book is different from, and preferably better than, any existing competitors. If you can also tell the publisher something about the size of the potential market for the book (don't exaggerate) that will be useful, especially if you have some available means of tapping that market, such as the mailing list of a society devoted to the subject. And if you can obtain a foreword or introduction from some eminent person whose name and reputation are likely to impress buyers of the book, that is another plus.

The Title

Does your title need revision? Some writers like to have a title before they begin writing; others leave it until the book is ready to go to a publisher. Some will tell you that it doesn't much matter, because the publishers will change it anyway (publishers as a whole always believe that they are better at finding good titles than authors), but in most cases they will happily leave it alone if it seems to be a good one. If you are trying to break into print for the first time, it is worth spending a lot of trouble on your title, because it is the very first thing that the publisher will see, and if it sounds dull and unattractive you will have already erected a little barrier in the way of acceptance. It may not be so important in this particular respect if you are an already established writer on the publisher's list, but you will probably still want to please everyone in the publishing firm by choosing a title which is unusual and eye-catching and which really fits the book. It doesn't matter at all whether your chosen title is short (*Rebecca*) or long (*The Spy Who Came In From The Cold*), although I think there is some prejudice in favour of something which is not too much of a mouthful – apart from anything else there may be some problem, if it is very long, in fitting it on to the jacket or the spine of the book – but you should try to find a name for your book which is appropriate, interesting and, if possible, original, but not so obscure that it is off-putting.

Finding good titles does not normally cause as much trouble for non-fiction as it does for fiction. The most important consideration is the appropriateness of the title, and a straightforward description of the contents may suffice. Sub-titles are often used to pinpoint the nature of the book and the readership for which it is intended. A title such as *Revision: An Author's Guide* may not be very exciting or original, but it does tell you what the book is about. This is not to say that, given the right subject, you cannot be rather more imaginative (*Wild Swans* or *The Great Railway Bazaar*), but usually the prime requirement is that a non-fiction title should be informative.

In most cases it is fairly easy to find a title for a novel which is not dull but is appropriate. Often it is simply the name (*Lolita*) or a description (*The Once and Future King*) of the main character. It can be a quotation (*Far From the*

146

Madding Crowd) – although most of the best ones have been taken. It can be anything at all except that of a book which is already famous. There is no copyright in titles, but you would be foolish to choose one which has already been used for a bestseller, which would lay you open to prosecution for 'passing off' (giving your book a well-known title in the hope that people would buy it in mistake for the celebrated one – and it's no use pleading that you had no such intention, because the law won't believe you). So just do your best to find something which might possibly intrigue a jaded editor.

Revision of the Book to Meet a Publisher's Requirements

If your work is accepted for publication without any ifs or buts, either you are a genius, or at least a born writer, or, like most of us, you have needed to learn your craft, but have taken everything in this book to heart, with the result that your own book is not merely well written, but has been well rewritten too. Frequently, however, the letter you will receive from an interested publisher will suggest that various alterations will be necessary before any commitment to publish will be made. You may be asked to go to the publishing house to discuss the matter, or the publisher's letter will specify in some detail the changes which the editor thinks should be made. I am not referring at this point to copy-editing, which will come later and is likely to be concerned mainly with the kind of points covered in Chapter 6. The criticisms that an editor makes at this early stage are far more likely to be structural or to do with the plot or characterizations, or certain aspects of your storytelling technique.

So how do you react to the suggestion of changes? If your first thought is that the editor has a cheek to want to mess about with your masterpiece, then you are not living in the real world. You might consider, first of all, that it is very difficult to get published these days – publishers are very selective and take only those books which they believe in and which they think they can sell, and they have an enormous number of new books to choose from – submissions pour into every publisher's office by the hundreds, and sometimes the thousands, every year; many of them, even from first-time writers, with a bit of tinkering, or possibly some more drastic rewriting, are often publishable, so the publisher has plenty of choice, and will not be much distressed if you refuse to listen to any editorial suggestions – the probability is that another equally publishable book will turn up in a few days' time. Secondly, you should disabuse yourself of the idea, which some writers cling to, that in seeking to alter your work, the editor is indulging in an ego-trip. All editors, you may think, are authors manqués, resentful of anyone who can do something which they cannot, and therefore prepared to show just how clever and how powerful they are by refusing to take on any book until they have messed about with it. It isn't true. There may be one or two such editors, but they are rarities, and in most cases the editor's one aim in suggesting changes is to improve both the quality and saleability of the book.

However hard you have tried to detach yourself from your own work, you can never succeed in doing so, and the opinions of partners or friends are quite unreliable. Unless you have paid for a criticism from one of the freelance advisers (many of whom are extremely helpful) who advertise in journals such as *Writers News*, the first truly detached, independent reading that your work has had is likely to have been by the editor, who may well see faults that you never knew existed. When editors like a book and believe that anything which is wrong with it could be put right, they will go to great lengths to help you to make the adjustments which will allow them to publish you with pleasure and confidence. I have been very grateful to all the editors I have had – they have asked for changes which have saved me from a number of stupidities, they have rightly suggested that I should soften my approach when I had gone over the top, they have pointed out omissions. I have often told the story of my fifth novel, *The Cast Iron Man*: my editor shocked me by saying it was unpublishable, and when I asked why, pointed out that the hero was a pompous prig, a bore, and a male chauvinist pig to boot; I took the typescript home, re-read it, and realized that she was absolutely right, although I had previously seen him only as a charming, likeable young man; I worked on the book, de-pompousing, de-prigging and de-boring him (mainly by giving him a sense of humour and making his dialogue less formal) and removing all his chauvinist remarks and actions; the result was that he became much more like the character I had intended him to be, my editor was happy, and the book was successfully published.

The moral is that you should always listen carefully and in an equable frame of mind to any comments that your editor gives you. You may feel that you have been unlucky and have come up against an idiot who doesn't understand your book and who is asking for changes which will totally ruin it. But before you make your mind up about that, it's a good idea to re-read your book, to think about what has been said, and see if you can perhaps begin to believe that the editor has a point. If you still cannot accept the comments, it is your privilege to do so, and in that case, you simply walk away from the possibility that the firm in question will publish the book, and try somewhere else. You may then get a totally different reaction, because editors are human and have their likes and dislikes and their different views of the strengths and weaknesses of a given book. Alternatively, you may be able to see that the suggested alterations will enhance the book without damaging your intentions, and you might even admit that they will make an enormous improvement. Yet again, you may like some of the editor's proposals, while others fill you with horror, in which case the best procedure would be to seek an interview with the editor and try to work something out together; she or he may be obdurate, but is more likely to be reasonable.

When you have agreed on any changes to be made, you will have to embark on yet another stage of revision. It is important to take this seriously, and to do a thorough job, if that is what is required, rather than just tinkering. One of the problems is that editors may not always be totally specific in their comments – you might be told, for instance, that your novel sags a bit in the middle, and needs tightening up. It is not sufficient to delete a couple of paragraphs and think that you have dealt with the problem; instead you need to analyze the whole story and work out why the comment has been made, and which parts are slow-moving and dull, and what you can do about it, which very often will mean a considerable amount of restructuring and the addition of new twists and turns of the plot to keep the interest flowing. If you are told that your hero is a pompous prig, then the problem will not be solved if you alter a couple of his speeches and tell the reader that he has a great sense of humour; instead you must look at his every appearance in the story, his every action, his every line of dialogue, and alter him quite radically throughout. When you have finished it is useful to go through the third and fourth stages of revision as described in Chapter 7 again.

Copy-Editing

Your book will probably receive the attentions of a copy-editor before it goes to press, although not all publishers use copy-editors nowadays (more's the pity). Good copy-editors are invaluable, and many an author is grateful for their efforts, which have resulted in facts being checked, infelicities of style amended, material made consistent, problems of headings and sub-headings and the like sorted out, and spelling, punctuation and grammar put in order. If you have a copy-editor it is worth listening carefully to all that she or he says, which will not only improve your book, but probably help you by example to become a better writer in future. However, if you have followed carefully all the precepts in this book, there may not be a great deal for her or him to do.

Why Books are Rejected

If your book has been rejected without comment – with just a rejection slip, perhaps, or a form letter – you will almost certainly be thinking that it wouldn't hurt the publisher to explain what is wrong, which would be very helpful to you. Few publishers are willing to take the time to make constructive comments on the books they turn down, and it may therefore be worthwhile to look at the reasons why so many authors do not receive an offer of publication for their books. 'Our list is full,' the rejection letters often say. It is a polite way of telling you that the publisher doesn't want your book, but it is rarely true – publishers can always find room for a book which is outstanding. In fact, the most frequent reason for rejection is that the book is badly written, and in that condemnation I include not only poor construction, with a complete absence of technique, and total incompetence in the areas of spelling, punctuation and syntax, but a lack of interesting, not to mention original, elements in the plot, if it is a novel, or in the thoughts if it is non-fiction. It never seems to occur to far too many would-be authors that writing is a craft which needs to be learnt before it can be practised successfully. The next main reason for rejection is that the book is adequate, but no more than that, and does not have the excitement that can fire an editor's enthusiasm; it may be a nice little story, or it may be an account of a journey to Timbuktu, but there is nothing really unusual about it, no quality to distinguish it from all the other novels or travelogues, or whatever it may be which other authors have submitted to that publisher. A non-fiction book may in fact be better than adequate, but is still rejected, but this time because there are too many competitive titles already available, and the one under consideration does not have a sufficiently different approach or new material which will make it stand out. Thirdly, books are rejected, often against the hopes of the editor, because no one in the publisher's sales department can see the possibility of selling sufficient copies at an acceptable price, or because there seems to be little chance of publication in paperback, which would make the project economically viable. Yet another regular reason for rejection, and here we are talking largely of fiction, is that the genre is out of favour; historical novels are currently in the doldrums, and so are war novels, and the glitzy 'sex and shopping' novels are far less in demand than they were a comparatively short while ago. Genres become unfashionable, and once that verdict is announced by one or two publishing houses, it seems to be adopted throughout the industry. In the case of historicals, I would guess that the wheel will turn in due course, and publishers will be looking for them again, and glitz may work once more, but war novels seem rather more unlikely to return to popular favour unless, God forbid, we have another major war; but it is always difficult to forecast trends. A final frequent cause of rejection is that the author's market research has been poor, and the book has been sent to a publisher which does not bring out books in the genre concerned. There are just about as many reasons why books are rejected as there are kinds of books – other possibilities are that the book may be libellous, or politically incorrect, or too long, or too short, or inordinately expensive to produce, or it may be simply that the editor got out of the wrong side of the bed that morning and was in a foul mood.

Even an apparently well-established writer can be shocked to be told that, although there is nothing wrong with it, the publisher does not want to publish his or her latest book, and indeed that he or she will not feature on the publisher's list again. There are three principal reasons for this kind of rejection: a change in the publisher's list, poor sales, and 'mid-list syndrome'. Publishers do sometimes make a decision to move out of a particular genre of publication, perhaps because they find it difficult to compete with publishers who specialize in that field, or simply because public interest in the subject has declined. Poor sales of the author's previous books is perhaps the most frequent cause of rejection, and it includes failure to sell subsidiary rights; the books of an author who suffers declining sales are terminally ill – the condition will worsen with each new book that is published, and at some stage the publisher will call a halt. 'Mid-list syndrome' is somewhat similar, and the term describes the situation of an author who produces perfectly respectable books which sell at the same unexciting, and barely profitable level, with the author never achieving the reputation which would produce continuing sales of the backlist titles, let alone project each new book into a greater success than its predecessor, which is what publishers always hope for, and which would take the author out of the mid-list and promote her or him into the position of a major seller. Both poor sales and 'mid-list syndrome' can usually be cured only, if at all, by the author moving to another publishing house, which can re-launch her or him.

Revising Your Book After Rejection

If you are trying to break into print and your book comes back to you after submission to a publisher with a formal rejection slip or a letter which tells you nothing of the reasons why it has been turned down, you will probably simply try another publisher or several other publishers. You may get a succession of rejections, without any comment from the publishers, and this will probably mean that there is something fundamentally wrong with the book. You should look at it again, very carefully, to see which of the reasons listed in the first paragraph of the section immediately above are likely to apply to it. Reading your book again may be very instructive; since it will almost certainly be some weeks since you last read it, you may be surprised to see clearly a number of faults which were not apparent to you earlier. You should not be dispirited, but must embark on a further process of revision, following the precepts of this book, but concentrating on what you believe may have been the weakness which led to its recurring rejection.

On the other hand, you may have had letters from publishers which, while firmly turning the book down, have offered some kind of encouragement in the form of complimentary remarks or perhaps a suggestion that you should send your next work to the editor concerned, or even sometimes that you should try a specific publisher which the editor thinks might be interested. If that happens you should be pleased – editors don't normally hand out compliments to unknown authors unless they mean it. Mind you, the book has still been rejected, so you obviously cannot be too delighted, and once more the answer may be, before you send it out again, to see whether a further stint of revision would sharpen it up, make it more appealing, generally improve it.

A third possibility is that the rejection will explain why the book has not been accepted, not in vague publisher-related terms, such as 'our list is full', but explaining what is wrong with the book. The comments may not be very detailed, so you may have to try to expand a brief remark into a far more extensive criticism, but even a hint can be very revealing when you read the book again after not having looked at it for some time. Once more, you embark on revision, and you may be able to make real improvements.

Re-Submissions

Should you ever re-submit a book to a publisher who has seen it and turned it down? In some instances an editor will actually ask you to send in the book for a second time after you have revised it, and of course you would be foolish not to do so (unless in the meantime some other publisher has made an offer for it as it stands). But in the majority of cases, which consist of formal, uninformative rejections, the answer is probably that you should try elsewhere, rather than go back to someone who has already turned you down, even if you have altered the book in the meantime. On the other hand, if you have received advice about what was wrong and have done your best to eradicate the fault, then you could re-submit, and the more encouraging the note that you received with the first rejection, the more firmly you should be advised to try the same editor again. Even in that case, however, I would suggest that you should never re-submit unless the work has been fairly substantially changed. The alteration of a few paragraphs is not enough – you need to be able to write an accompanying letter which will justify in advance the editor's time in re-reading your book, because you will explain all that you have done to improve it. You will send such a letter with it, of course, because one thing that you should never do is to re-submit a book without saying that the publisher has already seen it once, in the hope perhaps that it will land on a different editor's desk – even if it does, and the second editor likes it, when the book is discussed at an editorial meeting the first editor will undoubtedly recognize it, and will put in a few damning words. Even worse than a re-submission without coming clean about it, would be to change its title, use a pseudonym, and then send it in again. If you ever thought of doing that, your ideas need a bit of good old revision.

Revising at Proof Stage

If you are thinking that you can give your book yet another revision when the proofs arrive, forget it! Proof corrections are very expensive, and unless you have already agreed with the publisher that changes may be made to ensure that the book is as up-to-date as possible, amendments at proof stage should be limited to the correction of typographical errors and those few alterations to the text which are absolutely essential.

Revision After Publication

Most contracts for non-fiction books which are perhaps likely to become out-of-date in part or in full will contain a clause committing the author to revise the book (or, if unwilling to undertake the task or incapable of doing so, to allow some competent person to make the necessary alterations). The idea of a revised edition may originate with the publisher or the author may propose it, but in the latter case the publisher may have to be convinced that a sufficiently large market exists for the proposed new edition. In either case the whole matter will have to be discussed and agreement reached on the extent of the revision required, which might consist of a few essential sentences here and there or might mean a complete rewrite. The amount of new material may be restricted by the space available (a new sentence will perhaps have to fit precisely into the space taken by the sentence it replaces in order to avoid expensive resetting of the type – although modern processes make this problem much simpler).

Once everything has been agreed with the publisher, the author can start working – and guess what he or she must do when all the rewriting has been completed. You are right – it's revision time again.

Index